seán óg

His Own Story

by

seán óg o ceallacháin

BROPHY BOOKS
DUBLIN & LONDON

© Seán Óg O Ceallacháin 1988
First published November 1988
ISBN 1 85405 050 8

Typeset by Wendy A. Commins, The Curragh
Make-up by Paul Bray Studio
Printed and bound in Ireland by W. & G. Baird Limited

Published by

Brophy International Publishing Limited
108 Sundrive Road
Dublin 12
Republic of Ireland

Acknowledgements

Writing this book would have been impossible without the kindness and cooperation of old friends and colleagues. To all who helped in any way I am most grateful. I am especially thankful to Máire Ní Mhurchú and her staff in the RTE Reference Library, and also to my colleague Mick Dunne for access to his personal — and comprehensive — sports files. A special word of thanks is due also to Tom Woulfe, who read the manuscript and gave freely of advice and information. I am more than grateful also to my daughters, Caitríona and Sinéad, for putting my typing errors right and to my son, Finín, for his assistance with the photography.

I am extremely grateful to the following for their help in supplying and checking material and information:
Gerry Arthurs, former Ulster Provincial GAA Secretary; Pat Cashman, (*Irish Press* Art Dept); Mary Clarke, Archivist, Dublin Corporation; Jim Connolly; Sean Coyne, Librarian; Jim Cullen, 42nd Battalion, LDF; Margaret Dowling, "Walkinstown Players"; Sean Diffley, *Irish Independent*; Mick Dunne; Edward Fitzgerald; Mick Fitzpatrick, *RTE Guide*; Eamon Gaffney, *Anglo Celt*; Philip Greene; David Guiney; Paddy Hickey, Dept. of Education (Records Section); Tom Holten, RTE; Lensmen (Andy Farren); Cormac Liddy, *Limerick Leader*; Con Martin; Eamon Morris, Secretary, Football League of Ireland; Con Murphy, Cork GAA Board; Bridie McManus; Ray McManus (Sportsfile); Jim McNeill, *Irish Press*; Seamus McCluskey: *History of Monaghan GAA*; Gerry McLoughlin, RTE; T & D Norton; Mícheál O Laochdha, Dublin GAA Board; Tom O'Riordan, *Irish Independent*; Breandan O Tighearnaigh, Maurice Reidy, RTE; Tony Reid, *Evening Herald*; Con Shortt: *History of Ulster GAA*; Tony Sheehan; Eugene Timmons, T.C.; Thom Wardlaw, 42nd Battalion LDF.

Seán Óg O Ceallacháin

Dedication

To My Wife, Ann

Seán Óg O Ceallacháin

Contents

*My father turned the key in the front door and stepped into the hall.
He motioned me to remain quiet. He hung his coat on the hall stand
and placed his hat on top of it, as he always did. "We're home," he
called out.*

*My mother answered from the dining room, "How did they get
on?" "We won," I said.*

*My father signalled me to keep still. He walked ahead of me into
the dining room. My mother was on her knees polishing the floor,
her Saturday morning chore. She started to rise to her feet, looked at
me, and her face froze in horror. "Good Jesus, what happened to
him?" She could not take her eyes off my face. I had a huge plaster
across my nose. "He got a bit of a knock," said my father and before
he could utter another word I blurted out, "I got three stitches." My
poor mother collapsed into the chair and started to cry. I couldn't
understand what all the fuss was about. All I wanted to do was to
get out of the house and show off my stitches to my pals. I was 12
years of age at the time . . .*

*My mother was very upset. "That's it," she said. "That's it, he'll
never take a hurley in his hand again." My poor innocent mother,
little did she know that many years later she would be sitting in the
Hogan Stand in Croke Park watching me being carried off the field,
unconscious, with a far more severe facial injury . . .*

Chapter 1
Beginnings

Newcastle West, Co Limerick, lies in the heart of the rich farming and dairy industry. It is also a noted horse-breeding area and has become acclaimed for its special mineral water which has attained world prominence on the commercial markets.

Newcastle West has many other claims to fame, historically, culturally and sporting, perhaps the least being the fact that I was born there. On 12 May 1923 the population was 2,579, and when I was born early that morning my arrival added one more digit to the statistics.

My coming was unheralded and didn't cause even a ripple on the gentle waters of the Deale river which flowed down near its main street. My name wasn't on the lips of the affluent people of that fair town as they flicked their whips at lively ponies drawing traps and carriages on the roads to Rathkeale or Abbeyfeale or even to Limerick itself. The mood of the town was one of unease as the effects of the Civil War had left an indelible imprint on families and property. The *Limerick Echo* carried a prominent notice issued by the ruling government's Publicity Dept, signed by Eamon de Valera and his Chief of Staff, Frank Aiken. "To all Ranks. Soldiers of Liberty — Legion of the Rearguard. The Republic can no longer be defended successfully by your arms. Further sacrifices on your part would now be in vain and continuance of the struggle in arms unwise in the National interest. Military victory must be allowed to rest for the moment with those who have destroyed the Republic. Other means must be sought to safeguard the nation's rights. . . ."

The national newspapers also ignored my arrival that morning and

confined themselves to the more mundane events happening at home
and abroad. The *Irish Times* in its main news story announced that
the King and Queen were sightseeing in the Campagne and that a big
drive was on foot to collect income tax arrears (nothing has changed
in that regard!). Another heading claimed, "John Dillon Pessimistic".
The *Irish Independent* gave prominence to the finding of 10,000 rounds
of ammunition in a dump in Dundalk. Other headlines screamed:
"Drastic Licensing Proposals", "Total Closing on Sundays in Belfast"
(the wheel has come full circle, the pubs are open again on Sundays
in Belfast). The big attraction at the Abbey Theatre in Dublin at the
time was the St John Gogarty comedy, *Mary, Mary, Quite Contrary*
while Jackie Coogan was the star of the film *Oliver Twist* in the
Metropole cinema.

My father was born between Stewartstown and Mousetown, near
Coalisland, Co Tyrone. Many believed he was born in the South and a
certain amount of credence was given to that view because he travelled
in the course of his business to Limerick, Clare, Tipperary and Cork.
He was educated in the local national school and secured a King's
scholarship, which entitled him to take up a position in the Civil
Service, but he declined. After the death of his father, a small farmer,
my dad came to live in Dublin with his widowed mother and his
brother. He accepted an apprenticeship with Gilbey's, the wine merchants, and having worked for that firm for a number of years, left
to take up a job with Mineral Water Distributors in Henrietta St, off
O'Connell St.

Dad was a complex person. He had the ability to succeed in any
undertaking but somehow missed the bus in acquiring the material
rewards of life. He would throw himself wholeheartedly into various
schemes, invariably in the role of innovator, and having set matters
in motion would move on to other things. He was a marvellous racon-
teur, helped by a distinctive voice which immediately captured the
attention of his audience. He loved company, was a great mixer and
enjoyed his "jar". Mam knew very little about dad's early political
affiliations, except to say that he would go "missing for days and give
no reason for it." His job as a traveller entailed weekly visits to the
South by train. He was always reticent about his political activities
in his younger days, and when I would press him, he would say, "we
did our bit".

Being curious, I would persist in questioning him but I got little satisfaction. His brother, Tom, had been a member of the Old Dublin Brigade of the IRA, and when he died in 1949, he was given a military funeral in Glasnevin cemetery. Only then did I learn about my father and Tom's involvement with the IRB (Irish Republican Brotherhood). Both Tom and dad had been members of the Intelligence section of that organisation. His strange reluctance to talk about that side of his earlier life stirred my curiosity about the IRB. Who were they? When did they operate and how? What was their purpose? The prime objective of the IRB when it was launched in 1858 was to end the British occupation of Ireland, ultimately by force. From the beginning it was an oath-bound secret society and each member had to pledge "to do all in my power to establish the independence of Ireland and to keep secret all things relating to the organisation."

The historian and Irish language enthusiast, Dr Leon O Broin, has dealt in depth with the IRB at home and abroad in his books *The Revolutionary Underground*, *Fenian Fever*, and *Dublin Castle and the 1916 Rising*. The founder of the organisation was James Stephens, who was born in Kilkenny of a bourgeois family. He founded the IRB on St Patrick's Day, 1858, in Dublin. Initially, it was known as the "Society", the "Organisation" or simply "Brotherhood". It wasn't until 1873 that it became known as the IRB. It was mainly an urban organisation; only ten per cent of those arrested after 1867 were farmers, farmers' sons or farm labourers. Members of the organisation were encouraged to infiltrate various national bodies, such as the GAA, Gaelic League, Land League, etc., apart from political parties.

The coming into being of the national army following the signing of the Treaty more or less pre-empted the objects of the IRB, which no longer included the obligation to train and equip a military body for the purpose of securing an independent republican government by force of arms. Leon O Broin, writing in T.W. Moody's book *Nationality and the Pursuit of National Independence* said that "after 1921 the organisation appeared to die, but in 1923 as the Civil War ended, an attempt was made to revive it, and the constitution was once more rewritten". My dad and his brother Tom were very close and rarely spoke of their actual political involvement. Tom was to join the Old Dublin Brigade of the IRA and Dad became involved with the GAA in the city. When the time came I was to follow a similar path, though in my case, the circumstances were different.

My mother, Frances (Fanny) Madden, came from Ballyhahill,

West Limerick. Her father had died from pneumonia two months before she was born, the youngest of eight children. Her father and mother had taught in the local national school in Ballyhahill. Mam was the dominant force in our house, making most of the major decisions. She had a great sense of humour but she remained strict in our upbringing. She had strong religious beliefs and we had to toe the line in that regard.

Mam went to boarding school and completed her secondary education by spending a year in Ring College, an all Irish-speaking college run by Seamus O hEochaidh, an Fear Mor, a noted gaelic scholar. Afterwards she spent six months teaching in Adare, Co Limerick, but teaching life held no great attraction for her. She found herself drawn inexorably towards Dublin, which she had visited from time to time, and found exciting compared to the quiet of country life. Her brother, D.J. Madden, who had strong Cumann na nGael ties, and was later to become a Fine Gael TD for West Limerick, yielded at last to persistent pestering by his younger sister, and succeeded in getting her an apprenticeship in McBirney's drapery house, off O'Connell Street. She worked there for a couple of years until a better job came up in Gorevan's drapery house in Camden Street, which she took. She was later to be made buyer of the millinery. The hours were long and the wages at the time were small, but other trades and professions were equally poorly paid. In 1913 matters came to a head when James Larkin, who had founded the Irish Transport and General Workers Union to cater for all working people, gave an order to the tramway workers to abandon their trolleys on Sunday August 26, the first day of the Horse Show.

The Show was one of the big social events of the year. Deprived of public transport, those who supported the Show had to walk to the RDS. Larkin organised a mass rally in O'Connell Street to take place the following Sunday, 31 August. The authorities banned it but Larkin vowed to speak at it anyway. A huge crowd poured into O'Connell Street on that Sunday morning to see whether he would keep his word; Mam went along out of curiosity. She remembered with great clarity the roar that rang out when Larkin, disguised as a bearded clergyman, stepped out onto the balcony of the Imperial Hotel. Just as he began to speak, he was dragged back into the room by the police. That was the signal for the police to charge into the crowded street, wielding their batons, and the brutality which followed left hundreds with serious injuries.

When the tramway workers refused to sign a pledge that they would not join Larkin's union, this precipitated the General Strike which dragged on through the winter and into the early months of 1914. The strike and the behaviour of the police on Bloody Sunday did have one positive result: it led to the formation of Connolly's Citizen Army. The bulk of the recruits were Dubliners and they were to form the backbone of the forces that fought in the 1916 Rising in Dublin.

Social life in the city was non-existent for dad and mam during their courtship days. There were frequent gun battles and with curfew from midnight to five in the morning, movement around the city was a prime risk for those who attempted it. Sean O'Casey captured the mood of the time in his *Autobiographies* when he wrote, "Armoured cars clattered through the city, lorries caged with wire and crowded with Tans pointing guns at everyone's breast cruised through the streets; and patrols with every rifle cocked to the last hair crept along the kerb. Every narrow lane seemed to be the dark, dazzling barrel of a rifle . . ." The infamous Black and Tans, hated even by the British soldiers, made life a misery for the people of Dublin and elsewhere as they carried out atrocities at will.

The year before the Treaty was signed, my dad and mam married and went to live in Munster Street off the North Circular Road, not far away from Mountjoy Jail. My sister Maire was born in December 1920, and mam told her in later years that when she was born, bullets were flying around the house. The city was still in turmoil. There were frequent raids by police on houses suspected of harbouring Republicans and the much hated Black and Tans gave the police backing in manpower. A gun-battle had broken out near Cross Guns Bridge, not a great distance from our house, and my dad told us of the fear he felt when bringing the local doctor around back streets, to help in the birth of my sister. The *Irish Times* that day reported how 150 soldiers from the Berkshire Regiment came back to barracks from the Theatre Royal and were in truculent mood. As they walked along Burgh Quay they shouted "Down with Sinn Fein" and "Down with de Valera". When they reached their barracks in Portobello the real trouble began as crowds gathered, and the troops were subjected to jeers and stone throwing. The sequel was inevitable: the troops charged along Montague Street, nineteen people were badly injured, and a van driver and a young domestic servant were killed. By the standards of the time, the casualties were not high.

The Treaty was signed in December 1921 and my brother Seamus was born around the same time. Dad continued to work but his wages were small; his main income depended on commission on sales of mineral waters, and Dublin at the time was not very mineral-water conscious. Fate stepped in at that stage and made a major decision for him; the firm he worked in went out of business. The entire premises, along with others in Henrietta Place, was completely gutted by fire. My dad was out of a job.

Dublin was a sorry sight after six years of violence, and O'Connell Street was still largely in ruins while many government offices were surrounded with sandbags. Business life was in chaos and the prospect of dad getting another job was really hopeless. My parents were realistic about their circumstances. They just could not survive with dad out of a job. Mam made the decision to return to Limerick to her relatives. Dad had contacts in Nash's Mineral Waters in Newcastle West and learned of a vacancy on the sales staff. Mam was anxious to settle in Limerick and when dad accepted the job in Nash's they decided to set up home in Newcastle West. I was born in May 1923 and my brother Michael arrived one year later.

I retain only very vague memories of my childhood in Newcastle West. In later years I spoke to my mother about a couple of recurring memories. I remembered sitting in a pram while a big sheepdog sat close by. She told me it was her practice to put me sitting in a pram outside the door of the house, and we did, it seems, have a dog of the kind I had mentioned. My second recurring memory was about funny men wearing masks, and I ran in terror from those funny faces peering into our living room from the street. Mam identified them as the "Wren Boys", who were a common sight in the town on St Stephen's Day. My old friend Sean O Siochain still brings back that memory every time I hear him sing "The Boys of Báir na Sráide", who as the song goes, "went hunting for the wren".

Dad travelled a lot in the course of his business for Nash's and made frequent visits to Dublin. Life was gradually returning to normal in the capital city and much of the desolation of the previous years of turmoil and strife had been cleared away under the Irish Free State. Many of the well-known buildings, such as the Custom House and the General Post Office, were rebuilt and O'Connell Street, which had borne the bulk of the battle, had a complete facelift. Business life in the city had also improved and there was a noticeable air of hope and

An early photograph of the Coalisland John Boyle O'Reilly GFC. Back row, third from right, is my uncle Tom. Front row, second from left, is Bertie Donnelly, one of Ireland's greatest cyclists, and third from left is my dad.

The house on South Quay, Newcastle West, Co. Limerick, where I was born.

optimism about. My dad's trips to Dublin had a happy outcome when
he was offered a very attractive job by a leading soft drinks manufacturer. He immediately returned to Newcastle West and when my
mother heard the details of the job offer, she agreed to him taking it.

Dad's next problem was to find a suitable house in Dublin and again
luck was on his side. Dublin Corporation had built a huge scheme of
houses in the Fairview-Marino area. The houses were tenant-purchase
and they were built to ease the terrible housing problem in the inner
city. The new houses were a model of their kind, three bedrooms,
living-room, dining-room, kitchen and bathroom. Many of the unfortunate people living in overcrowded tenements in Gloucester Street,
Parnell Street and other inner city areas availed of the chance to move
away from their miserable existence. The houses were one-third sub-
sidised by the state, one-third by the Corporation and the tenant paid
the balance at a reasonable rent. The scheme was the pride and joy
of Dublin Corporation and was to be the forerunner of other such
developments around the growing capital. But like all good schemes,
there were drawbacks, not the least being the human element, and
the Fairview-Marino scheme was to be no exception. Most of the
families housed still had relatives living in the inner city and contact
had to be maintained but that could only be done by walking to the
nearest tram route and taking a tram to town. A trip of that kind
cost money and time, and pounds, shillings and pence were in short
supply. It was felt that "living in the country" in their new houses
was too far removed from their relations, so the trek back to the inner
city began and many of the new fine houses were left vacant.

The population of Dublin was increasing rapidly with people
arriving daily from outside counties, adding to those who had already
gained employment, and who had married and taken up residence.
They too were living in overcrowded accommodation and trying to
raise families. The new housing complex in Fairview and Marino was
a godsend and civil servants, teachers, Gardai and tradesmen quickly
availed of the chance to become tenants. In October 1926 my dad
paid a small deposit on a house in Fairview Avenue and shortly afterwards the family left Newcastle West and took up residence in our
new home, which was only a stone's throw from the main road to
the city, served by a regular tram service. My dad's business brought
him into contact with licensed vintners and that led him to becoming
involved with a new hurling club which had come into existence,

Outside our house with Mam in Fairview Avenue, prior to heading off to school with my brother Michael.

Young Irelands, the president of which, James McEvoy, lived a short distance from our house.

The Young Irelands club was founded on 23 October, 1923, at John O'Brien's public house on the corner of Liffey Street and Bachelors Walk, Dublin. Its members consisted of players from the Grocer and Rapparees clubs. Thirty-nine members attended the inaugural meeting. The first Chairman was Paddy Kenefick; Philip Kennedy was team captain; Pat Conway was elected Secretary; Dan Canny was the club Treasurer. Two teams were affiliated, Senior and Junior in Dublin competitions. As the club grew in strength it attracted players and supporters from practically every county. On its first appearance in the senior championship at Croke Park on Sunday 9 March 1924, the club played Faughs, beat them 4-2 to 3-2 and went on to qualify for the final, but they were narrowly beaten by a very strong Kickhams team. The first honours did not come their way until 1927 when they won the Intermediate championship. On that team were Phil Kennedy and Willie Conway, whose sons, Phil and Willie, were to win championship honours with the club forty-seven years later. The lack of a club ground and the failure of the club itself to concentrate on under-age players in order to build up its playing strength, were the prime reasons why the club is not as formidable today as it was during the 1930s and 1940s.

Dad's involvement with Young Irelands took on a new dimension. He arranged for players, who were unable to train early in the evening for important matches, to call to our house after work. A number of them worked in pubs and they trained after closing time. Most of the outdoor training took place in the "Circle", in Marino, a large local playing field used extensively by teams from Scoil Mhuire, Marino, and St Joseph's CBS, Fairview. That preparation paid off in 1932 when Young Irelands won the senior hurling championship title for the first time. My father was chairman of the club that year, and it was a great feather in his cap. Young Irelands beat UCD in that final and I sat on the sideline in Croke Park, collecting the broken hurleys which would be put to good use by my playing pals. The club had many top players, intercounty stars such as Charlie McMahon, a very imposing figure because he wore a black patch on the side of his head to cover a patch where a "ricochet" bullet had lodged during the "Troubles".

At seventeen years of age, Charlie had been involved with the

Dublin Brigade of the IRA in the raid on the Custom House on 25 May 1921, led by Oscar Traynor and Harry Colley. The buildings were completely gutted and valuable documents and records, useful to the British government, were destroyed. The IRA party came under fire from the British Army, who had arrived on the scene, and in the subsequent exchanges Charlie was hit on the head by a stray bullet. He was picked up by the British Army and brought to St George's Hospital (later renamed Bricin's Hospital) where his wound was dressed by the doctor, who informed him that the Army were calling back to imprison him. Charlie, grateful for the hint, slipped out of the hospital and returned home. He continued to serve the cause but suffered from blackouts. In 1925 he was operated on by Surgeon William de Courcy Wheeler, who removed the bullet from his brain. A steel plate was made, covered in black leather, which Charlie wore on a headband as a protection during games. He wore a cap playing matches and always looked a rather fearsome figure. He went on to play with Dublin and helped them to win the All-Ireland title in 1938.

There were other well-known household names on that successful Young Irelands team, such as Mick Hough and Christy O'Brien of Limerick All-Ireland fame, Tommy Treacy, All-Ireland winner with Tipperary in 1937, Eddie Byrne and Dan Dunne, All-Ireland winners with Kilkenny, Sylvester Muldowney, Joe Bannon, Eugene Coughlan, Mattie Bruton, Mick Cleary and Brendan Kenna. The team trainer and masseur was "Joxer" Kavanagh, who was also associated with O'Tooles Football Club in Seville Place. Joxer's son James was a brilliant hurler with Crokes, and is now Titular Bishop of Zerta and Auxiliary Bishop of Dublin. When I joined Eoghan Ruadh hurlers and O'Toole's footballers, Joxer was trainer and masseur for major competitions. Young Irelands beat UCD in that 1932 decider by 4-2 to 2-2 in a very exciting game and much of that success was attributed to the hard work and special training undertaken by the players operating from our house in Fairview Avenue.

The transition from country life to that of the city presented no real problems for our family. We loved it. Mam dispensed justice in our house, she was a strong-willed person and we had to answer to her for our wrongdoings. She was an ardent Republican and both herself and dad were great admirers of Eamon de Valera. Dad soon became a supporter of Fianna Fail and joined the local Tomás O Cleirigh cumann. My sister Maire and I were to make contributions later on

at concerts and social evenings staged by the cumann. Maire recited
Irish poetry and I sang. Mam was a great lover of ceili and set dances,
and we often had set dances in the house at Fairview; she played the
melodeon.

Most of the boys and girls we grew up with had parents who were
born outside of the city but who were very much part of Dublin life.
Money was scarce. There was a lot of unemployment and social assistance was virtually non-existent until the government brought in the
1933 Unemployment Assistance Act. Payment started in 1934 and it
proved a boon for those families who were desperate and in need. The
Act meant that a single man received 9 shillings (45p) per week; a
man and his wife 13 shillings (65p); with one child 14 shillings (80p);
with three children seventeen and sixpence (87½p) per week; four
children nineteen shillings (95p) per week and five children one pound
(100p) per week. The amounts look small compared to today's values,
but families had to survive on what they got in those far-off days,
even though for some it meant living in dire poverty. The introduction
of that particular piece of legislation helped to relieve the pressure on
the St Vincent de Paul Society, who were always very much in demand.
Dublin people are very proud people and do not like to impose on
others. Much tact had to be used in order to help those whose needs
were greatest. Later in my college days at Colaiste Mhuire I was part
of a St Vincent de Paul group which distributed fuel vouchers in
tenements and houses in the inner city. The fuel vouchers, two
shillings and sixpence (12½p), were life-savers, and from time to time
we were reminded by the recipients to visit some unfortunate family
whom we had missed the previous week. "Don't forget to visit Nolans
on the second floor, she hasn't had a bit of coal for weeks", was a
familiar cry. We often found that fuel vouchers given to one family
were handed to another more desperate. There were some families
who were too proud to take St. V. de P. handouts and who would
sooner starve than be seen admitting a member of that Society into
their houses or homes.

It was Dublin of the gaslights, and nearly every tenement room or
house kept the picture of the Sacred Heart or statue, with the "colzoil"
lamp and red shade burning before it. If all else failed, there was
always prayer. Hard times called for harsh measures and many were
forced to beg, like the old woman who stood on the roadway every
Friday night, just beyond Grogan's Lane on Lower Fairview Avenue,

Young Ireland, Senior Hurling Champions, 1932—*Back row:* C. McMahon (wearing the black protection band), T. Ryan, D. Dunne, S. Muldowney, Ed. Ryan, D. Coughlan, Ml. Cleary, James McEvoy (President). *Middle row:* Joe Bannon, T. Treacy, P. Kealy, E. Lloyd, Ed. Byrne, M. Bruton, E. Hetherington, J. Moriarty, "Joxer" Kavanagh (Trainer), Sean O Ceallacháin (Chairman). *Front row:* B. Kenna, E. Ryan, Seán Óg, C. O'Brien, M. Hough, Ed. Maher.

not far from where we lived on the Upper Avenue. She stood on the same spot, her black shawl covering her head and shoulders, a frail lonely figure. She sang the same song, if you could call it that, winter and summer. There was no rhyme or rhythm to the tune, a dirge-like wail which went on endlessly, only broken off to acknowledge the coppers dropped into the outstretched hand which protruded from under the black canopy. The coins were quickly transferred to an inside pocket and she continued her singing.

I stood at the end of our avenue every Friday night waiting for my dad. It was paynight for him and paynight for me, his ten year old son. Dad invariably called into Gaffney's pub in Fairview for his nightcap. There were some nights he did not appear, as his "night-caps" stretched to one too many and I was forced to forgo my vigil. Pocket money at that tender age was soon converted into sweets in Mulligan's corner sweet shop; if you wanted to buy the *Hotspur* or *Beano* or *Wizard* it meant a trip to Gogan's shop at the corner of Fairview Avenue. There was a great variety of sweets to choose from, my favourites being NKM toffees (ten a penny), Bull's Eyes, Lucky Balls (they had a farthing or maybe a halfpenny inside), Liquorice Lines, or Peggy's Leg, which cost only a halfpenny. You could call to Johnston Mooney and O'Brien's bakery shop in Marino Mart for "gur" cake; that delectable fruit cake, laid out on a slab, could be bought for as little as a halfpenny or penny a slice. Sometimes the slab had a covering of pink icing which added immeasurably to the taste. Mam was not too keen on spending money on "gur" cake, she said it was made from bakers' leftovers, but for growing boys out playing all day, it was a feast.

Mam was doctor, nurse and adviser on all kinds of problems. Cuts and bruises she treated with the penny tin of antiseptic ointment, and she also used iodine which stung the blazes out of you, and you had to hold back the tears as she applied it, with the comforting words, "be a brave boy now". For other ailments there was the popular Mrs Cullen's Powders, a panacea for all kinds of ills and disorders including "complaints peculiar to women". Vaseline soothed every-thing from a pulled muscle (there were no hamstrings then) to sunburn.

Milk was delivered to our avenue by a local milkman, Paddy Hughes. He had a horse and cart, and on it a large chromium milk churn. Paddy would pour the milk into family jugs and he always gave a "tilly" for the cat, a "tilly" being an extra squirt of milk or in another sense, the thirteenth of a baker's dozen. Coal was supplied by bellmen, with weighing scales, and you bought it by the weight required. There was always the familiar cry of "Co-al, Co-al Blocks" in the neighbourhood and a bell on the horse's harness would alert people that the coalman was on his round. Friday was fishday and we had a visit from the fish woman, wheeling a pram with the fish laid out on a bread board, "borrowed" no doubt from Johnston Mooney's or Kennedy's Bakeries. There was no mistaking her loud Dublin accent as she called out "Howth Herrins, Dublin Bay Herrins, Lovely bit of Mackerel and White-nen".

There was plenty to occupy us in our neighbourhood. You could whip a spinning top along the path and force people to hop out of the way, or roll marbles along the gutter or bowl a hoop to the local shops, if sent there by your mam or dad. The hoop was a discarded bicycle wheel, and if you managed to get one with a tyre still on it, it was luxury stuff, it made very little noise on the path. As we grew older the games changed. The girls played "Piggie Beds" on the paths with squares or circles marked out in chalk, and you hopped on one foot, tipping the "Piggie" (normally a shoe polish tin box filled with stones or clay) from one square to another. If you tipped the "Piggie" into the wrong square you lost your turn or you were out of the game. I must confess the girls were more skilful at it than the boys. We had a favourite game too, "Mind the Thread". Two boys, one at each side, would sit on the path holding an imaginary thread between them. It was held about six inches off the ground. The game would start as a man or woman came walking by and as soon as they came near us, we would start shouting "Ah, Mrs, mind the thread". Normally, the poor woman would lift her leg, thinking there was a thread on the ground, and she would hop over the thread. Most of them knew they were having their legs pulled and they would enter into the spirit of the game, and go through the motions of hopping over the imaginary thread. "Relievio" was another popular game. Half of the gang would go off and hide, and the other half would have to search them out, and once tapped on the shoulder, you brought your discovered opponent back to the "den", a specific lamppost. When you heard the cry "All in, all in, the game is broken up," you knew someone had broken the rules, and the game was at an end. "Follow the Leader" was another game we used to play. You followed the leader and did everything he did, kicking rubbish bins, ringing doorbells or knockers, running into gardens and out again. By the time the last boy, at the end of the line, got to the hall door, the owner of the house stood waiting, and you got a clip on the ear or a kick on the backside.

Football, hurling and cricket were the popular sports. There was always a supply of hurleys in our house, if spares were needed. Hurleys broken at matches by Young Ireland players were given to us. Paddy Hudson's father was a carpenter, and he pared the broken hurleys to size. As soon as my brothers Seamus and Michael and I appeared on Fairview Green, it was a signal for the Clarkes, Dessie and "Lal", and the Ellises, Paddy (Scrapper) and Peter, to appear along with Tim Rigney, the brothers Shields, John and Jim, Des O'Donoghue, the Delaneys Mick, Fran and Tom, Billy and Paddy McGurk, Noel Bonner and Mick Healy. They were soon joined by Paddy Hudson, Paddy, Johnny and Mike Fogarty, Brendan O'Carroll, Miceal and Paudie Cosgrave, the O'Loughlins, Sean and Kevin and Paddy McCabe. We had the makings of two teams, and a game would be soon under way. Selecting sides took only minutes; the hurleys were placed in a pile, and one of us would be chosen to throw a hurley to each side until there were two small heaps; thus we had opposing sides. Other boys would join in and be allotted to the team losing the match at the time, to help correct the imbalance. The houses behind our makeshift goals (the "posts" were jackets placed in two heaps) were always very vulnerable, especially the Fogartys' house, and from time to time the odd window was broken, but as Johnny, Mikie and Paddy Fogarty were involved in the game, the repairs were carried out and no questions asked. We learned our hurling on the "Green". There was no such thing as coaching, we aped the big name players of those days who figured in big matches at Croke Park, and naturally no two boys could claim they were each that particular star — someone had to yield. We learned to pick and hit, both sides, solo and improvise generally and we became very proficient. Our matches on the "Green" were watched and followed with great interest by the neighbours. We played gaelic and soccer, with a ball supplied by dad, courtesy of Martin O'Neill, the Leinster provincial secretary, who gave it as a present around Christmas time. If a kickabout started on the road we had our own alarm system should a member of the Gardai make his appearance. The cry "L.O.B., L.O.B." (lookout boys) was a signal for a disappearance trick. We hid in side passages or behind high garden hedges until the danger had passed. If you were unfortunate enough to be caught playing football on the road by the limb of the law, he would dispense his own punishment, a clip on the ear or a toe in the backside (not too hard).

The older boys played cards on the "Green". A game called "Dawn" was very popular. The nine of trumps was known as "Big Fat" and the five of trumps as "Little Fat" and you played with partners. You had to give subtle hints to your partner about the suits or hand you were holding: "I should be digging the garden" (Spades) or "I hear Joan Carroll is getting married" (Diamonds) or "Did you ever have a pain here" pointing to your chest (Hearts). "Pitch and Toss" was very popular, mostly played by the older boys. Pennies were placed on a comb or a "feck", as we called it, and flicked into the air, and the winners were those who had bet on harps or heads, when the coins hit the ground. A "boxman" was used to look after the bets to ensure that nobody cheated. An American, the story goes, having watched a large "pitch and toss" school in the Phoenix Park, on a Sunday morning, said that Ireland was truly a very religious country. He had watched a group of men standing in a circle: one man stood alone in the centre and threw money into the air, and all would look up to heaven, and then they would look down to the ground, muttering in unison the word "Jaysus".

Visiting the seven churches and the annual Mission were part of the big events in our religious upbringing, and mam saw to it that we fulfilled our duties. We visited the seven churches on Holy Thursday as part of the Easter ceremonies. My brothers, Seamus and Michael and I were taken in charge by older sister Maire. Our first stop was at our parish church in Fairview, then on to North William Street on the North Strand. We walked to Gloucester Street Convent (which was always nicely decorated by the nuns) and then to the Pro-Cathedral in Marlborough Street. From there it was on to the quays to Capel Street Bridge, cross over to Adam and Eve's on Merchants Quay, and then to SS Michael and John some yards further on. We always finished at Church Street which had, without doubt, the most beautifully dressed altar, covered with flowers and candles, which left the most lasting impression on young minds. Sadly, the visit to the seven churches is no longer part of the present-day Easter ceremonies but in my growing up days we looked forward to it.

The annual mission in our parish church in Fairview was always very well attended and its success was invariably determined by the reaction to the Thursday night sermon on "Sin". Among Seamus's pals was a Protestant, John Beatty, who went along with us to the mission. Of course, he was told that he had nothing to lose, as all Catholics went to heaven while the Protestants went you know where. John looked forward to the Thursday night sermon if only to watch us squirm and shift in our seats, as the missioner called down the wrath of heaven on those boys who brought innocent girls up dark passages and lanes to do the "work of the devil". The good priest had us all quaking in our boots as he spelt out our fate and the punishment which would follow in the next world if we didn't mend our ways. John was enthralled with the sermon content but it left us bloody worried. John insisted on remaining with us till the close of the mission in the hope that some other "goodies" might emerge. Even when Seamus would go "missing" John came along with us and was able to put Seamus in the picture about that night's sermon, should he be questioned later by mam.

Sunday was a busy day in our house because it meant going to a hurling or a football game in the morning and to another game in the afternoon. Sunday morning also marked the visit of the old cornet player to the avenue. It was said he was an old soldier down on his luck, a Great War victim. He arrived early and took up his position on the roadway between two rows of houses and proceeded to give his rendition of "Roses in Picardy". It was a painful performance which did not endear him to the inhabitants of Fairview Avenue, especially those unfortunates who were suffering from hangovers or sore heads from the night before. I'm sure they echoed the sentiments of my dad, who, when the first unholy strains of that popular piece of the time broke the peace of the morning, cried out, "that son-of-a-bitch is back again". The cornet player was a shrewd man. He kept playing "Roses" in long bursts, stuttering in notes that were never intended by the composer. As the recital continued, bedroom windows opened and coins were flung at him. He didn't waste time once the coppers ceased to be thrown, he collected the coins and beat a hasty retreat, knowing that he would be back again the following Sunday. After Mass dad would cycle to a local match, myself perched on the crossbar. It was back for dinner and off again to a game in Croke Park. He collected the results for his radio programme and for the *Evening Mail*, for which he was to write a GAA column in later years. Holidays were a bit of a luxury but we did manage to spend a week in Bray or Greystones and on those trips dad would insist on a swim before breakfast. Every morning he went through the same ritual of chasing Seamus from one end of the beach to the other to get him into the water — Seamus hated the cold water.

Having country relations was very useful, and mam would pack us off to Ballyhahill to her sister Gretta, who taught in the National School in Glin. After a spell there we headed off to Rathkeale to her brother David, a farmer and a publican in the town. My brother Michael and I spent long summer months in the company of the Maddens and Foleys, my other cousins in Rathkeale. One of my most memorable holidays was on Ned Cregan's farm in Ballyshane, with his brothers Jim and Mike, and sisters Maureen and Ita. I also got the fright of my life on that holiday. It was during milking time, and I ran to open the gate of the farmyard to allow Ned drive in on his motor-bike. As I ran towards the gate, one of the cows charged at me so I ran hell for leather and jumped into a ditch which was covered in nettles. I must have howled for an hour as Ita and Maureen tried to comfort me. Ned won an All Ireland senior hurling medal with Limerick in 1934. His son Eamon carried on the family tradition and won an All Ireland with the county in 1973, and later became the Limerick senior hurling team manager. But I spent many an enjoyable evening pucking a ball around a nearby field in Ballyshane with Ned, one of Limerick's great defenders. Then it was back to Newcastle West for a spell with the Cremins and my Aunt Theresa where we idled away the long summer days. Looking back on those years revives pleasant memories of happy, carefree days when a postal order for two shillings and sixpence (12½p in present value) would last a whole week or even longer. Your range of purchase might have been restricted, but what you got was marvellous value for money.

Chapter 2
Schooldays

I started my schooling days with my sister Maire at Scoil Mhuire, Marlborough Street, and went from there to nearby Scoil Colmcille, also an all Irish-speaking school. My mother loved the Irish language and Irish dancing and she taught us patriotic songs and recitations. Her favourite party piece was "The Old Fenian Gun" which she recited with suitable gestures. We daren't laugh during those recitals; she took it all very seriously. For some reason best known to herself, she decided to send me to Scoil Colmcille and my brothers Seamus and Michael to Scoil Mhuire, Marino. I must confess I spent a very unhappy time in Scoil Colmcille, although mam had told us on many occasions that the happiest days of our lives would be spent at school. That may have been true during my secondary education at Colaiste Mhuire, Parnell Square but it did not apply during my national school stint.

The principal was a Kerryman, yet he was different in many ways from those from the kingdom I was to meet later on in life. I spent four years in his classes along with thirty other boys and on leaving, I danced a little jig going out the school gates. He was christened "Caner" and he certainly lived up to his nickname. He was a teacher given to strange impulses and decisions. One of his silliest instructions was to order the class to learn the catechism by heart during the summer holidays. Ours was not the small penny catechism but a very thick translation so it would have taken a lot of hard learning. On our return from holidays "Caner" could find only one boy of the thirty pupils with any knowledge of the catechism answers. So the rest of us were marched down to "Seomra na gCotai" where he gave each of us six biffs with the cane, breaking three canes during the punishment session. The next day some of the parents of the punished boys arrived at the school to lodge protests and threatened to report him to the Department of Education. There were other occasions when he punished boys cruelly for small indiscretions and sent them home with swollen hands and fingers. It was an era when corporal punishment was fully administered and accepted unflinchingly. There was no control and some teachers who overstepped the bounds of normal behaviour got away scot free.

I entered for the boys' solo singing at Feis Atha Cliath. On the day of the competition "Caner" insisted that I sing the two chosen songs for the benefit of the class. He stood at the back of the room while I tried manfully to sing the songs seriously. But human nature being what it is, I just couldn't stop giggling at some of the faces being made at me. "Caner" marched down the room, grabbed my arm and pushed me back into my seat with the warning "don't you put your nose near the Feis this evening". When I arrived home after school and told my mother about the teacher's warning, she was furious. "You are going to sing at the Feis, I paid your entry, he didn't and that's that." My mother brought me to the Feis that evening and in the Round Room of the Mansion House I competed against at least twenty other boys from various schools. I won the competition, helped no doubt by the fact that I had chosen the harder of the two song choices, the only entrant to do so.

Twelve months later I was back again at the Mansion House competing in the Boys' Solo singing competition, which I again won. A few days later the manager of the Gaiety Theatre called to the school and asked the principal if the young boy (mise) who had won the solo singing competition would like to sing on the Gaiety Show. I was thrilled at the suggestion. The principal asked him if the songs he wanted sung were to be Irish songs. The manager told him he hadn't Irish songs in mind, they would have to be popular songs of the time. The principal exploded. He told the unfortunate man in no uncertain terms that no pupil from his school, an all Irish-speaking school, would stand on the Gaiety stage and sing English songs. Without further ado he ordered him off the school premises. When I arrived home from school that day and told my mother about the visit of the man from the Gaiety, she nearly lost her temper. She then and there decided to bring me to the Gaiety herself and take up the offer. But my tears and pleadings won the day. I mentioned to her that I would have to bear the brunt of "Caner's" anger if I went against his wishes. It was only in later years did I wonder had I turned down the chance of becoming a famous singing star. Dad brought me to Dr Vincent O'Brien, the Musical Director at Radio Eireann, who after hearing me sing recommended that I join the Gardiner Street choir, under the direction of his son Oliver. This I did for twelve months. I don't know if it helped my singing voice, but I do know I learned a lot of new hymns.

The Eucharistic Congress of 1932 was an occasion I have never forgotten. Scoil Colmcille had no special plans for it, unlike all the other schools in the city. My brothers Seamus and Michael had to get new white trousers and shirts for the big day, so mam got a similar outfit for me to wear, and I went along with the other boys from Scoil Mhuire, Marino to the Phoenix Park. It was to be a sight never to be forgotten. There were hundreds of thousands facing the huge High Altar. The Congress had opened in the Pro-Cathedral in Marlborough Street on the Wednesday and there had been Pontifical High Mass on Thursday and Friday with ceremonies in the evening in Phoenix Park. We went there on the Saturday. There was a choir of 2,700 boys and girls, led by the famous Irish tenor John McCormack, who gave a wonderful rendering of *Panis Angelicus* during the High Mass. I had never seen so many priests gathered together in the one place, thousands of them in white vestments. We couldn't get a tram home to Fairview after the ceremonies so we walked home, buying chips on the way with our tram money. I performed the same walking feat many years later with my wife Ann, and children, Finin, Caitriona and Sinead, when Pope John Paul II made his historic visit to our shores in 1979.

My schooling did have one redeeming feature: it gave me my taste of radio broadcasting on 2RN, at the tender age of twelve. Mr O Cathain was asked to provide a small choir for a programme on *Children's Hour*, which was broadcast from 5.30 pm to 6.30. The choir consisted of Sean O Ceallaigh, Mairtin O Broin, Sean O Conghialla, Miceal O Colla, Brian Mac Aindreis, Seamus O Ciosain, Cian O Cathain, his sisters Eithne and Niamh and myself. We fulfilled other engagements on radio programmes in *Children's Hour*, including Irish plays for young listeners. I was asked by the then station announcer, Mairead Ni Ghrada, to appear with her sons, Briain and Seamus, in a few of her plays, in English and Irish. In 1935 I had the part of the young

St Patrick in a play written by her, and my coach and tutor was Ian Priestly Mitchel. (Ian later became synonymous with the Irish Hospital Sweepstakes request programme.) Mairead was a wonderful lady, kind and helpful, apart from being one of the finest newsreaders ever employed by the broadcasting authorities. She retired from her job in 1935 but she continued to serve the station well with her plays in Irish and English for many years after. She was also the lady who gave my father the opportunity of becoming a well-known radio voice.

I left Scoil Colmcille for the last time in the summer of 1936. I didn't meet Mr O Cathain again until many years later when he came into my sports shop in Talbot Street. He was going to Canada to take up a teaching position. I wished him luck! 1936 ended on a high note for me when I was sent on a Coiste na bPaiste holiday to the Kerry Gaeltacht. The scheme was the brainchild of Miceal O Maolain and Seamus O Tallamhain, prominent members of Conradh na Gaeilge. It gave young Dublin boys and girls an opportunity, a marvellous one at that, of improving their knowledge of Irish. One of my local playing pals, "Lal" Clarke, and I were sent to Fearan, near Ballyferriter, where I stayed with the Buidleir family. Staying with me, also from Dublin, was Noel Mahon, a noted boxer and a member of the CBS Boxing club. One afternoon he was showing me how he once knocked out an opponent. He demonstrated the blow, swung a right and caught me flush on the chin and put me on my back. I certainly believed every word he told me after that about his boxing prowess in the ring!

We spent our mornings at the local school learning Irish under Miceal O Concubhair. The afternoons were free to swim, fish or go climbing. The Buidleir family were really wonderful and they made sure our holiday with them was enjoyed to the fullest. I recall buying snuff for the *bean a' ti* in a shop in Ballyferriter, as a gesture for her many kindnesses to us, for she treated us like her own sons. One of my treasured memories of that holiday was a visit to the Blasket Islands by boat from Dun Caoin to the famous Peig Sayers, who lived on the island. She made us very welcome and gave us griddle cake, which she had just baked, with tea. Her cottage was spotless, a traditional Irish cottage with just the bare necessities. Peig was a very warmhearted woman who spoke only Irish to us. She gave us little mementoes of our visit.

In 1987 I returned to Fearan after all those years and met Seamus

Buidleir, son of the *fear a' ti*. Nothing had changed in nearly fifty
years. The Sacred Heart picture was still in place, with its little red
lamp in front; so too the old grandfather clock, still ticking away.
All the old memories came flooding back, those happy, carefree days
which had left so many vivid imprints on my mind. Seamus was able
to recall a lot of incidents and scrapes we had been involved in, some
of which I had forgotten. His parents had long since passed away, but
they left behind for me, a complete stranger, memories I have treasured.
Seamus Buidleir's own family have grown up and are working in
America and at home, but he hasn't changed. There is still that
twinkle in his Kerry eyes, and he looked so innocent when he posed
a parting question in his native tongue: "will the Dubs ever catch up
with us in football?"

It was in the natural order of things that I should go to Colaiste
Mhuire, Parnell Square, for my secondary education; the College had
become the choice for most of the boys leaving Scoil Colmcille. It
was established in 1931 as the first all-Irish post-primary school for
boys in Dublin. Among the people who figured very prominently in
the foundation of Colaiste Mhuire were Earnan de Blaghd, Minister
for Finance at the time, General Dick Mulcahy and John Marcus
O'Sullivan, also government ministers. When the Christian Brothers
were asked to establish an all-Irish school in Dublin they responded
immediately and the government provided a building, 6 Harcourt
Street, as a temporary premises for the College. The house had been
the residence of Cardinal Newman during his time as provost of
St Mary's Catholic University. Because of this name, the name of
the new College became Colaiste Mhuire.

On 5 October, 1931, Colaiste Mhuire was officially opened. The
new building was blessed and a Mass celebrated in the College. On
the following day classes began, with eighteen pupils enrolled. Before
the end of term two classes had been formed. The principal was an
Brathair M.R. O Tathain and his assistant was an Brathair O Flaithile.
When the second year commenced, in 1932, seventy pupils enrolled,
three classes were formed in the College and two new teachers were
recruited — Tomas O Floinn, who later became Assistant Secretary
in the Department of Education, and Mairtin O Fearchair. In 1933
the government provided a new building for Colaiste Mhuire at
27 Parnell Square. By 1940 the number of pupils had increased to
300, and as the numbers increased Numbers 25 and 26 Parnell Square

Bishop James Kavanagh (right), Titular Bishop of Zerta and Auxiliary Bishop of Dublin, whose father, "Joxer" was in demand as trainer for Dublin and club teams, O'Tooles and Eoghan Ruadhs, chatting to An Br. P.U. O Néill, Ardmháistir, Coláiste Mhuire.

Two of my former teachers taken at a Coláiste Mhuire Past Pupils Reunion function — Padraig O hUadhaigh (left) and Tomás O Floinn (right), who later became Assistant Secretary in the Department of Education.

were added to existing accommodation. That continued until the College took possession of No. 28, in 1972, and an extensive school library was added. Colaiste Mhuire has currently over 500 pupils and since 1931 over 4,000 boys have received their education through the medium of Irish at the College. These past pupils are well represented in all walks of life, all over the world.

I entered the hallowed halls in the autumn of 1936 and it was to be my alma mater until I left to take up a job in 1940. Academically, I wouldn't rate with the great scholars the College has produced. I struggled through my Intermediate examination because I was more obsessed with hurling and football than with my studies. We had a wonderful teaching staff during my period there which helped. Ollamh Tomas O Floinn (The Toff) taught us English and I can still rattle off poems by Shelley, Wordsworth, and Milton, apart from Shakespeare, all a legacy of his industry and patience. Ollamh Padraig O hUadhaigh (Hookey) taught us Irish, and his methods helped me enormously in the writing of Irish plays for radio. My favourite Brathair was M.H. O Murchu (Franco) a Kerryman, who was in charge of games and also taught Maths, while Ollamh Seamus O Caomhanaigh (Chaveo), who hailed from Dingle was a wonderful Irish teacher and no mean footballer either. Completing the staff were Brathair T.C. O Murchu (Tich) for Latin and Science; Ollamh Diarmuid O Brosnachain for French and Art; and Ollamh Anraoi Saidleir, who was to join the staff later and taught Maths, French and English.

Presiding over the College was an Brathair M.R. O Tathain (Tats) a unique man in every sense of the word. If a student stepped out of line during classes, he was sent to "Tats" for punishment. A classmate of mine, Podge, was sent to "Tats" and arrived back holding his hands under his armpits in obvious pain. "Chaveo" was very concerned, insisted on seeing the injured hand and quickly realised that Podge was faking (he hadn't gone at all). "Chaveo" escorted Podge personally, and when Podge returned we knew he wasn't faking the pain from the strap.

Tats turned up now and again at our matches where he would use his superb vocabulary to chastise opposing players whom he felt were using unfair tactics against Mhuire players. I remember Domhnaill O Scanail benefiting from Tats' presence on one occasion in a hurling tie between Colaiste Chaoimhin and ourselves at Croke Park. The Chaoimhin full back was giving Domhnaill a lot of stick but Tats took

Coláiste Mhuire, Metropolitan Cup Winners, 1938. *Back row:* M. O Comhraidhe, D. O Scanaill, L. Garland, S. O Siocháin, P. Mac Óistin, S. O Sciatháin, M. O Loinsigh, C. O Broin, M. O Colgáin. *Middle row:* C. ÓhÉanáin, R. MacUráin, S. Brugha, F. O Fagáin, P. O Maoldomhnaigh, S. Prestage. *Front row:* B. O Braonáin, Seán Óg O Ceallacháin.

up a position behind the full back's goal and proceeded to berate him about his unsporting behaviour. The poor lad became confused as Tats kept up the harangue, and started making mistakes which Domhnaill made very valuable use of to pick off match-winning scores. I was pleased too because I picked off a few scores which also helped. Domhnaill went on to become a priest in the Dublin archdiocese, one of over seventy priests, many scattered all over the world, who were educated at Colaiste Mhuire.

We won the Metropolitan Cup in hurling in 1938, beating a very good St Vincent's School, Glasnevin side in the final. It was a memorable victory as the "Mhuire" had won very little by way of major trophies prior to that. St Vincent's had many great players, some of whom I was to play, both with and against, in later years. On that side was Gerry Glenn, who was to star on Dublin county teams, and with me on the Eoghan Ruadh teams; Con Martin, a marvellous dual player, and of course, an international soccer player. Included also were Paddy "Beefy" Kennedy, who was to join up with Young Irelands in hurling and Peadar Mackens in football and win an All Ireland medal with Dublin in 1942, John Newcomen, Iggy Handibode, the Cunningham brothers, the Hunts, the Darcys and Ned Dowling. St Vincent's produced marvellous teams around that time and we were perhaps fortunate that we had a number of the players which had won the Dublin Colleges Special senior hurling title in 1933. (That was captained by Peadar McMahon, who was later to make a major impact on the county scene with Young Irelands and O'Tooles in football). We had Finbar Fagan, a towering defender, who captained the side, and other stalwarts in Kevin Byrne and Mick Lynch, both of whom later played with the Kevin's club, Peadar Muldowney, Brendan Brennan, Sean Prestage, Michael Colgan, Seamus Brugha, Malachy Curry, Peadar Hueston, Liam Garland, Bob McGuran, Liam Skehan, Michael Weafar and Sean Sheehan. At fifteen, I was a bit young for senior colleges hurling but I managed to acquit myself favourably enough. It was a splendid final and the fact that we contained Gerry Glenn at midfield helped us to a narrow victory. It was my first important outing at Croke Park and I loved every minute of it. We had a very vocal supporters club, Tats had issued a stern warning that any boy who failed to turn up to support the team would incur his displeasure, and that was warning enough.

Colleges competitions kept us busy on Thursdays and Saturdays and I was also involved with the St Vincent's hurling club in Fairview. This club had been launched in 1931 by Fr Willie Fitzpatrick and Brother Ernest Fitzgerald; my dad was Chairman of the Dublin Junior Hurling Board at the time, and lived in Fairview, so he was involved in the original setting up of the club machinery. He was to assist the new club too at Board level, where his support was invaluable in those early years. St Vincent's started in the Fingal League, but because of transportation problems to that far-flung outpost it was decided in 1933 to apply to the Dublin County Board for permission to compete in their competitions. Naturally my dad was in a position to ensure that the St Vincent's application was supported. The club drew its players from around the Fairview-Marino area and I too became a member of the Juvenile team, coming under the influence of Fr Fitzpatrick, the driving force behind the club. We played on Sunday mornings and invariably met at the junction of Griffith Avenue and Malahide Road, where we were taken to other city venues. I moved on to minor ranks and won my first medal against Eoghan Ruadh in the final of the 1937-38 hurling league; that marked the end of my involvement with the club, for reasons I relate later in this book. It was a particularly good St Vincent's team, with the wily Chris "Budger" Kealy and Joe, his brother, Sean Shouldice, Sean McAuliffe, Dermot and Dan Hanratty, Liam McConkey, Billy McGurk, Andy Dwyer, Jimmy Shaughnessy, Kevin Moore, Eamon Foley and my brother Seamus. But the grounding we got in the finer points of the game was put to good use during those minor years, and quite a number of that team were to figure prominently on Dublin senior teams in later years.

They were busy times with not enough hours in the day to pursue all your favourite sports, and we had plenty of choices. Cricket was a popular game in the neighbourhood and it was played mainly in the "Circle" in Marino because of the wider expanse of the playing area. Brian Road had a particularly strong team which included the Byrnes, Sonny, Billy and Pat, George "Spud" Murphy, Peadar Doyle, James "G" McDermott, Joe McLoughlin, Bobby and John Hamill. My team from Fairview comprised the lads who played regularly on Fairview Green. "Spud" Murphy held the record of 86 not out and I was trying desperately hard to beat it. It was near tea-time and I had reached 80 and I was confident of passing Spud's record. My brother Michael appeared and roared at me, "Mam will kill you, the tea is over, so you better get home quick." Had he left it at that I would not have minded, but he kept harping on what my mam would do if I didn't make tracks for home. Spud Murphy slipped in a full toss, I skied the ball and Billy Byrne caught it. I was out, and gone was my chance of breaking Spud's record. The only reason I didn't kill my brother that evening was he was able to run faster than I — and that truly saved his bacon.

I quickly forgot my disappointment and challenged the Brian Road boys to a football match the following evening. No punches were pulled in those epic tussles and no referee was in charge to decide on rights or wrongs. It was a case of the fittest surviving and you had to take your bloodied nose or black eyes as part of the growing up process. Our Fairview Green team was a good one, and apart from the Clarkes, the Cosgraves, Paddy Hudson, the Fogartys, Mick Healy, the Ellises, the McDonnells, we had Bobby O'Neill and Charlie Walker, who lived on Fairview Green. Charlie was to become well-known later in life as a soccer team manager with St Patrick's Athletic, while Bobby developed into a star goalkeeper with Parnell's gaelic football team, with whom he served for many years. His two sons, Dermot and Alan, are now goalkeepers of stature in League of Ireland football. We also played against boys from Marino Green, Croydon Green and Aidan's Park, and survived.

I pass by my old stamping ground occasionally. The "Green" no longer rings to the whoops and hollers of young voices at play. There are no football or hurling matches being played and not a kid to be seen on the roads around the playing area. The Corporation has to cut the grass a couple of times a month, if not more, where once a blade wasn't let grow because of activity on it. To add insult to injury, the Corpo have now planted small plantations of trees, in the four corners of the playing patch, which will prevent generations in future years from playing football or hurling on the patch. You can well ask, as in the popular song, "where have all the children gone, long time passing". It's perhaps a sign of the times we live in. We had no television in our growing-up days, we made up our own games, not having the luxury of pocket money either, but we were happy and contented, and the word "vandalism" was unheard of.

In 1939 Colaiste Mhuire produced a marvellous team which carried off the Special Senior Colleges football trophy. We met old rivals, O'Connell Schools, in the final. The Mhuire side was strengthened by the inclusion of Sean and Martin Hely, and the team was captained by Micky Judge, a prolific score taker. All-round footballer Bobby Nutty, Paul O'Sullivan, Malachy Curry and myself completed the forward division. Goalkeeper was Frank Ryan, who was very prominent at the time with Home Farm, and he fronted a defence consisting of Kieran Cuddihy, Brendan Herlihy, Sean Moore, Kevin Byrne and Hugh McEntaggert, while Sean Hely and Mick Weafer were at midfield. It wasn't a particularly good O'Connells side that year and we won the game quite easily, 6-6 to 3-4; I had the good fortune to score 4-2. "Mhuire" had previously won that trophy two years earlier with the help of Colm Heenan, Finin Monaghan, Tom Comber, Charlie McDonnell, Joe Fagan, Gerry Scully and Seamus Lennon, all talented players. It wasn't until many years later in RTE that I was reminded of that particular match by well-known actor Brendan Cauldwell. I asked Brendan why he remembered the game so well. "Because I was the bloody goalkeeper," he said, "and I had to pick the ball out of the net six times, and you didn't help with your four." Brendan claimed he was only doing the school a favour, as they were short a goalkeeper, and he volunteered his services. The experience cured him of ever offering to be the "man in the gap" on later occasions.

The College figured prominently in Irish plays and competed in Cumann Dramaiochta na Scol. In 1939 we carried off first prize for a play *Hercules*, in which I played a part. The drama competition was held in the Peacock Theatre and at the end of a busy week, we were declared winners, much to our great delight. I was approached by Earnan de Blaghd and he invited me to attend the Abbey School of Acting. I said I didn't think my family could afford the course. He told me that there was no fee involved but that I could try it for six months. I spent two years in the School of Acting and it was to be the most rewarding period of my life. I learned voice production, voice projection, articulation, stage presence, make-up and all the ingredients which go into the making of a stage actor. The course was to prove invaluable to me later in my radio and television work. To help articulate words, you were given a small block of wood, measuring one inch by a half-inch, with a "vee" cut out of top and bottom. You placed the block of wood between your teeth, and you had to practise speaking with the block held between the teeth. You were made to persevere until such time as you spoke coherently, which wasn't an easy thing to do.

The Director of the School was Frank Dermody and he was assisted at times by Cecil Forde. Many well-known actors and actresses were to become products of the School during my spell there. Among them were Harry Brogan, a great pal of mine, who moved on to greatness on the Abbey boards and films, Kathleen Ryan (who starred in many fine films), Sheila Manahan, Maureen Kiely (later to marry Cyril Cusack), Joan Dalton (who also went on to join the Abbey Players, and was to wed Joe Linnane), Isobel Couser (who later joined the Gate Theatre), Sheila Carty, Eithne Dunne (who played with the Abbey Players, and later with the RTE "Rep" Company), and Peter Kavanagh, a brother of poet Paddy. We often had a visit from the Monaghan bard, who would bounce into the rehearsal room, which was adjacent to the Peacock stage, give a lecture on acting, the Abbey and playwrights and quickly disappear out the door again. My sister Maire won an acting scholarship from Scoil Caitriona in Eccles Street, and that was a boon to us, as we were able to perform our parts at home before going to the School that night.

Towards the end of the acting term it was the practice to put on excerpts from plays which would involve all the players, for the benefit of the Abbey directors. I was keen to play the part of Bartley in Synge's *Riders to the Sea* but the part was given instead to Harry Brogan. Harry knew I was disappointed but told me not to worry. On the night that the Abbey directors were sitting in judgement on our acting efforts, Harry told producer Frank Dermody that he was feeling the effects of a cold and he could hardly do justice to both Bartley in *Riders to the Sea* and Joxer in *Juno and the Paycock*; he suggested that I be given the part of Bartley. Dermody agreed. I also had the part of Donough in the *Whiteheaded Boy*. Later that night Lennox Robinson and Earnan de Blaghd sat in judgement on our efforts as we tried to impress them in our various roles. My sister Maire and I were not among those actors and actresses who were to go on and make a living from the stage, but then, we were the youngest players in the School, and I was still attending college. Both of us did use the good grounding we got at the Abbey School many years later when we became involved in amateur dramatics. The only privilege we had at the School was a free night at the Abbey itself. We were allowed to sit in the gallery and watch a production, provided of course, that seats were available. If not, we had to sit on the aisle steps. It was the time of the great Abbey players, F.J. McCormack,

Eileen Crowe, Arthur Shields, M.J. Dolan, Denis O'Dea, May Craig, Maureen Delaney, Willie O'Gorman, Fred O'Donovan, Eric Gorman, and of course my old pal Joe Linnane, with whom I was to renew old acquaintance many years later on radio.

One thing acting schools teach you is clarity of diction and the ability to pitch your voice. It teaches you proper breathing and voice control which is so essential for stage and radio careers. I must say I wince at times listening to some of our radio and TV presenters drawing in copious gulps of air before delivering their lines. Some of our newsreaders on radio and TV can change the pitch of their voices to capture the pathos of the story they may be reading, while others simply deliver in a monotone fashion regardless of whether the stories have a dramatic, joyous or sad content. It is very obvious listening to some programme presenters, on radio particularly, that they have not been given proper voice training or breath control, and can be heard daily, sucking in breath through the mouth instead of the nose, in quite irritating fashion. There is definitely room for improvement in that aspect of broadcasting on our national air waves.

War was declared on Sunday morning, 3 September, 1939 and the news was on everybody's lips coming from Mass. Incessant overnight rain had flooded parts of the city, augmented by a frightening intensity of thunder and lightning. The Oireachtas, recalled from the summer recess the day before, sat through the night before adjourning at 4.50 am on that Sunday morning, having passed the emergency legislation presented to it by the Taoiseach, Eamon de Valera. Dev told that august gathering that a "time of war" as defined in the Constitution, covered the emergency which then threatened the country. No one was prepared to argue against that interpretation of the circumstances, and legislation was quickly passed. When the news of the declaration of war gathered momentum, panic buying broke out all over the city and stocks disappeared quickly, much of it under the counters, to be sold subsequently at far higher prices. Elsewhere in the country the infamous Border was to be sharply defined, resulting in villages and houses being bisected between Northern Ireland and "Eire", as we were then known. The village of Pettigo in Co Donegal was to be divided in half, one side in a "war" situation and the other in an "emergency", the latter description undoubtedly one of the great euphemisms of the century.

My Limerick relations arrived at our house in Fairview for a quick snack before walking to Croke Park for the All-Ireland hurling final between Kilkenny and Cork. Frequent radio bulletins announcing that a state of war existed between Britain and Germany failed to dampen the enthusiasm of those with only hurling on their minds. The rain of the early morning had eased but the sky was leaden and the rumbling of thunder and distant flashes of lightning were only a foretaste of what was to follow after the game had started. The heavens opened and the rain began to cascade down in sheets, accompanied by thunder and lightning. I watched it all from the steps of the stand, where I sat beside my dad at the press box. In spite of the conditions the game was a thriller, and Kilkenny sneaked a win when Jimmy Kelly of Carrickshock fired over the winning point with a minute remaining, too late for Cork to save the match. Spectators left Croke Park after that 1939 final saturated to the skin. My country cousins fared much better, because we were able to borrow old clothes, trousers, jackets, socks, shirts from neighbours when our own stock had been exhausted, and they at least had dry clothes going home in the train.

In 1940 I suffered a major disappointment when Dublin lost the Leinster minor hurling championship title to Laois, on an objection. A few weeks earlier I had played on the Dublin minor football team which lost to Meath in the championship at Navan, so I was hopeful of better rewards with the hurlers. My club, Eoghan Ruadh, had selection of the minor county hurling team following our victory over Colmcille in the county final. Two of their players, Paddy O'Grady and Dan Kinnane, were asked by Ruadhs to attend at the Phoenix Park for training with the Dublin panel. Both O'Grady and Kinnane had played for New Irelands, who only had a senior team. They were persuaded to join Colmcille, who were building up a very strong club at minor level. When the team to play Wexford was announced, both of the Colmcille players were chosen on the selection; I was picked at left half forward. Wexford had a formidable team, which included Nick Rackard, Paddy Keogh and Padge Kehoe. Wexford were leading by a point in the closing stages, and I remember chasing after Nicky Rackard, who was soloing upfield with the ball on his hurley. I tapped the handle of the hurley and the ball dropped. I quickly scooped it up, moved away a few yards and lashed it over the bar for the equalising point. A few weeks later we beat them easily in the replay. We

The Dublin Minor Hurling team which lost the 1940 Leinster title to Laois on an objection. *Back row:* Tom Fitzpatrick (selector), Martin Healy, Paddy O'Grady, Dan Kinnane, Mick Wallace, Jim Whelan, Maurice Keane (selector), Sean Shouldice, Batt O'Rourke, Brendan McShane, Ned Maher (selector). *Kneeling:* Gerry O'Connor (selector), Chas. Darcy, Paddy Hudson, Sean McDonald, Dick Molumby, Kevin Matthews, Sean Hickey, Seán Óg O Ceallacháin, Paddy O'Grady, Brendan Casey.

Left: Earnán de Blaghd, on whose invitation I spent two fruitful years at the Abbey School of Acting.

played Kilkenny in the semi-final and won readily enough to qualify for the Leinster final against Laois. Now, Paddy O'Grady had been born in Kilmallock, Co Limerick on 4 July 1921, but his birth wasn't registered until April 1922 because of the "Troubles". When Paddy explained his worry about his birth registration to a well-known Board official, he was assured that his eligibility wasn't in question. Kinnane and O'Grady were picked on the Dublin team to play Laois in the Leinster final. It was considered one of the best Dublin minor hurling teams ever to represent the county. Charlie Darcy was in goal, the full back line was Martin Healy, Dan Kinnane and Batt O'Rourke; the half line, Kevin Matthews, Seamus Whelan and Paddy Hudson; midfield, Brendan McShane and Sean Shouldice; half forward line, Dick Molumby, Paddy O'Grady and myself; full line, Mick Wallace, Sean Hickey and Seanie McDonnell. We beat Laois comprehensively, 10-5 to 3-5 in a very one-sided contest. Full-back Kinnane was a towering figure, well developed, over six feet in height and looking older than his actual years. The Laois officials were obviously suspicious of Kinnane's credentials and decided to look up his birth details in the Custom House in Dublin, where they discovered that all was in order. It was only when they were doing a random check on the other Dublin players that it was noticed that O'Grady's birth was not on file, which led to a more detailed search, and the subsequent error of O'Grady's registration came to light. It must be said that the Laois officials acted perfectly within their rights in the matter, and did what most County Boards invariably do when checking on the legality of underage players.

Laois lodged an objection against Dublin on the grounds that Paddy O'Grady was an overaged player. The Laois objection was upheld at a subsequent Leinster Council meeting and Dublin had to forfeit the Leinster crown. When the matter cropped up for hearing at the following Dublin Board meeting the chairman, Sean O Braonain, said that those responsible for the selection of the Dublin team should have ensured the legality of the team. It was decided to summon the player concerned, officials of the Ruadh club (which had charge of the team) and the Secretary of the Minor Board to the following week's meeting. The Board heard the evidence concerning the constitution of the minor team for the Laois match, and the Board was satisfied that on the evidence tendered by Laois, Dublin had to admit guilt, although it was a technical error to have included Paddy O'Grady on the team.

By seven votes to four O'Grady, who stated that he believed the date of registration was the date of eligibility, was found not guilty of supplying false evidence to the Minor Board, and the Eoghan Ruadh club, who were responsible for the county selection, were exonerated. I can say there were bitter feelings in Dublin over the loss of the match, and the events surrounding it. Laois didn't help matters when they faced up to Antrim in the All-Ireland semi-final and were duly beaten by the Ulster champions, the first Leinster team ever to lose to Ulster opposition at that grade. Limerick hammered Antrim in the All-Ireland final that year. But it wasn't all gloom that year because in late September I was offered a job, which I promptly took.

Chapter 3
Work and Play

After the Intermediate exam I had gone into Fifth Year, which was the "rest" year before preparing for the Leaving examination. During the summer holidays my dad decided he wanted a new suit of clothes and dropped into Padraig O Glasain's store in O'Connell Street, which sold *earraí Gaelacha amhain* (Irish goods only) and was patronised by Irish speakers. Dad's knowledge of Irish was very limited but he believed in supporting goods of Irish manufacture. In the course of buying the suit, Mr O Glasain mentioned that he had that day advertised for a young apprentice. Dad immediately put forward my name for the job and Mr O Glasain suggested that I appear for an interview the following day. When the interview was over Mr O Glasain offered me the job with starting wages at five shillings (25p) per week. The wages were the norm for those times, but young girls being employed in the drapery trade were charged apprentice fees by some employers. In the case of O Glasain's, young girl apprentices were also paid five shillings a week, but they were told that ten shillings was being deducted per week to pay for their training; we got a five shillings increase in wages every year.

The first thing I had to learn in my first week in the shop was the cost code for the purpose of marking up the prices of goods, shirts, socks, woollens etc. The code was simple enough; the letters "A Discovery X" represented numbers from 1-11 (A=1 D=2 I=3 S=4 etc.). When marking the cost of a shirt at 12 shillings and sixpence, you simply wrote AD/O and underneath you wrote the retail price of the garment (25% profit was added). The working hours were long, 9 am to 6 pm and on Saturdays 9 am till 9 pm. As goods became scarcer, the hours were shortened to 7 pm on Saturdays and 5.30 pm on week-days. But they were exciting times in those early years of the 1940s, and I enjoyed every moment. Mr O Glasain was a very pleasant and good humoured employer, and was also very efficient as a salesman. It was a house rule that if you were unable to please a customer in his choice of article, you called the "boss" over to deal with the prob-lem. As often as not, he sold the article which the customer had earlier turned down. O Glasain's shop, situated beside Kingstons in O'Connell Street, was also famous for kiltmaking. Many famous Pipe Bands wore O Glasain kilts, which were made on the premises, and we also made for individuals who wore the Irish kilt.

One such person was Claude Chevasse, a noted gaelic enthusiast who lived in Paris, and who had his kilts made by O Glasain. We had his measurements on file so it was a simple matter to have a kilt made up and ready for him when he called to the shop. A letter arrived from Paris one morning from Chevasse stating that he was coming to Ireland and he needed a new kilt. The day the letter arrived O Glasain was out sick and his wife took charge in his absence. She handed me Chevasse's letter and told me to make the necessary arrangements to have the kilt made up, which I promptly did. The following afternoon, a Saturday, was very busy but over the din of voices and cash registers came Mrs O Glasain's strident voice, "Sean, what did you do with that French letter?" Every head in the shop turned in my direction, as I immediately dived under my counter on the pretext of searching for something. The poor innocent woman again called out, "Sean, did you follow up that French letter?" as I quickly searched through my order book, found the letter and, holding it high for everyone to see, marched down the shop and handed it to her. A "French Letter" in those days had an entirely different meaning!

Despite the fact that coupons were required for all wearing apparel, nobody was prevented from buying goods if they failed to produce coupons. Our best customers were from the North and everybody vied to serve them because they slipped you a quarter pound of tea with every purchase. Tea was a very scarce commodity at the time, and could be bought on the black market in certain houses in the city at a pound a pound — it normally cost fifteen pence. Oranges and lemons had long disappeared from the shops; there were no ships available to bring them to our ports, because of the risks involved due to the war and because of the deliberate policy of economic pressure by the

British government, who could exercise almost complete control over Irish overseas trade. This pressure was designed originally to force the country to abandon neutrality, but it also arose from a natural resentment on the part of Britain at risking the lives of their seamen carrying supplies to a neutral state. Yet Irish beef and drink was being exported in large quantities to Britain, also canned rabbit and other meat products, which were vital to their existence. There were great fears in Northern Ireland that the supply of Guinness was to be cut off because of Britain's intransigence to our own needs on the supply of certain materials. The threat passed and the North got their Guinness. As the war went on more stringent laws were brought in affecting wearing apparel, in an effort to stretch supplies of material. Fewer pockets were allowed in suits and trouser widths were drastically reduced from 24" to 20", but there were ways of giving the customer an extra 2" on his trouser width by stitching a seam down the legs of the trousers, called a "flapping seam". There was also an acute paper shortage which eventually led to the wrapping paper used in shops being made from straw, which of course tore at the least amount of pressure. Ads appeared in the papers requesting exchanges of goods; a pair of shoes was bartered for tin goods, while women's wearing apparel disappeared from the shelves. Silk stockings were unobtainable: what small supply there was went under the counter. Artificial silk stockings replaced them at even higher prices, till eventually an enterprising firm brought in a lotion which could be painted on the legs to give the effect of stockings, but which unfortunately didn't stand up to rain showers.

We had no shortage of woollen suiting in O Glasain's. Foxford Woollen Mills supplied us with the orange and green kilt material and rugs. It became common practice, as suiting material became more scarce, for clothing manufacturers to use multi-coloured rugs as ladies' coating material. Old suits were turned and some of those firms provided a twenty-four-hour service. Despite all the shortages, the lack of foodstuffs, the curtailment of gas and electricity, the absence of proper transport (the trams had long ceased to operate), everybody went about their business and accepted their lot. No doubt the poor suffered, but the poor always will in those circumstances. There was no whinging or griping, you just accepted your situation.

In June 1940 the Taoiseach, Eamon de Valera, broadcast to the nation, announced the establishment of the Local Security Force and appealed for volunteers. By June 44,870 members had enrolled, and on the 22nd of the month the new force was divided into two sections; "A" to act as auxiliary to the Army proper, and "B" to assist the Gardai with auxiliary police duties. Training and control for both groups was placed in the hands of the Garda Siochana. I joined the "B" with my next-door neighbour, Paud Cosgrave, and we spent several nights per week patrolling from Fairview along the sea front to the Bull Wall, Dollymount. We had to check the doors of shops and premises to ensure that they were properly secured, and watch out in particular for anything which seemed out of place, such as "parachutes falling from the skies", etc. That followed reports that German pilots, who were engaged in aerial battles with the RAF (they could be seen at times on a sunny day from the top of Howth Head, but far out to sea) were seen to bail out. It was all very serious stuff.

One night, as Paud and I started our midnight patrol, we checked the door of Gogan's shop at the corner of Fairview Avenue (Larry, the son, does a bit of work on Radio 2, I believe) to discover it was unlocked. It was a great feather in our caps, and we immediately got in touch with the Gardai in Clontarf station. One hour later a Garda arrived on a bicycle "to take control of the situation". He praised us for our attention to duty and brought us into the shop. He asked us did we smoke, and we said we did. He went behind the counter and came up with a packet each of Sweet Afton cigarettes. "Off you go now, lads, on your round," said the very generous arm of the law, "I'll look after the shop," and away we went. Cigarettes were very scarce at the time and were "under the counter", given only to regular customers. I had often tried to buy cigs in Gogan's and always got the same answer, "We only have the Three Nuns — nun yesterday, nun today and nun tomorrow."

I remained a member of the Local Security Force until an event happened which made me change over to the Local Defence Force, under Army control. On the night of 31 May, a fortnight after my eighteenth birthday, a German bomber dropped three bombs in the vicinity of the North Strand and North Circular Road. Our house in Fairview shook with the blast. We rushed to the bedroom windows and watched flames shooting skyward. Our next-door neighbour, Jim Foley, a Garda, said the bombs could have fallen on Amiens Street railway station, and so it looked from our vantage point. I immediately put on my LSF suit, a blue denim jacket and trousers. Hundreds of people were already making their way towards the North Strand area, where flames had lit up the early morning sky. Between 1.28 and 2.05 am on that Saturday morning, four bombs had fallen, but the biggest bomb of all had fallen on the North Strand Road, straddling the tram lines at the city side of Newcomen Bridge. It was in that area that the most appalling damage was done. Only when I got to the top of Newcomen Bridge did I realise the horrific devastation which had taken place. Ambulances were dashing up and waiting, with engines running, to bring the dead and dying to hospitals. Children were running from houses nearby crying for their parents as the rescue workers worked frantically to extricate people from their fallen houses. Glass had strewn the streets and gas was escaping as masonry crashed into the road, creating more havoc for the ARP and rescue workers. People from nearby streets helped the nurses and doctors to comfort and calm the women and children; many took them to their homes.

Everybody wanted to help but it was a job for the men who had been specially trained for such emergencies, and we were told to keep everybody who was not in the rescue services behind ropes. A Garda asked me if I knew where Dr Cusack lived. I made my way to the doctor's house at the corner of Charleville Street, opposite the Strand cinema. Dr Cusack had been working non-stop at the scene and had been relieved for a brief spell. I gave him the message that more bodies had been taken out of the rubble and more could not be moved until seen by a doctor. He asked me an extraordinary question, "Are they mortally obsessed?" Without wishing to delay the good doctor, I said, "I think so." I hadn't a clue what he meant and to this day I am still in the dark about the actual meaning of the question posed on that morning. I only presumed he meant were the people being taken out of the rubble already dead. Rescue work continued and at the final count, thirty-seven were killed. That number included the entire Browne family, Mary Browne (75), Harry, her son, Mrs Mary Browne (33), his wife, Maureen (7), Nan (5), Edward (3½), and Angela (2). There were other families wiped out in that terrible catastrophe, which left eighty badly injured. Twenty-five houses were destroyed and a further 300 made unfit for habitation. The noise of the explosions was heard as far away as Mullingar. I knew every shop on that particular stretch of road; I also knew the people who served in them and owned them, as I had passed them every day on my way coming from school. It was hinted that the pilots of the German bombers, chased by fighters over the Irish sea, dropped the bombs because they saw glints of water below them. A bomb fell on the Dog Pond in the Phoenix Park, again in error, beside water, while other bombs dropped in the city were not far away from water. The German government eventually paid the Irish government £325,000 in compensation for the loss of lives and for damage done to property in the North Strand area.

There were a number of sad twists to the losses of life in the bombing on that fateful May morning. Mr Patrick McLoughlin had removed his wife and children to 157 North Strand Road after a bomb had fallen on their home in Summerhill. Shortly after he left them to get some clothes from their old home, the big bomb fell on North Strand and Mrs McLoughlin and one of her children were taken to hospital. It could not be ascertained at the time whether Mr McLoughlin had returned with the clothing before the bomb fell, but his body and that of his two-year-old son were found in the debris. A man's body was taken from the roof of a cottage in Ossory Road. It was said he had been walking on Newcomen Bridge when the bomb fell, blowing him forty yards to his death. There were other stories too which emerged from that very sad occasion which helped to bring home to the people the horrors of war. More bomb shelters were erected in parts of the city; they were unsightly but very necessary. Thank heavens those shelters did not have to be used for the purpose intended, as they became distinct health hazards, being used as toilets by late night citizens. Business returned to normal in the city and there were no more bombings.

My brother Michael worked in the woollens in Clery's in O'Connell Street, while Seamus was in the Blackrock Tailoring Co in Chatham Street. My sister Maire was well established in the Irish Folklore Commission, which had its premises at the time in UCD, Earlsfort Terrace. Denis Guiney, who had an extensive drapery store in Talbot Street, caused major shock waves in drapery circles in the city when he bought Clery's of O'Connell Street in November 1940 for £250,000. In the months which were to follow he sold off all the goods in the store at virtually half price, and it was said, cleared the initial purchase price of that well-located store. He immediately introduced his low cost selling in the store, a policy which had paid off so handsomely in his original shop in Talbot Street. As the war progressed, goods became very scarce but Denis Guiney was able to use his great influence in procuring import licences from the government, and that preferential treatment allowed him to bring in a whole range of goods by ship. Clery's store kept many small, and indeed large, manufacturers in business in the city, who otherwise would not have survived because of the shortage of materials.

A well-known practice at the time was for a small shirt manufacturer to get samples of shirting in one department in Clery's and bring the samples to the buyer of the shirts in the same store. The shirt-maker would then get an order from the buyer for a full range of shirts, colours and sizes, etc. to be delivered by a certain date. The manufacturer would walk back to the shirting material department and give them an order to cover the making of the shirts already ordered from the shirt department. Once the material was delivered to the shirt maker he got on making up the order which was duly delivered back to Clery's. The same practice was followed by other manufacturers, who had to rely on Clery's for the goods which kept their factories open during the scarcity. Nylon stockings had replaced silk ones and Clery's had a big monopoly as they were able to import them in large quantities. Smaller stores like O Glasain's had to buy them from Clery's and resell them at their buying price. Mr O Glasain was eventually offered a chance of purchasing nylons. He placed a huge order for them, worth over one thousand pounds, which was a lot of money then, and they were delivered to the shop on a Friday evening. We spent a number of hours transferring them to the upstairs stock room. When the shop closed on the Saturday night, the nylons were safely locked away in the stock room. When the shop reopened on the Monday morning, not one nylon remained on the shelves. Thieves had broken in over the weekend and stolen every blessed one. Good work by Garda detectives eventually led to the capture of the thieves but the nylons were never recovered.

Two events of note happened to me in 1943; I was promoted to the Ruadhs senior hurling team, and I transferred from the LSF to the LDF, which had been handed over from the Garda to Army control in order to create a more military-type force for use in the event of an invasion, either by the Germans or the British. Patrolling along the sea front had become very mundane anyhow; a number of my pals had joined the Local Defence Force, and at least it offered more exciting prospects. The transition went smoothly; I presented myself at Company Headquarters in the old DWD Distillery on Richmond

Road, was given the army number 230265 and was allotted to "D" Company 42 Battalion, under Company Sergeant Tommy Wardlaw. The Company Commander was Matt Flynn, who lived near us on Shelmartin Avenue, Fairview. His Seconds in Command were Harry Wolverson and Jim Cullen. We spent weeks drilling and marching and quickly became proficient in the use of weapons. There wasn't a great choice of arms. Our issue was the old American Springfield rifle which used a 300 calibre bullet; later we got the Lee-Enfield with a 303 calibre bullet. Many felt that the old Springfield was more accurate because it did not have the normal V-sight at the tip of the barrel; instead you had to sight your object through a small peep-hole at the tip of the barrel. Naturally, both rifles had bayonets as part of issue. Slipping on a bayonet as part of arms drill didn't present any real problem, though you always had an inward fear that it might come unstuck at parade time. When the order came to "fix bayonets" you clipped it to the gun barrel (it took only a matter of seconds) before getting the order to "slope arms". There were times when the bayonet did get stuck on the "grip" at the tip of the gun barrel; when that happened, you were in trouble, as I found to my horror on one occasion. We had assembled in Griffith Barracks on the South Circular Road on Easter Sunday, prior to taking part in the Easter parade with the regular Army and the other services. My Lee-Enfield rifle had a worn bayonet "grip" and when we got the order to "Fix Bayonets", I found great difficulty clipping it to the gun barrel. Eventually it gripped but I wasn't happy that it was properly secured. Our platoon sergeant, Martin Kavanagh, kept scurrying up and down asking "Is everyone ready?" It wasn't the time to tell him that I wasn't happy with my "bayonet fixing". We got the order to "Slope Arms" and in that movement my bayonet shot off and hit the helmet of a colleague four rows behind; you could hear the clang a mile away. Sergeant Kavanagh was furious, "What bastard did that?" as he marched up the ranks to see which rifle was missing a bayonet. As he moved to the end of the column, my bayonet was quickly returned, and this time I clipped it on properly, just in time, before the sergeant came back down the ranks. All was ready when the order came to move off, as we headed for O'Connell Street and the parade platform, where the Taoiseach, Eamon de Valera was taking the salute. The bayonet problem never arose again, I made sure of that.

I must say, in all modesty, my arms drill was impeccable, because

I had the added advantage of getting extra drilling from my brother-in-law, Noel Dillon, an Army officer attached to the Anti-Aircraft Brigade, which had a gun position at the end of the extension at the Bull Wall, in Dollymount. Noel gave me a thorough going-over in arms drill. I impressed the Company Sergeant, Tommy Wardlaw, at a dress parade one evening, and he gave me a small unit to train. I was also made Company Interpreter that same evening, when the Company Commander, Matt Flynn, asked if there was anybody with a knowledge of languages in the ranks. I still had a smattering of French from my college days, but thinking that he meant German, I said in an aside to our sergeant that I knew French. He immediately told me to fall out, and marched me straight to the Company Commander. I explained that I knew French, he said it was sufficient and promptly named me as Company Interpreter. I don't know what I would have done had the Germans invaded this country at the time; I doubt if my French would have measured up to the challenge. I was made an NCO (a non-commissioned officer) and given a section to look after, which gave me a degree of importance. One of the lads jokingly called me "Frenchy" one night; I gave them a forced march round the Distillery yard for a half an hour with full pack, and never after did I hear the word "Frenchy" used in my company. We paraded on Thursdays and Sunday mornings but the squad leader Harry Wolverson gave me permission to miss the Sunday morning parade if I had a morning match with Eoghan Ruadh. "Swish" Quigley assured me that the Germans would respect the country's religious beliefs, and would definitely not invade us on a Sunday morning — he was the joker in our section. We had to put up with a lot of ribbing on those Sunday morning marches. A small gang of locals would congregate at O'Leary's corner at the junction of Malahide Road and Marino Mart, and we got the "bird" as we passed by. One such morning our Squad Commander, Matt Flynn, halted about twenty of us in front of a gang of locals who had been doing their whistling acts. We got the order to "fix bayonets". The gang took one look and ran like the hammers of hell, and never after were we troubled with snide remarks or cat calls — they had got the message. We took night manoeuvres very seriously. The "Blackout" was in operation and street lamps only showed a small glimmer of light. There was no bag snatching or mugging of elderly people in those days and you could go about your business without fear of being harmed.

There were fine soldiers in the LDF and they trained with primitive weapons; but during the "mock" battles with the Army there were no punches pulled. One night we were doing night manoeuvres in St Anne's Estate, near the old Mansion, and my section was deployed to attack it and take it. Another section was deployed to defend it, and after much inching around, flitting from tree to tree in the well-laid-out gardens, we came face to face with the defending section, to be told that they were a machine gun post, and they had mowed us down as we attacked their position. Swish Quigley, one of my section, told them in no uncertain fashion that we were "tanks" and we had just knocked the "whole bleedin' house down and yis were all kilt". Luckily, one of our squad leaders, Jim Cullen, was on hand to make a ruling; he told the other section, "You just don't argue with a tank," and that ended the battle of rights for that night.

There were combined exercises between the Army and the LDF from time to time, which both sides took very seriously. I was involved in the "Battle of Tolka Road" (off Clonliffe Road) one weekend. The Army, having battled its way from the south, had arrived at the outskirts of the city, and the LDF was given the task of defending their own areas against the "invading army". We wore white arm bands, while the Army had red ones. The umpires were invariably Army brass, who wore white and red armbands, and they scorched around in army cars or motor cycles, adjudicating on claims made by the opposing sides. We had taken over the defence of the Ballybough area, which included the bridge, and our instructions were to prevent the Army from advancing from Fairview and Poplar's Row. The Drumcondra side was well covered by the local LDF, and they were lined up along the banks of the Tolka river, from Ballybough back up to Drumcondra. We were visited from time to time by our section leaders, Jim Cullen and Harry Wolverson, and they briefed us on the possible routes the Army might take in an attempt to break through our lines.

I was instructed to take up a position with two of my unit at the end of Clonliffe Road, and at a given signal we were to go through the motions of firing mortars to destroy the bridge and render it impassable. There were all kinds of rumours about the whereabouts of the Army, but nobody knew from which direction they might strike, least of all the defenders of Ballybough. Most of our section had taken up positions on Orchard Road and Tolka Road and we had a lookout posted at every vantage point. The kind-hearted residents of the road were insisting on us "dropping in for a cup of tea, ye must be all famished", etc. All such invitations were stoutly declined; there was a war on, and you dared not desert your post.

The manoeuvres took on a measure of reality when word came down the line that the Army had broken through the outer defence lines. It seemed the Army had stopped a train around Balbriggan, commandeered it, filled it with troops and had roared unchallenged along the lines at Fairview Park, hidden from the view of the LDF who were deployed along the banks of the track. The train stopped at East Wall bridge, the Army poured out and overran all the defending positions in the immediate area. I got an order to "blow the bridge at Ballybough", which we did. By this time the Army had broken through our defences at the top of Clonliffe Road (Drumcondra side) and the excitement of the occasion was heightened by young kids running up to our positions -- "I seen them, I seen the Army, they're up the road, I seen them." Very shortly the Army did arrive; we could see them running from garden to garden, and we started on command firing off our blank ammo. We had been issued with ten rounds starting off that morning. The exchanges between ourselves and the Army lasted until the ammo was exhausted, and the Army began to withdraw. When the local residents saw the Army pulling out, they took it we had won, and people came out of their houses cheering and congratulating us for "beating the Army". Naturally, we claimed that we had held our positions through the attack, and had in fact beaten off the Army, but we never discovered the real result of the exercise, and the "Battle for Tolka Road".

Swish Quigley was in no doubt who had won the battle and claimed that it was the blowing up of Ballybough Bridge, the master stroke, which had led to the defeat of the Army. Swish was inclined to exaggerate a little, I must say. That particular manoeuvre between ourselves and the Army dominated conversations for many days, and some of the tales which emerged got better in the telling. In one particular engagement, a Field Ambulance unit was asked to pick up a few "casualties" and bring them by stretcher to the nearest dressing station. The stretcher party had a long way to go from the battle area, carrying the "injured" soldier, and it was thirsty work. So the stretcher party stopped outside of Gaffney's pub in Fairview, placed the "casualty" on the ground and hopped inside for a few quick ones. After about a half hour they came out to find an empty stretcher, pinned to which was a note, "Bled to death, couldn't wait, gone home".

There were many aspects of our training scrutinised after the Army confrontation and it was felt that some of the units involved were lax in their approach to the whole exercise. We heard that the Army had entered from the top of Clonliffe Road virtually unchallenged, and that the LDF positions had been overrun in a matter of minutes. There were other rumours suggesting that some positions had been let unguarded while the local defending soldiers were in "having a cup of tea" at the time, but those rumours remained unsubstantiated. I do know our platoon covered itself in glory and performed as well as any on that day. Matt Flynn praised us for our diligence and fortitude, and for the manner we had conducted ourselves throughout the whole operation. He also complimented our squad leaders, Harry Wolverson and Jim Cullen, for their excellent leadership in the heat of the "battle". While this praise was being lavished on us in the dispersal point in the old Distillery, on Richmond Road, some of the men were firing off all their unused blanks, and cheers greeted each round released. In the weeks which followed, all the sections were put through their paces while the NCOs were subjected to a thorough examination to see if they had forgotten anything from their training days.

The squad did learn a very useful lesson from the clash with the Army. We had been very impressed with the speed with which the regular Army soldiers moved from one hiding point to another, virtually unseen. Our sergeant, Martin Kavanagh, decided to try out a night manoeuvre in the grounds of Clonliffe College. The idea of the exercise, he told us, was to try and capture an "enemy post" as silently as possible. We gained entry into the College grounds by climbing over the boundary wall from the road. The sergeant pinpointed an old shed at the top of the field, and instructed us to wriggle along the ground, with our rifles cradled in our arms, making the least amount of noise, to complete the exercise by taking possession of the hut. So far, so good. The well-intentioned sergeant told us he would take up a position near the hut, and he would evaluate the entire modus operandi from his vantage point. He stressed the importance of silence; not a word was to be spoken during the exercise until the mission was completed. It was one of those dark, dry summer nights, and we could just make out our objective in the distant gloom.

The sergeant took up his position, and gave a soft whistle, which was the signal for the exercise to begin. Nobody, of course, had told us that a herd of cattle grazed on that particular piece of land, and that the whole area was littered with small mounds of cattle droppings. We had just travelled a few yards when the trouble broke out. The silence of the night was shattered by shouts of (appropriately, I suppose) "Holy shit, the place is covered in f..... cow shit!" Other voices had taken up the cry: "Ah, f..... this for a yarn, look at me bleedin' uniform!" From various positions there were howls of protest and the sergeant's voice could be heard shushing us, but there was no stopping the angry shouts of the men. "Shush, me arse, you're f..... alright, Sarge, you're not covered in shit." The poor sergeant tried to bring a bit of order to chaos and he didn't help the situation when he reminded the men that in a war situation, they would have to put up with that kind of discomfort. That only brought renewed protests from the men. "Look at me bleedin' rifle, Sarge, covered in cow shit, I'll never get it clean." Needless to say, the night exercise broke up in disorder. We all vowed that never again would we attempt a night manoeuvre of the Clonliffe nature without someone doing a recce beforehand to make sure there were no pitfalls. The only guy to miss all the action was Swish Quigley. He got short taken before the exercise began and was just rejoining the squad when all hell broke loose. He claimed afterwards that he had a second sense about those things.

For the last year of my LDF service I transferred to the 11th Cyclist Regiment (Irish speaking) based at McKee Barracks, and my transfer was prompted by the perseverance of Breandan O Tighearnaigh, a regular visitor to O Glasain's shop in O'Connell Street. He was a rep for the New Ireland Assurance Co., and most of the staff were clients of his, myself included. Breandan was very keen to have Irish-speakers in his squadron, and I eventually succumbed to all the inducements he was offering. The 11th Cyclist Regiment had been formed in 1942 by Commander J.N. Farrell, and comprised squadrons formed from the Cycling Clubs in Dublin (41st Squadron), An Oige members (42nd Squadron) and an amalgram of other interested parties, including many members of the Post Office staff (43rd Squadron). Early in 1944, an Irish-speaking Squadron was formed (44th Squadron). The Squadron Commander was Breandan O Seaghdha, a teacher in St Peter's National School, Phibsboro. Breandan O Tighearnaigh was one of the officers in the 44th Squadron, who subsequently became

Squadron Commander and retired from the 11th Cavalry in 1982 as a Commandant. The 11th Cyclist Regiment, which was mechanised in 1948 as the 11th Cavalry Regiment, became one of the best known units in the post-war FCA. Amongst those who served in its ranks in the early days were Tomas O Cofaigh, who became in time Secretary of the Department of Finance and Governor of the Central Bank, Tom Hardiman, who was later to be appointed Director-General of RTE, and Jim Tunney, TD who played with me on the Dublin football team for some years, was Chairman of the Fianna Fail Party and a Lord Mayor of Dublin. The unit was based at McKee Barracks for over forty years, but its headquarters moved recently to Griffith Barracks, where they are now two Cavalry Units, the 2nd Cavalry Squadron of the Permanent Defence Force and the 11th Cavalry.

The war didn't affect my sporting activities in any way. In 1941 I collected my third minor county hurling championship medal and moved to the Ruadh junior side. The bulk of the junior squad were products of the very good minor teams that had served the club so excellently in that grade. At the start of 1942 Eoghan Ruadh showed its strength by fielding a team that was to go on to win every competition at junior level. Those successes included championship, League, Corn Ceitinn, Miller Shield and Saturday League, the first time a club had actually made a clean sweep of all titles in the one season. It was a truly remarkable team, which had Mickey Banks in goal, and the full backs were Kevin Matthews, Paddy Walsh, and Jerome Coakley, a very strong line. The half backs were Sean Coughlan, Bobby Kane and Tommy Hickey. Dick Molumby and myself comprised the midfield partnership, and the forwards included Dessie Kilbride, Jackie Butler (Waterford), Tadgh Buckley, Sean Moore, Sean Hickey and Mick Currivan. My brother Seamus came on to the team later that year, and quite a number of the panel were to earn promotion to senior ranks the following year. The club had much to celebrate and went from success to success at under age and senior level. It meant the fielding of two senior teams in the League series in 1943. I was to play with the Eoghan Ruadh "A" team and Seamus figured on the "B" side. The war wasn't going too well for Britain that year and Lord Haw Haw, Irishman William Joyce, in his nightly broadcasts from Germany gave a list of all the British ships sunk by German submarines. Joyce was a bit of a folk hero and went down very well with those who held very strong anti-British views.

Regular visitors to O Glasain's drapery shop, where I worked, were Mrs Sidney Czira and her son Finian. She was a lovely person, small and ladylike in stature and she enjoyed chatting about the war and its effects. She was married to a Hungarian and two of her sisters were caught up in the national movement. Her sister Grace had been married to Joseph Plunkett in his cell the night before he was executed in 1916. Another sister, Muriel, had married Thomas McDonagh, also shot in 1916. Mrs Czira had been a very popular figure on radio from the start of the new station, 2RN, and presented many programmes featuring historical ballads. Indeed, her son Finian told me that she had a passion for ballads and had a huge collection. She broadcast under her pseudonym "John Brennan". Finian told me she had written a letter to the *Irish Times* protesting against a speech of a Senator who had referred to the Irish Volunteers in connection with the assassination of Kevin O'Higgins, at a time when men were awaiting trial on the charge of "conspiracy and murder", and some of them were known members of the Irish Volunteers. In the course of her letter to the *Irish Times* she said that "no evidence had yet been produced connecting them or the Volunteers with the attack, and if it were to become customary to attack prisoners in the Press and Parliament while their cases were still *sub judice*, trial by jury would become a mere farce." Finian said that his mother's concern was with the right to fair trial, rather than with the political aspect, but the letter was published a few days after the assassination, when feelings were running high. Within twenty-four hours of the letter appearing she was sent for by the Director of Broadcasting and told that her outstanding engagements were cancelled and she would not be used again. That exclusion ban lasted until the change of government in 1932, when the new Minister for Posts and Telegraphs had the ban removed. Indeed, any political views expressed by those who were involved in radio in the late 1920s which ran contrary to those of the government of the day led to their being kept off the air. The sentiments expressed by Finian Czira concerning his mother correspond with the version described in Maurice Gorham's book *Forty Years of Irish Broadcasting* on the banning of "John Brennan" by the then Director of Broadcasting.

Mrs Czira and Finian were regular visitors to O Glasain's in those early war years, selling a pamphlet called "News and Views", and most of the staff were on her selling list. I asked Finian what prompted them to set about printing and distributing "News and Views", which in the main was very much slanted in favour of the German war effort. He said his mother had been told by a friend of theirs that the German Ambassador to Ireland, Edouard Hempel, was interested in paying some person to collect news items about himself and about the Germans which were appearing in the daily papers. Mrs Czira went to the German Legation and met Herr Hempel, and told him she was interested in supplying the information he sought. She told him that she would use the reading facilities in the RDS, which provided all the daily papers, getting the British ones from Belfast. Herr Hempel decided she should join the RDS as a member and he agreed to pay her annual subscription. Mrs Czira extracted the information which she felt met her brief and conveyed it to Hempel. She also proceeded to put together the pamphlet "News and Views", which laid great stress on the German gains in the war, and with local nationalist fervour running very high at the time she found a ready market for her printed publication. No secret was made of the fact that a sizable volume of opinion in this country favoured a German victory in the war, which they hoped would lead ultimately to the unification of the country. "England's difficulty, Ireland's opportunity" was the popular cry at the time. The Cziras sold the pamphlet at other outlets and Finian told me that they left a bundle with one of the porters in Dail Eireann, who proceeded to drop pamphlets in the letter boxes of Fianna Fail TDs. The Cziras continued the service until the war began to turn in favour of the Allied Forces and gradually they ceased to print the pamphlet.

Eoghan Ruadh, Dublin Senior Hurling League and Boland Cup winners in 1946. (Other trophies won that year were Corn Ceitinn, Intermediate League, Saturday League, Linesman Cup). Seán Óg, the captain, is sixth from left in front row.

Mrs. Sydney Czira ("John Brennan") interviewing Maud Gonne McBride on Radio Eireann on the setting up of her 'Inghinidhe na hÉireann" in 1900. Mrs. Czira's sister Grace married Joseph Mary Plunkett in his cell before he was executed in 1916. Another sister Muriel had married Thomas McDonagh, also shot in 1916.

Chapter 4

With Eoghan Ruadhs and Dublin

In 1943 my club, Eoghan Ruadh, broke new ground when they invited the famous Limerick club, Ahane, to Dublin to play a senior hurling challenge in aid of the Merrion Church Building Fund, the parish priest being Father Pat Flanagan, founder of the Ruadh club. It was the first time for the Limerick champions to play in the capital, and the first time for any club outside the city to be invited to appear at GAA headquarters. Ahane were famous in their own right; they included many famous household names, such as the Mackeys, Mick and John, the Herberts, Tony, Mick and Sean, Timmie Ryan and Jackie Power. Both Timmie Ryan and Mick Mackey had captained Limerick teams to All-Ireland victories. The match took place on Easter Sunday at Croke Park. The weather was unkind for a start, which affected the attendance, and the fact of it being a major holiday didn't help either. When all expenses were paid, the princely sum of £20 was left to go towards the Church Fund. The club later ran a special function which netted a very tidy sum and that made up for the disappointment of the Croke Park gate returns.

The Ahane game signalled my first match with the "Ruadhs" at senior level and I was pleased enough with my debut. The Ruadh side was exceptionally strong, with Jimmy Donegan of Kilkenny fame between the posts. The full-backs were Jack Maher, Dan Nicholl, and Dixie O'Brien. At half-back were Jim Byrne, Martin Dunne and Jimmy Whelan. Tommy Jenkinson and Gerry Glenn paired off at midfield, and they had to contend with Timmie Ryan and Tony Herbert. Tony was to join Faughs some time later, and became a leading figure on Dublin teams. Our half-forward line was Kevin

Matthews (later to become one of the great goalkeepers in the game at county and inter-county level), Mick Leahy and myself; the full line, Joe Hickey, Mick Connolly and Sean Moore. The Limerick defence was powered by Jackie Power, acknowledged as one of the best in the position. Paddy Byrne was the goalkeeper and the full line Tom Conway, Mick Hickey and Philly Byrne. Flanking Power were John Mackey and Paddy Kelly. The Ryan-Herbert midfield was a striking one and played a significant role in the eventual result, despite the stiff opposition presented by Tommy Jenkinson and Gerry Glenn. The Ahane half-forwards were Sean Herbert, Mick Mackey and John McGrath, and the full line was comprised of Jim Hassett, Paddy McMahon and Gene Fitzgibbon.

The game itself was a real thriller and Ahane edged the verdict in the closing stages when Mick Mackey broke through the Ruadh defence on a solo run, brushing off all kinds of challenges, to slam the ball to the net from twenty yards, leaving his side winners 2-7 to 3-2. The game itself did my confidence an awful lot of good because of the calibre of the opposition. Eoghan Ruadh were no slouchers on the field, they stood up to the toughest opposition in city competitions, but Ahane showed their strength in no uncertain fashion that afternoon. Mick Mackey typified the mettle of the visitors. When he grabbed possession anywhere within thirty yards radius of the Ruadh goal, he immediately made a beeline for the goal, brushing aside by no means gentle efforts to dispossess him, before unleashing a shot for goal. Lucky for us that Jimmy Donegan was in brilliant form between the posts; he stopped everything in sight. We would have been hammered but for him that day. Both Gerry Glenn and Tommy Jenkinson played their hearts out in the middle of the field against a pairing which was regarded as being one of the best ever to represent the Ahane club. Jackie Power was virtually a one man defence; very little got away from him despite the fact that he was marking one of the slickest centre forwards in Dublin hurling in Mick Leahy, and Ruadh's best forward that day. It was a marvellous contest all through the hour and the game hung on a thread until Mick Mackey got the winner, which deprived us of a morale-boosting success. I must say, I learned a lot from that experience. The club was satisfied too with the overall display of the team in matching the highly-vaunted Limerick champions, who had a long history of successes at county senior level. The "Ruadhs'" lead in bringing a top club from another county to play in Croke Park set the fashion, and other clubs followed suit.

Later that year I was chosen on the Dublin team for the National League campaign, and I was to remain a regular player until I retired from the inter-county scene in 1953, in a League game against Kilkenny. I mention that game particularly because it also marked the retirement of one of Kilkenny's household heroes, Jimmy Langton. I had played against Jimmy many times during my stint on the county team. He was, in my estimation, one of the truly great hurlers, who could coax a ball onto his stick in a flash and whip it over the bar in one movement. I remember chasing after Jimmy in a League game in Croke Park. He got to the ball first, picked it into his hand, and as I came charging in to block hurley and ball he stepped back a few paces as I went sailing past, and calmly stroked the ball over the crossbar. As I turned back towards him, he gave me a wink and said "Sorry, Sean," and turned away. It wasn't meant to be a jibe, but he knew how I felt, having bought the "dummy". I was to pull the same ploy many times during my career on the hurling field; it was just part of the game.

In 1944 I was part of a "connivance" which had been instigated by my father. His job as traveller for J.J. McCarthy's and Sons of Cork, Wines and Spirits Merchants, took him to County Monaghan, where he had customers in Scotstown (Moynas), Castleblayney, Carrickmacross and of course Ballybay and Monaghan town. The chairman of the Monaghan County Board at the time was Jim Cahill, a Garda Sergeant, who took over the office in 1941, with Leo Burns of Donaghmoyne as County Secretary. Cahill was a Tipperary man who loved hurling, and he had played it with no little success in the county of his birth. He and my father struck up a great friendship and many a "good night" was had whenever the pair met in Monaghan town. It was during one of my father's visits to that fair town that the question of hurling cropped up.

Sergeant Cahill was very keen to get hurling moving in the county, which was dominated by football. The Ulster Council that year had launched a senior hurling championship in which only four counties took part, Monaghan being one of them, and Cahill was anxious that the county would perform well enough to incite interest in the game. The problem was there were so few players good enough to play at senior level in the county. My dad suggested that he "borrow" a few players to augment his selection, explaining that he knew a few players

who would be willing "to help out". Cahill agreed, and considered
the suggestion an admirable one. On his return to Dublin dad set
about selecting his players for the trip to Monaghan a few weeks later
to play Down in the Ulster semi-final. My brother Seamus and I, Joe
Hickey, Gerry Glenn and Tom Shortall, from Eoghan Ruadh, Paddy
Hudson, an old pal from Fairview, who was a member of St Vincent's,
Joe Butler, who played with New Irelands, Paddy O'Brien (Kilkenny),
Chunky's father, and a few De La Salle brothers made up the Monaghan
team, with Jim Cahill himself operating at full forward. Jim was
nearer fifty than forty at the time, but was solid as a rock. A huge
crowd flocked to see the new look Monaghan team in action on the
hurling field, and they were loud in their praise of the skills displayed
by the "young players" on the team. In the end, Monaghan provided
the shock of the year by beating the fancied Down men by 3-7 to
1-10. There was great jubilation in the town after the match, and we
were told that even well-known "Orangemen" had been shouting their
heads off during the match in support of the home team.

My dad and Jim Cahill thought the whole exercise was very worth-
while, and after the Dublin contingent had been well wined and dined,
we headed home. Antrim had qualified for the final, and the game
was fixed for Monaghan town two weeks later. I had a problem. I
had played against Antrim in the League earlier in the year, and I was
well-known to their players, so it was decided to leave me out of the
team altogether. It was just as well, as I had reached the finals of the
mixed tennis doubles at the Fairview CYMS, and the final was fixed for
the same day at the Ulster senior hurling decider. Seamus McCluskey,
in his excellent *History of Monaghan GAA*, captured the whole mood
of the occasion in a chapter on that historic breakthrough in hurling
when on that auspicious day in Monaghan town, the home team held
the much-fancied Antrim team to level scoring, thanks to the brilliance
at midfield of Gerry Glenn. Joe Hickey created his own piece of history when he scored from a penalty. It must have been the first time
ever that a penalty had been awarded in the game of hurling. The
referee, John Vallely (Armagh) gave Monaghan the penalty, and
insisted that only the Antrim goalie stood on the goal line. Joe Hickey
slammed the ball to the Antrim net. At the end of a hotly contested
hour, scores were level, Monaghan 6-4 to Antrim's 5-7. The Monaghan
goalie that day, Paddy Callan, was one of the side's heroes. My brother
Seamus cleared everything in sight at full back and even impressed

one of the Antrim officials, who assured him, leaving the pitch, that he would keep him in mind for a place on the Ulster Railway Cup team the following year.

If the town had celebrated well for the initial victory over Down, there was nothing to equal the excitement at having held Antrim to a draw. Hurling had at last made an impact on the Monaghan people and one of the heroes was centre back Joe Butler, a chemist, who had worked in Castleblaney. (Joe was later to join Faughs and gain his place on the Dublin team for the All-Ireland final of 1948 against Waterford.) The replay between Monaghan and Antrim was arranged for Corrigan Park the following Sunday. The performance of the Monaghan team had attracted a lot of attention and the word filtered through to the county selectors that "certain officials" from certain counties would be in Belfast for the replay. That presented a bit of a problem for Jim Cahill and my dad, as they were forced to drop most of the "borrowed" players, but my brother Seamus, Gerry Glenn, Joe Hickey, Tom Shortall and Paddy Hudson decided to see things through. It must be said that the replacements for the borrowed players were definitely not up to standard, and despite all the hard work of Glenn, Hickey, O'Callaghan, Hudson and Shortall, Antrim led 7-3 to 0-0 with about a minute remaining, when Monaghan were awarded a 21-yard free. Joe Hickey went to take it; one of the players suggested that he try for a goal. Joe did a quick calculation. If he went for the goal and it was saved it meant that the Monaghan score-line would have remained blank. Joe took the major decision of going for a point; he was not leaving the field with a blank scoreline. He lashed the ball over the bar, and out of the ground. When the final whistle sounded seconds later, Antrim had won 7-3 to 0-1. Later, Jim Cahill gave Joe Hickey the ball which had scored his side's only point, and Joe has that ball to this very day.

It wasn't to be the end of the story for me. A few weeks later I was summoned before a special meeting of the Eoghan Ruadh committee to answer charges that I had played illegally with Monaghan in senior hurling, on the date of the drawn Ulster final. The secretary Jimmy Donegan told the meeting that he had it on very good authority that I had played on that date with Monaghan. I assured the committee that I had not played on that date, and they could get confirmation by ringing the Fairview CYMS and asking for the well-known St Vincent's club official, Andy Hanratty, who had actually umpired my Mixed Doubles match (we won). I was asked had I played on a later date (the replay date) against Antrim, and I again was able to offer evidence of having been in Dublin on that particular day. I was asked had my brother Seamus played on those dates, so I had to tell the club officers that I could not answer for him (my dad had briefed me well). The chairman, Mick Connolly, told me that they were giving me the benefit of the doubt though they had grave suspicions about the whole matter, adding that "there was no smoke without fire", or words to that effect. Now, had they pinpointed the date of the Down match in which I had played, I would have been forced in all conscience to admit my wrongdoing. But as that date wasn't mentioned, I had answered the other questions truthfully. I cannot say my trip to Monaghan cured me of rule-breaking on later occasions, but that's another story.

The following year Monaghan again figured in the Ulster senior hurling series, but this time their forces were genuinely drawn from local talent. They beat Fermanagh in the semi-final and were beaten by Antrim in the final 7-7 to 2-5, but at least the spark had been lit and hurling still survives in the county. Jim Cahill was made an Ulster selector that year and when the side was being chosen to play Connacht, he was asked about some of those very "good players" who had played in the previous year's Ulster final against Antrim. Jim, without batting an eyelid, told his fellow selectors that all the good players "had emigrated". Chosen on the Ulster team for the visit of Connacht that year was Paddy Murray (Armagh), a big strapping lad, who may not have been the most stylish of players but was strong and fearless. It was said that Paddy's fearless tackling led to some of the Connacht players having to leave the field for medical attention. At half time, Jim Cahill was reported to have said, "Good work, Paddy, keep it up, they have only one sub left."

I resumed my official duty with Dublin teams. We did not win any provincial titles, in spite of the fact that we could beat all the top teams in the country at League level. In the 1946 National League semi-final at Croke Park, we beat Cork 8-7 to 1-7, a Cork team with such stars as Tom Mulcahy (goal), Billy Murphy, Con Murphy, Alan Lotty, Jim Young, Jack Lynch, Con Cottell, Christy Ring, Sean Condon and the Riordans, Gerry and Mossie. We had a fine Dublin side, and but for the declaration rule, the county would have won a far greater number of All-Ireland titles. Once the Leagues had concluded, most of the good players who had served Dublin so well throughout the League campaign would declare for the county of their birth, for championship purposes. It meant that the Dublin selectors had to field virtually new teams for the championship. One of the strange features of hurling in those days was the emphasis on goal-scoring, and totting up eight goals against such formidable opponents as Cork was no mean feat. I scored 2-3 on that occasion, while Donal Cantwell, Mickey Lyons, Mossy McDonnell, Ned Daly and Ned Wade were the other marksmen. Christy Ring was the main threat for Cork. He tried every trick in the bag but he was unable to break down a Dublin defence which was truly brilliant on the day, with Sean Coughlan, Andy Dwyer, Ned Dunphy and Gerry O'Leary rocklike, fronting a steady Mickey Banks between the posts. Harry Grey and Paddy O'Brien stole the honours at midfield.

We met Clare in the League final at Limerick and I got a right roasting from the Clare right half-back, Dermot Solon. Dermot was really the star of that Clare performance and he inspired them in a second-half recovery to earn a share of the honours. Clare beat us by five points in the replay but this time the hero of the Clare team was Dermot's brother, Jackie, at midfield. He played a stormer and it was too late in the game when I was moved out in an effort to curb him; the damage was already done. At least I made amends for my indifferent display in the drawn match; I played really well in the Croke Park replay. I did ask the selectors at half-time to move me out to midfield on Jackie Solon, whom I had played on when he was with UCD, but by the time they did make the move Clare were well on their way towards winning that League crown. It was unfortunate that very heavy rain fell in the opening quarter, and I found great difficulty holding a grip on my hurley. I remember attempting a line ball and as I swung at the ball, my hurley flew from my grasp, missing a couple of players in front of me. At the end of the day, Clare deservedly had won the game and with it, my last chance of a League title. Jackie Solon was the prime marksman for Clare, totting up 1-5 points out of 1-10, and gave a masterful display at midfield.

The Leinster senior hurling final that year, 1946, was played in Croke Park. My brother Seamus was established in defence, alternating between corner back and left half, and he had played extremely well when he was brought on in the drawn League final against Clare at Limerick. He was retained for the replay and never looked back after that. Seamus was a fearless defender; once he had committed himself to a tackle, there was no drawing back. His best game was against Christy Ring in the 1952 All-Ireland final against Cork; he actually held the Cork ace scoreless from play until Ring was moved out to the wing later in the first half.

I wasn't picked on the Dublin team for the 1946 Leinster final against Kilkenny; I was in the subs, but an injury to Peadar Flanagan after fifteen minutes gave me my chance. Dublin hit an inspired spell when Ned Wade pointed and that was followed by a goal from Ned Daly and three great points from Tony Herbert, which left us in front by eight points. I had earlier scored a good point shortly after taking the field. Inexplicably, we allowed Kilkenny back into the game with a Jack Gargan goal and points from Jimmy Langton and Paddy O'Brien. Dublin's lead was cut to two points at the interval. The second half was a thriller, and I was fortunate to pick off a few more scores, but once again Kilkenny came back with a great goal from Tom Walton with minutes remaining. I still have vivid memories of those closing moments. I fired in a low ball but Kilkenny goalie Jimmy Donegan turned it round the posts for a 70. We were playing injury time. Harry Grey lobbed the ball to the Kilkenny square but Willie Walshe cleared it to safety. Mick Gill (Dublin) gained possession; he had come on as a sub in the second half. He soloed towards the Kilkenny goal and passed the ball to me. I moved forward a few steps before cracking the ball head high towards the Kilkenny goal. As it sped on its way the ball lifted in flight, struck the top of the crossbar, and over for a point. A few inches lower, as I had intended, it would have finished in the net, and we would have drawn. Kilkenny goalie Jim Donegan told me weeks later that he didn't see the ball once I had struck it, as his view was obscured by one of his defenders. My disappointment wasn't eased as I pushed my way through the crowds on the way to the dressing rooms, then behind the old Hogan Stand, when a Dublin voice said, "O'Callaghan should have gone for the goal". I didn't look back. Cork beat Kilkenny in the All-Ireland final that year.

Later that year we travelled to Fermoy to play Cork in the National Hurling League, and it developed into quite a contest. Mick Hassett was my partner at midfield and Christy Ring was also in the midfield berth for Cork, one of the few times he had played in the position for the county. Ring was a most difficult player to mark. He would

Action from the Eoghan Ruadh-Young Ireland Dublin Senior Hurling Championship Final in 1946. From left: Seán Óg, Philly Ryan (Young Irelands) and Jack Ryan (Young Irelands); in the background on left is Sean O'Neill (Eoghan Ruadh).

remain static for a few moments, and when you looked for him, he had taken off in quest of the ball. If Ring got his nose ahead of you in a race for the ball, you were doomed. His powerful forward thrust invariably got him away from the danger of being "hooked" from behind, and he was deadly when he got within scoring range. Ring had powerful hips and he used them to advantage. I remember one particular moment in that game when he raced up to me with the ball on his hurley; he feinted to the left, but I was not drawn. He was forced to play the ball, and as I moved towards him to block his shot, he hit me a glancing blow with his hip. I stumbled, and when I looked up the umpire was signalling a Ring point. Undoubtedly he was a perfectionist; he possessed powerful wrists which helped him to propel the ball with lightning speed, and he was adept at striking, right- or left-handed. He was ruthless too. If you put your hand up to catch a dropping ball, Ring did not stand on ceremony; he just pulled on the ball, regardless. His lack of inches made him vulnerable against taller opponents in a contest for a dropping ball. Still, it was a pleasure to play on Ring. He had a lot of little tricks, quick feints, and of course superb ball control on solo runs. Cork beat us that day by a couple of points, but I can honestly say I was more than pleased with my own performance against one of hurling's "greats".

1946 was a particularly good year for Eoghan Ruadh as I captained the senior team to win the League and Boland Cup; but we lost to Young Irelands in the senior championship final. I would have achieved the grand slam had we won the championship, and it would have been a first for the club. I was reappointed captain for 1947, and we again won the League and Boland Cup, but the much coveted championship again eluded us. The Ruadh club received its most representative honours early in 1947, when six players, Sean Cronin, Ned Dunphy, Mick Banks, my brother Seamus and I, and Jimmy Donegan were chosen on the Leinster team to play Connacht in the Railway Cup semi-final. Seamus was chosen at left half-back while I was paired with Dan Kennedy (Kilkenny) at midfield. Seamus and I became the first Dublin brothers to be selected on a Leinster hurling team. Gerry O'Connor, a Dublin selector, was also one of the provincial selectors, a factor which may well have influenced the inclusion of so many Ruadh men on the Leinster side. Connacht defeated us in that semi-final. It was a well-drilled Connacht team, with Jimmy Duggan in goal, and the defence included M.J. "Inky" Flaherty, Jim Brophy, Willie Fahy and Bernie Power. Dan Kennedy (Kilkenny) and I had our hands full at midfield against John Killeen and Paddy Gantley, two very polished hurlers. In the attack were such household names as the Gallaghers, Stevie and Josie, Hubert Gordon, Tommy Kelly and Pat Jordan. Connacht went on to record a historic first-ever Railway Cup title win against a Christy Ring-captained Munster team in the decider. That Connacht win eased our own disappointment at having lost the semi-final to them.

It was Dublin and Kilkenny again in the Leinster senior hurling final in July 1947 at Portlaoise, and I was picked at midfield with Mick Hassett. This was another classic, and the match was evenly balanced with about ten minutes to go when Kilkenny's Terry Leahy cut loose to score 2-2 points in a great spell, ending our hopes of victory. Mick Hassett and I had a great first half against Dan Kennedy and Jimmy Heffernan. Just before half-time, as I had delivered the ball, I got the handle of a Kilkenny hurley in the ribs which nearly turned my insides out. The Kilkenny defence was brilliantly marshalled by Jimmy Kelly, whom I had played on the previous year, when I was called in at left half-forward. I was switched on to Kelly midway through the second half but Kilkenny were in full flight. Liam Reidy was the inspiration in attack which started the game without Jimmy Langton and Jack Mulcahy. In the end, Kilkenny had won with a safe margin to spare and went on to contest the All-Ireland against Cork, a final which taught me a lesson I have never forgotten: never gamble on GAA matches.

I was never a gambler really but I got involved in a situation that year which cured me for all time of the gambling urge. Con Murphy, a renowned rugby international full-back, and a Corkman, persuaded me to accept a £10 bet on Kilkenny to beat Cork in that famous 1947 All-Ireland final. I was earning a little over a fifth of that per week at the time, so I thought I would lay off part of that bet. I slipped into Tommy Moore's pub in Cathedral Street and asked Mick Butler, the manager, a former Kilkenny full-back, would he cover half of the bet (£5). He told me that he had staked every penny he could muster on Kilkenny, and there was no way he could possibly place another penny on his native county. Indeed, he said, if Kilkenny were to lose that particular final he would be working for his boss for six months for nothing. I was stuck with Con Murphy's tenner. It meant that if Kilkenny lost, I too would be working for my boss for nothing for a month. The 1947 All-Ireland hurling final between Kilkenny and Cork turned out to be a classic, a heart-palpitating affair, which was decided by a last-minute point from thirty yards from Terry Leahy to give Kilkenny the title. I never enjoyed one minute of it. Visions of losing that £10 bet had kept me in such a state of nerves that the splendour of it all was lost on me. I winced every time Cork scored, I groaned every time Kilkenny missed and when Terry Leahy got the ball in his hand prior to scoring that all-important winning point, my head was already down between my knees, I just hadn't the nerve to look up and watch him score. Never after did I suggest or accept a bet on a match. I had learned a very object lesson.

I won my first Leinster senior hurling championship the following year, when after a whole series of upsets Dublin and Laois qualified for the Leinster decider at O'Connor Park, Tullamore. The appearance of Laois in a final brought a huge attendance to the Offaly venue, which, unfortunately, led to chaos on the sidelines. Spectators encroached on the pitch at times and play had to be stopped to enable sideline cut-ins to be taken. We had won the toss and played with a stiff breeze in the opening half. We dominated the play and quickly built up a safe lead in the first quarter. A Dublin player was injured, and this led to a free-for-all in which players and hundreds of spectators became involved. Stewards, the referee, Gardai and players eventually succeeded in getting matters under control and the game restarted. Dublin led 3-8 to 0-1 at half time and despite a very plucky and wholehearted effort by the Laois men in the second half, Dublin won easily. Best for Laois that day were Paddy Lalor, Harry Grey, Paddy Hogan, Billy Bohane, Joe Stynes and goalkeeper Tom Fitzpatrick. Dublin met Antrim in the All-Ireland semi-final at Croke Park in August and we won in a canter, 8-13 to 2-6. The Antrim side had many fine players, Noel Campbell, Dessie Cormican, Sean McDonald, Hugh Sheehan, Kevin Armstrong, Willie Feeney and Seamie Mulholland. At no stage did Antrim pose a threat and we won as we liked. On that same day, Waterford were creating a major shock, toppling Cork in the Munster final, and there were loud gasps of surprise around Croke Park when the final score was announced. The Deise men beat Galway quite convincingly in the semi-final a fortnight later and so, after a lapse of ten years, Dublin and Waterford faced each other in an All-Ireland final on the first Sunday in September.

The 1948 All Ireland Senior Hurling Semi-final at Croke Park, Dublin v Antrim. Dublin are in darker strip; second from right is Seán Óg.

Dublin Senior Hurling team beaten by Waterford in the 1948 All-Ireland Final. *Back row*: P. Donnelly, S. Cronin, J. Butler. D. Cantwell, D. Walsh, N. Dunphy, M. Hassett, L. Donnelly, G. Sutton, Seamus O Ceallacháin, D. Dillon. *Front row*: C. Keeley, J. Kennedy, K. Matthews, Seán Óg O Ceallacháin, T. Herbert, F. Cummins (capt), J. Prior, M. Williams, J. Drumgoole, Chris Keeley.

Waterford All-Ireland Senior Hurling Champions 1948 – *Back row (players only)*: M. Hayes, M. Healy, M. Hickey, E. Carew, A. Fleming, J. Allen, V. Baston, J. Keane, D. Power, T. Curran, J. Murphy, P. Neville, W. Galvin. *Front row*: J. Cusack, J. Goode, N. Daly, K. O'Connor, J. Ware (capt), C. Moylan, M. Feeney, P. Waters, J. O'Connor, L. Fanning.

In their previous meeting Dublin had taken the honours, so Waterford were thirsting for revenge. John Ware (goal), Mick Hickey, John
Keane, and Christy Moylan were the only players who had figured in
the 1938 final between the two sides. It was certainly the highlight
of my career to be contesting an All-Ireland final. It was an objective
achieved, even though the game itself was not my best by any stretch
of the imagination. Waterford half-back Mick Hickey held me scoreless from play for most of the game until I scored a goal near the end,
which came too late to affect the issue. The coveted Liam McCarthy
trophy was already on its way south. I must say, I loved every minute
of that final. I remember the roar of the crowd as we trotted out on
the field; the silence as we stood for the National Anthem; the cacoph-
ony of sound all during the game as the fortunes of battle ebbed
to and fro. I must say playing in an All-Ireland final has a very significant effect on a player. It gives him a sense of participation which
no other occasion engenders. Only those who have been part of it
can appreciate its humbling effect in defeat — or its uplifting grandeur
in victory. One way or another, it's an occasion to be savoured, and
that 1948 All-Ireland senior hurling final will always be something
special for me, because I was part of it. It was also a special day for
Waterford, celebrating their first ever Senior All-Ireland success, and
Tommy Moore's pub was packed to capacity on the day before the
match with Waterford supporters. For a GAA man not to have visited
that famous hostelry was like a Muslim who hadn't visited Mecca.
It — Tommy Moore's, I mean — was the place to be seen during the
week before or after an All-Ireland. The story has been told many
times about an Italian Cardinal who got disorientated in the vicinity
of O'Connell Street during the Eucharistic Congress in 1932. In halt-
ing English, His Eminence asked a Kerryman, up for the Congress,
for directions to the Pro-Cathedral. Quick as lightning came the
response: "Sure, 'tis up there opposite Tommy Moore's".

I joined Clanna Gael football club around 1945 and soon rubbed
shoulders with one of the great inter-county stars of the time in Frankie
Byrne (Meath), one of the best forwards, pound for pound, competing at senior level. Frankie was an uncanny marksman. He took just a
couple of steps, and could point frees from any angle. He may have
been small of stature but Frankie could outjump taller opponents. I
remember him beating Phil "Gunner" Brady of Cavan in fielding in
Croke Park. Included in the Clans line up at the time was Tim O'Keeffe

in goal, "Weeshie" Murphy (Cork), Maurice Leahy, Brendan Corcoran, Seamus O'Dowd, Miceal Ferriter, and great midfield stars in Jim Morris (Carlow) and Mick Kilkenny. In attack were Nick Rackard, Tommy Mulhall (Kildare), Art O'Leary, Frankie Byrne, the Houlihans, Paddy and Mick, and myself. Sean O Siochain, who had captained Clans to win the 1937 championship title and who also, as captain, had a very distinguished run on the Dublin team, had eased out of club football when I came on to the senior team. But there was Liam McAuliffe, who was still playing top-class football, and a great club character. Clans produced many fine players and there was a very heavy emphasis on teachers. In later years, Clans supplied Mickey Whelan, Paddy Holden and Gerry Davey to the Dublin team which won the All-Ireland senior football title in 1963, Mickey Whelan having earlier won an All-Ireland with the 1958 senior side.

One of the problems about playing for Clans came around championship time. Being a strong club with many county ties, it attracted leading players, so those of us living in the city who had slogged it out in the league series, in all kinds of weather, were passed over at championship time, and replaced by bigger-named players from other counties. Matters came to a head for me when I was relegated to the subs for the senior championship game against Peadar Mackens, which was played at Croke Park. Clans had acquired a number of new faces for the championship, and it always felt strange togging off beside a player who was a complete stranger to you. Mackens had a very formidable team, with such well-known players as Paddy "Beefy" Kennedy, Matt Fletcher, who had won an All-Ireland senior medal with Dublin in 1942, and Mickey Richardson, and they proceeded to build up a comfortable lead in the game with about six minutes to go. I was pressed into service as a sub and in the space of five minutes I scored two goals, which was a good way of proving that I should have been on from the start. I was pleased when C.P. (Charlie Perry), writing in his weekly column in the *Evening Herald*, made that point too. I had decided, however, to join up with my brothers Seamus and Michael, who were playing with O'Tooles, along with some of my Eoghan Ruadh colleagues, Tommy Jenkinson and Kevin Matthews. I was to enjoy my football with the famous Seville Place Parish club and win many trophies with them. Perhaps it proved the difference between playing with a club drawing its strength mainly from local talent, and one which depended on well-known players born outside the city.

The only "outsiders" on the O'Toole team which I joined were long-time members of the club, Turlough Murray (Armagh), Joe Power (Clare), and Al Breslin (Fermanagh), who had played with their native counties but who had given great service to the O'Toole club. We won the 1947-48 senior football league and the St Vincent de Paul Cup in my first year with a panel which included Jack Lombard (goal), Al Breslin, Joe Power, Bobby Kane, Leo Synnott, Kevin Matthews, Jimmy Barnes; Tommy Jenkinson and Turlough Murray at midfield; forwards, Peadar McMahon, Liam "Harrier" Roche, Mattie Killeen, Paddy "Spud" Murphy and Dermot Byrne, not forgetting Georgie Kilbride, Pat Bridgette, Tommy Cullen and Jimmy O'Rourke. St Vincent's were our main rivals, and we met them in the championship semi-final in Croke Park in 1948. Most of St Vincent's were dual performers against whom I had played with the Ruadh. That particular game was a thriller. The scores were level with about two minutes to go when I blocked a sideline kick on the Cusack Stand side of the field and lashed the ball over the Railway goal to put us ahead. From the kickout the ball was worked upfield and was caught by "Ra" Healy (St Vincent's). He was challenged in possession and referee Joe Leonard (Clanna Gael) awarded a free to the "Vins" about thirty-five yards out from our goal, which Kevin Heffernan pointed. The final whistle sounded immediately. We lost the replay in a gale at Islandbridge by the narrow margin of one point. St Vincent's had claimed that if they could get over O'Tooles they would win the championship. They lost that final to a very strong Garda side, but from 1949 onwards the "Vins" were to farm the football championship as the O'Toole challenge faded.

I was chosen on the Dublin senior football team for the following three years, until St Vincent's successes at championship level increased their representation on the county side to the exclusion of other clubs. Dublin teams, admittedly, fared none too well at championship or League level during my spell with them, even though the St Vincent's players who were later to go and make major impacts on the inter-county scene were included, Jimmy Lavin, Denis and Tim Mahony, Jim Crowley, Maurice Whelan, Ollie and Cyril Freeney, Kevin Heffernan, Liam Donnelly, Norman Allen and Des "Ra" Healy. The "outsiders" who played with me on those sides were Jim Tunney, Cecil Manning, Vinnie Russell, Noel Fingleton and Bobby Finnegan. Dublin regained the Leinster senior football crown

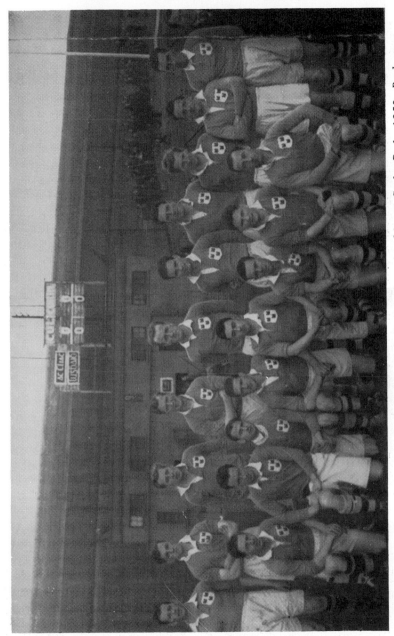

Dublin Senior Football Team versus Louth in Leinster Championship at Croke Park, 1950. *Back row:* Bobby Finnegan, Kevin Heffernan, Ollie Freaney, Des Healy, Jim Lavin, Liam Donnelly, Jim Crowley, Cyril Freaney, Mick Mangan, Jim Tunney. *Front row:* Cecil Manning, Denis O'Mahony, Seán Óg O Ceall-acháin, Norman Allen, Noel Fingleton, Maurice Whelan, Tim Mahony, Vinnie Russell.

in 1955, bridging a gap of thirteen years since winning the previous one. They went on to play Kerry in that famous final with twelve St Vincent's players, goalkeeper Paddy Flaherty, Jim McGuiness and Johnny Boyle. It could be said that it was one of the most emotional finals ever contested between the two great rivals; the game was built up to hysterical proportions by the media. It was a case of the old "catch and kick" versus the "new look" modern-day style. It could also be said that the "Dubs" and the "Hill" manifestation hadn't yet arrived. That was to come later, much later. But it was one final that Kerrymen still talk about as being the most gratifying win of all their triumphs over the "Jackeens".

Playing in an All-Ireland is, of course, every player's dream. It's a hope which is nurtured from a very early stage and the feeling gets stronger as one progresses up the various grades of competition. It was only natural for me to become obsessed with the idea of All-Ireland participation. I was literally born into that atmosphere. My father spent every Sunday at matches and I was brought to most of those matches. In 1948 my dream became reality when I played on the Dublin team against Waterford in the All-Ireland hurling final, and while I failed to win a coveted medal I was still part of that wonderful occasion. Some of the finest players ever to grace a GAA playing field sadly depart the scene without tasting the utter joy or the absolute sense of accomplishment which an All-Ireland final engenders. Sadly too, the advent of television came much too late to chronicle for posterity on film the many great skills of stars of former years, household names who became legends in their own times, players who weaved spells of magic with hurley and sliotar, and who are still talked about whenever hurling people meet. I have written and reported on All-Irelands, I have commentated on them on TV and radio, but I can honestly say that involvement as a player in an All-Ireland final has no equal.

I had played for Leinster in the Railway Cup competition, so to complete the line of accomplishments all that remained was a coveted Dublin senior hurling championship medal. My club, Eoghan Ruadh, had never won the county senior hurling championship title since attaining senior status in 1928. I had captained them to win the League and Boland Cup in successive years, but the main prize had eluded us. To put Dublin hurling in its proper perspective at the time, I must sketch in some of the background. There were only eight senior hurling clubs competing for the major titles, Faughs, (perhaps the strongest club), Young Irelands, (the club my father was associated with), UCD, Commercials, Civil Service, New Irelands, Kevins and Eoghan Ruadh. With the exception of the Ruadh, most of the clubs fielded players who were born outside the city. Faughs and Young Irelands had club members who were in a position to offer and provide employment for the many big-name hurlers who were then starring with leading counties. Getting a job in Dublin was something not to be ignored and many of those hurlers jumped at the chance when they were subsequently invited to play with Dublin clubs. Eoghan Ruadh depended mainly on players who had come up through the ranks from juvenile to minor to junior, then on to senior grade, and were born in the capital. There was no restriction on players who were not Dublin-born, and the club was very glad to have a number of such players who were loyal members. The standard of hurling in Dublin in the late 1930s and 1940s was as high as in any of the traditional hurling strongholds. The cream of talent was drawn to the Dublin scene and the competition and rivalry was fierce between the competing clubs. In some instances, inter-county rivalry bubbled to the surface and that factor was also reflected in local club clashes. It was against that background that Eoghan Ruadh had to pit their skills and talents, in their battle for survival at top level, and it was certainly a battle at times.

Eoghan Ruadh filled another void as well. Dublin needed a local team of some standing, a team which the ordinary native could follow and claim as his own, in an atmosphere where the bulk of the emphasis was being placed on the "country players". Ruadh supplied that need, and it was a very important factor in the rivalry generated by the city versus country clashes. Faughs were managed by Tommy Moore, whose licensed premises in Cathedral Street, off O'Connell Street, was the mecca for GAA enthusiasts visiting the capital city. Tommy was a former All-Ireland hurler, and he knew the quality required to keep his club at the top in Dublin competitions. Many famous stars had worn the Faughs strip, and Harry Grey, Mick Butler, Tony Herbert, Christy Forde, Ned Wade, Dan Devitt, Charlie Downes and Terry Leahy were the idols of the Faughs followers in the late 1930s. Young Irelands included Charlie and Peadar McMahon, Eddie Byrne, Tommy Treacy, Christy O'Brien, Mick Hough, Dan Dunne and Joe Bannon. UCD commanded a wide range of brilliant hurlers in Bill Loughnane (Clare), Jack Feeney (Waterford), Jim Cooney (Tipperary), and Dick Stokes (Limerick). I remember playing on Dick in my first year on the Ruadh senior team. It was a county senior hurling championship tie at Croke Park, and it was played as a curtain-raiser to an important national football league game. UCD were leading by a point as the game moved into the closing stages, but I was fortunate to pick up a loose ball and hammer it over the bar for the equaliser. As I moved away I got a tap on the shoulder, and Dick said, "Nice point, Sean". That was the kind of player Dick Stokes was.

Eoghan Ruadh had long battled to establish their right to be accepted as a mainly local team battling against the forces represented by the opposing star-studded teams. The Ruadhs then were powered by such as Mick Connolly, Gerry O'Connor, Mick Leahy, Gerry Glenn, Paddy "Mucky" Maher and Jim Byrne, the only Dublin-born player on the Dublin team which beat Waterford in the 1938 All-Ireland final. It was rumoured that well-known broadcaster Paddy Crosbie, a teacher in North Brunswick St. CBS (known as "Brunner"), based his character, Mucky Dunne, on the Ruadh player. Club rivalry at the time generated so much heat that even first round championship matches were certain to attract bigger attendances than those seen at county finals elsewhere. There was a prime reason. County stars who had come to live in Dublin could not opt to assist their home clubs in county championship matches. This meant that many inter-county stars played their club hurling and football in Dublin, with the result that many Dublin championship games came close to All-Ireland standards. Certainly the fact that the local teams in Dublin had to rely in the main on the native players eventually led to the making of the native-born county football team. Sadly, however, the same cannot be said of hurling, which remains the poor relation at present. But it was the period of great games and great players, and the competitions throve. The presence of Ruadhs as local standard bearers brought the crowds flocking, especially if Faughs provided the opposition.

Those were the days when the real aficionados gathered on the steps beneath the old Hogan Stand with the "Professor" silencing everybody with such pronouncements as "I see, gentlemen, that Jupiter Pluvius is in the ascendant again". Then there was old Devereux, the tall Wexford man, who was a life-long follower of the Faughs, and

never came to Croke Park without his faithful Kerry Blue. When the
opposition put the ball wide, he would tip back his old brown hat,
balance back on his heels, and announce happily, "plenty room for it
there". On football Sundays the scene was re-enacted under the small
Stand, when Paddy and Johnny McDonnell, the Synnotts, former
great O'Toole and Dublin players, would hold court; eager followers
listened in awe as "Macker", John, Stephen or Josie Synnott gave their
considered opinions about the football fare on view. Those big local
matches continued to make Sunday morning matches compulsive
viewing but the starting time, 11.45 am, brought rebukes from Mother
Church, who felt that many people were missing Mass, and suggestions
were made to have the games played later in the morning. A quiet
compromise was reached and the starting time was moved to midday,
thus allowing those attending 11.30 Masses to make it to Croke Park
(the Latin Mass was a great deal shorter, and evening Mass was still
in the womb of time). The new changes didn't please everybody,
especially those players who worked in licensed premises and who
had to be back for opening time. They had to adjust to the new starting time, even if it meant getting someone to work his day off to
allow a prominent barman to play an important game with his club.

Eoghan Ruadh remained the local favourites, and between 1939
and 1941 they contested three senior hurling championship finals in
a row against Faughs, failing each time narrowly in thrillers. The
Dublin County Board made an unprecedented gesture when they
presented the Ruadh club with a special set of medals to mark those
three games, an unheard-of gesture at the time.

Chapter 5
Great Dublin Games

Neither Faughs nor Eoghan Ruadh were concerned in the destination of championship honours the following years when Young Irelands stepped in to record successive championship crown victories. I made my first appearance in the county senior final in 1944 and our old rivals Faughs provided the opposition. A record attendance of 10,000, a fantastic crowd for a county final, watched a pulsating game. Faughs drew on all their well-known big names, Christy Forde (Dublin 1938 All-Ireland winning goalie), Ned Wade (Tipperary), Terry Leahy (Kilkenny), Harry Grey (Laois) and Mick Butler (Kilkenny), just to mention a few. The Ruadhs had their own favourites in action, Gerry Glenn, Jim Byrne, Mick Connolly, Jimmy Donegan (Kilkenny), "Mucky" Maher, Joe Hickey, Mick Leahy, Dixie O'Brien and Tommy Jenkinson, and I was picked at left half-forward. Most of the teams of that era had their "hard" men, and Ruadhs were no exception. The hurling at that time was tough and uncompromising, and if it exploded, which at times it did, the "hard" men were sure to be involved. There were no such incidents in that 1944 decider, which was one of the best finals between the two clubs. The press reports at the time paid a warm tribute to both teams, not alone for the exciting fare provided but for the sporting manner in which the game was played. I was pleased enough with my own performance, though I had to contend with one of the best wing-backs in the game in Dan Devitt, but at least I did score a goal and two points. Faughs, who led by four points at half time, led by seven going into the last quarter, but we staged one of our typical fight-backs to reduce the Faughs lead to a solitary point. In an exchange of scores near the end, Faughs added to their big collection of titles, winning by 2-11 to 2-8.

I really enjoyed those great battles with the Faughs, and those star players who wore the Faughs jersey. The games served to illustrate for me the importance of skill, speed and stamina when pitted against such formidable opposition. I learned a lot too from "Mucky" Maher, Dixie O'Brien, Gerry Glenn, Gerry O'Connor, Mick Leahy and company who had established Eoghan Ruadh as a strong hurling force. There was one annoying practice which was part of the hurling scene in those days, and that was the unnecessary stoppages of play. If a player went down and called for medical attention the referee had no option but to stop the match. It was frustrating from our viewpoint, because we invariably put everything into a last-ditch stand, reducing the opposition lead as the excitement built up. There were times when that late surge brought success, there were times when it did not, but when players deliberately feigned injury it helped to break the continuity of play, and that served the purpose for which it was intended. Ruadhs were often denied a well deserved victory because of those tactics, and Faughs, well within the rules, had perfected the gambit and brought it to a fine art. Frustration built up on those occasions, and some games got out of hand as certain clubs used the stop-start gambit to win major competitions. But they were still great times, great games and some were more memorable to look back on. The stoppages gambit would not be tolerated in present-day matches - the "non-stop" rule has seen to that.

I do remember one particular match which had Paddy "Mucky" Maher and Sean "Blondie" Roche at midfield. (We had another Sean Roche playing with the Ruadh at the time, so to distinguish them, one was called "Blondie" and the other "Blackie".) Sean "Blondie" never liked playing on a bright sunny day, as his eyesight suffered from the strong sun and he had a problem trying to anticipate a high dropping ball. He was a strong hurler and never flinched from a tackle or challenge. Unfortunately, on a sunny day he was lethal when a high ball was dropping down; he just pulled where he thought it might be. "Mucky" Maher, often as not, happened to be in the vicinity of the dropping ball and became a victim of Sean's wild pull. In the particular game I have in mind, "Mucky" fell to the ground and being nearest, I went to his assistance. He was alright, he wasn't injured, but he grabbed me by the arm and said, "For Jaysus sake, will you tell Gerry O'Connor to take Roche off before he kills us all"

— that meant friend and foe alike. Mucky was a marvellous character, fearless and strong, and his cherubic face gave the impression that butter would not melt in his mouth. Some opponents found to their cost that such was not the case. Gerry Glenn, another Dublin product, was a very stylish hurler who had figured prominently on Dublin teams in the early forties, and was noted for his fiery approach. If you were unfortunate enough to get involved with Gerry in a game, he would fix you with a steely glare and quietly say, "Are you fond of living? If you do that again, they'll be making a collection for your widow". Opponents got the message.

Ruadhs made their exit from the championship at various stages of the competition and we seemed further away than ever from winning the elusive title. Came 1951 and we met a very good Civil Service team in the quarter-final. It was a very touch-and-go affair but we struggled through at the end and that brought us a semi-final place against our old rivals, Faughs. The other semi-final pairing was more interesting, with an appearance of a new face at that stage of the series, St Vincent's, who were pitted against the defending champions Young Irelands. The inclusion of St Vincent's brought another dimension to the hurling scene. Like Eoghan Ruadh, they were drawn from local parishes, and the club the year before at their AGM had copperfastened a motion which stated that only those players who had come up from the ranks of underage competitions would be allowed to play for the club. Naturally, the appearance of St Vincent's in a county senior hurling championship semi-final was a completely new departure for them. St Vincent's had already acquired a sizable following at football level. They had captured the football championship title in 1949 for the first time, retained it the following year and were bidding for a notable treble in 1951. Naturally the big band of supporters which followed them in football threw themselves wholeheartedly behind the hurlers and there was talk of the "impossible double". There was another side to the scene from a Dublin viewpoint and that was the fact that a second club had come on the horizon to challenge the might of the "country" clubs . . . and that factor was to generate an extra edge to competitions at hurling level in the city.

For their semi-final against St Vincent's the Young Irelands had strengthened their forces with the additions of the noted Tipperary stars, the Kenny brothers Sean and Paddy, Pat Stakelum, Seamus Bannon and Phil Shanahan. Phil's brother Bill was already an established player on the team, along with the ageless Bill Walsh of Kilkenny fame. Tipperary also supplied Edmund Brown, who lived in the city; a well known tenor, he appeared regularly on the main Dublin theatre stages, and when appearing at times in the Royal, often sported a plaster from a knock he had received earlier in the day with his club. Edmund was a very stylish half-back and I played on him at times. The St Vincent's and Young Ireland 1951 semi-final was played on a Wednesday evening at Parnell Park, and the Donnycarney venue brought a huge crowd to watch the titleholders gain an expected easy passage. Even the most ardent St Vincent's fan held out little hope of a win against such a formidable array of hurling talent. But for once the big names did not have matters all their own way, and as the game wore on it was the more enthusiastic St Vincent's players who began responding to the crowd's exhortations. The exchanges were very exciting as the lead alternated on several occasions, but the more youthful St Vincent's won the day and the match in a blazing finish. For the first time ever, the St Vincent hurlers were through to a county senior hurling championship final, and having toppled the titleholders, they were really cockahoop.

With the reigning champions out of the title race the Eoghan Ruadh-Faughs march took on an entirely new perspective and it was natural to assume that the winners of that semi-final would be the prime fancy to take the ultimate honours. Both had the experience, the team ability and of course the big match temperament. That was the thought foremost in the minds of the Faughs and Eoghan Ruadh players as they lined out for the second semi-final at Parnell Park a week later. The game opened on a hectic note before one of the biggest crowds ever to throng Parnell Park. The early exchanges reflected the mood of the players and there were a number of incidents as tempers became frayed. As usual, both teams served up tremendous hurling and there were a number of bad misses on both sides. Harry Grey and Mick Maher began to dominate at midfield as Sean Dinny O'Neill and myself were forced to take a back seat. Faughs led by a goal at half-time, but the whole trend of the game changed in the second half as goalie Mick Banks, my brother Seamus, Sean Coughlan, Finbarr Molumby and Sean Cronin clamped down on the Faughs forwards. The old reliable Jack Finan started the Ruadh recovery with a goal, supplemented by a second goal from Tommy Norton, and with ten minutes remaining we enjoyed a four points lead. It was the turn of

Faughs to pull out all the stops for a change, and this they did, chipping away at our lead, reducing it to a single point. Ruadhs had what looked like a legitimate goal disallowed and an ugly scene looked like developing. Faughs broke away and pointed and seconds later, Harry Grey failed to score from a well-placed free, much to the astonishment of the Faughs followers. Our cup of misfortune was filled to the brim in the last second of the game when I doubled on a ground ball, and as it soared over the bar the referee whistled full-time and refused to allow the score. Bedlam broke loose, but all the remonstrations in the world failed to change the referee's decision and that was that — the match ended in a draw.

It was back to Croke Park for the replay and the tension was just as great as it had been for the drawn tie. The *Irish Press* captured the whole story of that game in the opening paragraph of the match report the following day. "If they never win the championship, Eoghan Ruadh's memorable fighting recovery, which whittled down a twelve points lead, and in the last pulsating moments of the game, levelled and scored the winning points, will go down in the annals as one of the best comebacks seen in Dublin hurling for some time." It was an extraordinary setback for gallant Faughs who had dominated the first half, where Harry Grey was again invincible in the centre of the field despite all my efforts, and they looked well in command at half-time when they led 4-6 to 1-4, a lead due mainly to Tony Herbert, who shot 2-3 of the Faughs total. Drastic measures were called for at half-time, so Dick Molumby was moved to midfield and I was switched to left half-forward, and as events subsequently proved, the switches worked wonders. Dick Molumby took over to dominate at midfield while I quickly shot a goal and added three further points and Ruadhs were on their way back. The impossible had happened. Ruadhs, calling on all the experience of previous great finishes against the "old enemy", were just not going to be denied, and sheer willpower and that indomitable Ruadh spirit once more carried the day; in a blazing finish we won 4-11 to 4-8. It was now Eoghan Ruadh versus St Vincent's in the county final, a pairing which even the most optimistic follower from either side could hardly have envisaged at the start of the series. More important still, it was now a local derby, and that added immeasurably to the fixture's appeal.

It had further significance for me. I had started my club hurling as a juvenile with St Vincent's and remained with them up to minor grade until an incident, which was not of my making, led to me changing clubs and joining Eoghan Ruadh. I had played with the St Vincent's minor team and helped them to qualify for the 1938-39 minor hurling league final, in which our opponents were Eoghan Ruadh. We were togging off in the dressing room at Croke Park on that Sunday afternoon when my dad was told by Father Fitzpatrick that I was being left out of the side; he was including a new player who had joined the club. My father was furious, and pointed out that it had been my marksmanship which had played such a big part in getting the team to the final. My father was supported by some of the other selectors and Father Fitzpatrick was forced to concede. As I was leaving the dressing-room my father grabbed me by the arm and said, "If you never play another match for Vincent's, I want you to play well today". The gods smiled favourably on me in that final. It was a misty day, the conditions were not easy, the ball was heavy, but we beat old rivals Ruadh by 4-5 to 5-1. I scored two goals and five points, my brother Seamus scored a goal and the winning goal was kicked to the Ruadh net by substitute Eamon Foley. I didn't get much time to celebrate because my dad rushed Seamus and me out of the dressing-room, and by the following day he had us sign a transfer form and we both became members of Eoghan Ruadh. My dad was a stubborn man, but he was well matched by Father Fitzpatrick, who was a very strong-willed person and liked to have his own way. I went on to win every honour with the Ruadhs, who had a senior team, whereas St Vincent's were still in the developing stages and didn't make the senior scene until much later.

The Dublin senior hurling championship final of 1951 was arranged for Croke Park on 24 June. The week before the match was pretty hectic, and as I lived in Fairview I was caught up in much of the atmosphere of the occasion, especially since the St Vincent's players were drawn from the surrounding parishes, including my own. Eoghan Ruadh, on the other hand, were based off the North Circular Road, in Aughrim Street and Oxmantown Road, in an area popularly known as "Cowtown" because of its proximity to the cattle markets in Prussia Street. Heavy rain fell on the eve of the game and again all that morning but it had cleared off before noon. We had a problem in our house. My brother Seamus twisted his knee the night before, and by Sunday morning it was very much swollen. I immediately drove him to a local masseur and he worked on it for quite a while before strapping it. The swelling had eased and Seamus felt that it would hold for the game. He was one of our key defenders and would have been a major loss to us. The final brought the crowds flocking to Croke Park and the attendance touched 22,000, the biggest ever. Among them were many who had never seen the clubs in action, but who had come out of curiosity. St Vincent's had the greater following because of their footballing background but ironically, most of the "country" clubs weighed in behind the Ruadh.

The atmosphere in the Ruadh dressing-room was pretty tense coming up to match time. No matter how experienced you are, you cannot hide the nervous flutters in the pit of the tummy. Even Kevin Matthews, the team joker, was silent but then Kevin had reasons to be quiet. Not alone was he one of the best goalkeepers in the country, he was also the county goalie. Unfortunately, Kevin had been suspended for playing soccer. Mickey Banks was his replacement and was shouldering a mighty burden filling the shoes of one of the best in the game. As events turned out, Mickey Banks was one of the heroes of the day. The pre-match speeches add only further tension to the occasion, players are hyped up enough, but there was no mistaking the tone of Gerry O'Connor's speech or the implications should we lose. Gerry had been through it all before, as indeed had the other selectors, Mick Leahy, Batt O'Rourke and chairman Mick Connolly. This was it, this was at last the opportunity the club had been waiting for to break the hoodoo. I was picked at midfield with Sean Dinny O'Neill as my partner. We knew we faced a very stiff challenge from our opposites, Norman Allen and Liam Donnelly. Midfield control was going to be very important and both Sean and I didn't have to be reminded of that fact. I had never trained as hard for any game as I did for that particular final. I felt it was my only real chance of winning that elusive championship medal.

You could feel the tension as the two teams lined up for the start of the game. St Vincent's, having toppled the titleholders Young Irelands, felt that the Ruadhs could also be beaten. In the early stages Sean Dinny and I got most of the breaks around the middle, and after about three minutes I snapped up a clearance from the St Vincent's defence and from about sixty yards hammered the ball over the bar for the first score of the game. That score really set the adrenalin in motion and lifted us. It brought a reaction from the "Vins" and pointed frees from Paddy Donnelly and Norman Allen

Eoghan Ruadh, Dublin Senior Hurling Champions, 1951. *Back row:* Willie Ryan (Trainer), Mick Leahy (Rúnaí), Seán Óg O Ceallacháin, Finbar Molumby, Sean Maher, Ned Dunphy, Maurice Burns, Batt O'Rourke (selector). *Middle row:* Mick Connolly (Chairman), Paddy Ryan, Jimmy Whelan, Mick Banks, Seamus O'Callaghan, Sean Coughlan, Paddy King, Martin Murphy, Gerry O'Connor (selector). *Front row:* Tadgh O'Donoghue, Jack Finan, Dick Molumby, Sean Cronin (capt), Kevin Matthews, Peter Whelan, Tommy Norton. (Not in picture – Sean D. O'Neill, Gerry Guidon, Tommy Ryan and Jim Donegan).

and one from Liam Hely put them in front. I shot a goal from a 70-yard free and we were back in the lead, and I gained possession from the puck out to land the ball back in the "Vins" square, where Jack Finan promptly finished it to the net to consolidate a lead we were not subsequently to lose. The tempo was at fever pitch, and tempers began to get frayed as the Ruadh got a firmer grip on the exchanges. Sean Dinny and I were enjoying ourselves at centre field; everything we did seemed to lead to a score. St Vincent's switched their midfield players, with Liam Donnelly coming to my side of the field, but by then we were in control. If the ball is running well for you it can help a player to scale any height; your judgement of the dropping ball becomes very sharp, you fall back instead of going forward and you gain possession and score. Fate can play the opposite too, and that happens when you are struggling with your game, trying to find your touch . . . it can be a cruel game at times.

Ruadhs had extended their lead and were comfortably ahead with about eight minutes to go before half time. I remember chasing after Paddy Donnelly on the Hogan Stand side of the field as he soloed with the ball, a favourite gambit of his. Paddy moved very fast and I was still yards behind him when he delivered the ball. I remember turning away, after that I remembered no more . . . My next recollection was wakening in the dressing-room surrounded by St John's Ambulance men, my father, some Ruadh officials, and Dr Joe Stuart of UCD, who normally attended injured players at major games at Croke Park. I had been unconscious for about twenty minutes, as they made frantic efforts to revive me. I woke with Dr Stuart slapping my face, waving a smelling salts bottle under my nose. I didn't know where I was but I had a ferocious pain in my right jaw. My dad, hovering over me, told me I had been struck by Paddy Donnelly. Then I heard booing and cheering and realised where I was. Dad, having satisfied himself that I had recovered all right, left to watch the remainder of the game. Dr Stuart told me that I was struck in an off-the-ball incident and that Paddy Donnelly had been involved in it. I just couldn't fathom it. Paddy and I had been team-mates on the Dublin team for a number of years, we had met many times in League and Boland Cup games, and we always had been the best of friends. I had admired him as a hurler and considered him one of the best half-backs in the game. I still don't know to this day what prompted the stroke which shattered my jaw. I joined my mam and my fiancée

Ann on the Hogan Stand; they had witnessed the whole incident and were very upset. My dad had assured them that I was all right. Only minutes of the match remained and Ruadhs were well in command. When the final whistle sounded they were comfortable winners, 6-6 to 2-8. The incident had dampened the excitement of the occasion and the usual after-match celebrations were on the muted side. As I was leaving Croke Park with my parents and Ann, club followers led by Paddy Fennelly were mounting a horse and cab he had hired for the day, suitably dressed in the Ruadh colours. The coveted trophy was placed on top and cheered on by hundreds of Ruadh supporters, and the big celebration cavalcade headed back up the North Circular Road to Stoneybatter and "Cowtown" where pent-up emotions were soon released.

I made a journey of a different kind. Such was the pain in my jaw that I was unable to speak. I wasn't able to eat or drink, and had only had a light snack before match time. My problem became far more acute late on Sunday night and early Monday morning. My face was now badly swollen and my parents became worried and sent for the doctor. When he arrived he said I was in a state of shock and suffering from concussion and ordered me into the Bons Secours Hospital in Glasnevin. The game had made a big splash in the Monday morning newspapers. The headlines ran "Deplorable incident mars Dublin final"; "Tempers lost at Croke Park"; "Player seriously injured at Croke Park". The match reports really added more tension to the situation and there were wild rumours that I was in a critical condition in hospital. That prompted a string of callers to my home in Fairview and so started a trying week for my parents. A number of St Vincent's players called, including Paddy Donnelly. He told them that nothing justified his actions and he was deeply upset about the whole incident.

The following Sunday an article appeared in the *Sunday Press* with a heading "I shudder to think of the Dublin final". The article in question was a cynical description of the county final and was far removed from the truth. Eoghan Ruadh wrote to the editor of the paper, complaining about the particular article and demanding an apology, but it was not forthcoming. Months later the paper offered to do an extensive article on the club, but the request was ignored. That *Sunday Press* offering on the county final annoyed a lot of people, apart from the two clubs. I include a portion of it.

The Dublin final was a "broken" day — broken heads, broken hurleys, broken weather, and broken regulations, this was my impression of the All Dublin final. It was the first final of its kind and unless there is efficient control, it is hoped that it will be the last. The "All-in Dublin final" would be a more apt description. The pulling was reckless and despite the few good spells, we were all pleased when half time came. At that period Eoghan Ruadh had established supremacy . . . The events up to then were so disturbing that one had little relish to see more of the game . . .

The article went on to make pointed remarks about the two clubs, making references to other games in which one or the other of the two sides were involved in past years.

The day after the match I was X-rayed to find out the extent of my injury. On Tuesday, the surgeon, Mr McCarthy came to see me wth the results of the X-rays. He told me I was lucky for two reasons. The X-ray showed a clean break in my jawbone. Had it been a splinter break, he would have had to take a splinter of bone from my shin and that would have involved facial surgery in the repair process. I asked him about the procedure of the operation and he told me he would wire my top teeth to the bottom ones and they would have to remain that way for approximately three weeks. It meant that I would not be able to talk. I would have to sip liquids through a straw and I would be unable to eat solids, as chewing food would be impossible because of the wiring. I learned, however, to poke small pieces of food into my mouth from the side, and swallow quickly. It certainly was the most uncomfortable three weeks of my life. The best way to understand my predicament is to press your top teeth to the bottom ones, and then try to communicate or worse still, try eating a crumb of food. I couldn't yawn or sneeze without being painfully reminded about the consequences of my situation. I woke several times at night because of the wire and on at least two occasions the surgeon had to do a re-wiring job because I had snapped the wire in my sleep. There were no visitors apart from my family, as I could not talk anyway.

The surgeon removed the wire after three weeks and he had the jaw X-rayed again. The break was no longer visible, and he told me that the jaw at that particular spot would be stronger than ever and that I would have no ill effects. As I was leaving hospital next day, I

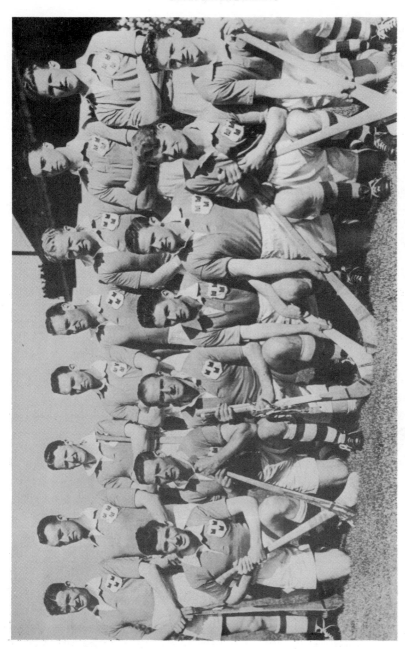

Dublin Senior Hurling Team which lost to Cork in the 1952 All-Ireland Final. *Back row:* Sean Cronin, Phil Ryan, Gerry Kelly, Seamus O Ceallachain, Alfie O'Brien, Tony Herbert, Connie Murphy, Tom Fahy. *Front row:* Sean Kennedy, Jim Prior, Kevin Matthews, Roger McCarthy, Norman Allen, Des Ferguson, Jack Finan.

reminded the surgeon of something he had said to me when he was showing me the X-rays. He had said that I was lucky for two reasons. The first reason was the fact that the break was clean, but I reminded him he hadn't told me what the second reason was. He smiled and said, "If you want to know, I'll tell you. The blow you received was a very hefty one. Had it been one inch higher, it would have caught the base of your skull, and it would have been fatal."

I returned to work in my sports shop in Talbot Street, which I had opened the previous year. It had been a struggle trying to compete against the bigger sports stores who gave the schools and colleges, some of whom I was dealing with, long-term credit, facilities I could not afford to give. (Lack of capital was to force me to sell the business at a big loss.) I had a visit from a Garda Superintendent from Store Street, who said he was calling in connection with the game in Croke Park in which I had received a facial injury. He asked me if I was taking any legal action in the matter, but I told him I was not. The incident was over and done with and best forgotten. He said he had been instructed to interview me on the direction of the Department of Justice. He further said that a question had been asked in the Dail concerning the lack of action taken by the Gardai following the assault on me in the hurling game. I reassured him that I was not contemplating any legal action, and in response to another question, I told him my club would not be taking any action either. That ended the matter.

Many years later my daughter Sinead was fussing about the house making last-minute preparations for attending a friend's wedding. "Dad, would you ever drop me down to Killester Church? I'm nearly late for a wedding." "Anybody I know?" I asked. "No, just friends of mine, Brian and Gay," she said. It had become a household joke in our family over the years how I would ask my daughters about their boyfriends, "What does he do and what does his father do?" On the way to the church I asked Sinead about the groom's father: might I know him? She said she didn't think so. "I think he played a bit of hurling when he was younger, he now plays golf." I asked, "What's his name?" "I don't think you know him, Dad, it's Paddy Donnelly."

It's a strange world.

Chapter 6
A Referee's Life

Gerry O'Connor stopped me as I was leaving the Civil Service ground in Islandbridge. We had played Young Irelands in a senior hurling league game, and Pat Stakelum, Seamus Bannon and the Kennys, Paddy and Sean, were having their first outing in the Young Irelands colours. I played on Seamus Bannon at midfield and we had a rare old battle. A huge crowd had turned up for the match, when it was mentioned in the morning papers that the Tipperary players were to play that Sunday. Ruadhs had to win the game to maintain our challenge for the League title, and we did. Gerry's message to me concerned refereeing. "I was asked to submit a name from the club for the referee's panel, so I sent in your name," he said. "But, I haven't ever refereed a match," I told him. "It will be no bother to you, you know all the rules, all you need is a good watch to keep the proper time," was Gerry's reply. I had long learned that it was no use arguing with Mr O'Connor, because he always had the last word. He then told me that the County Board were desperately needing referees, as there was a grave shortage in the county of those officials. A few weeks later I got a card from the Board Secretary, Ned Murphy, informing me that I had been appointed to referee a senior football league game between St Mary's, Saggart and St Margaret's, in Saggart. I was playing football at the time with O'Tooles, so I roped in my brother Michael, Billy Robinson, Liam "Harrier" Roche and John Monaghan as my umpires.

It was with much trepidation that I faced up to my first refereeing chore, ignoring comments from my umpiring friends; comments which suggested that no referee ever got home alive from the venue, and stressing the wisdom of having a will made. I must admit I would have preferred to officiate at a game where the competing teams played a gentler style of football, just enough to ease me into the business. Instead, I was controlling a game between two sides who were known to call a spade a spade and followed up with actions to prove it. I called the two sides together, told them precisely what would happen if anybody stepped out of line, and sent them back to their positions before throwing in the ball. Let me say there was never a more exciting match played on that sod at Saggart. The conduct of both sides was exemplary and not once did I have to admonish a player about his conduct. The game ended in a draw, which pleased everyone, myself included. Both sets of club officials were loud in their praise of my handling of the match so I left Saggart a very happy and relieved man. The extraordinary sequel was that while Gerry O'Connor had submitted my name as a hurling referee, I was never appointed to officiate at a hurling match.

For the next four years I was to referee football matches at all levels of the game. The Dublin County Board generally provided a curtain-raiser for important inter-county matches at Croke Park, and I was notified to referee a county senior football championship tie, which developed into a "needle affair", between Kickhams and St Finians, Newcastle. I sidelined two players for striking each other, and minutes later two more players became involved, so I sent them packing, including another player who vigorously questioned my decision to act in the case of the second two players. After that I had no problems. I then became the property of Martin O'Neill, Leinster Provincial Secretary, who began to pencil me in for his matches. Not alone did I have to referee the senior fixture but also the minor game, and he too stuck rigidly to giving me football fixtures — but none at hurling level. I progressed to the panel for the National League competition; the referees were appointed by Padraig O Caoimh. The Leagues brought me to many counties and I enjoyed the challenge which every game brought. In March 1951 I got a call from Padraig O Caoimh to say that he had appointed me to referee the Ireland versus Combined Universities football exhibition match at Croke Park. He said that officials from both sides had agreed to my appointment and he felt confident that I would do a good job. I was naturally thrilled; it was a very prestigious match. Mr O Caoimh mentioned that he would like to see the rules firmly applied and mentioned certain rules, like the pickup, the tackle and time-wasting, which he felt were being abused. Ironically, the pickup and the tackle problems are still with us, after all those years. He also emphasised that common sense should dictate all my decisions; and I was to follow those guidelines for the remainder of my days as the "man in the middle".

The Ireland versus Combined Universities football game on 5 March that year was one of the finest games seen at headquarters for many a long day. Both teams brimmed with household names and the standard of football was really remarkable. The Ireland team lined out as follows: Sean Thornton (Louth), Jas Murphy (Kerry), Paddy O'Brien (Meath), Sean Flanagan (Mayo, capt.), Jackie Lyne (Kerry), Henry Dixon (Mayo), Sean Quinn (Armagh), Con McGrath (Cork), Eamon Mongey (Mayo), Tony Tighe (Cavan), Mick Higgins (Cavan), Jim McDonnell (Louth), Brian Smith (Meath), Tom Langan (Mayo), and Edwin Carolan (Cavan). The Combined Universities had such splendid stars as Jim Brosnan (Kerry), Eddie Devlin (Tyrone), Hugh McKearney (Monaghan), Sean Purcell (Galway), Mick Gould (Cork), Denis Bernard (Cork) and Peter Solon (Mayo). The match itself was a thriller and the football displayed elevated the contest to one of real brilliance. Sean Flanagan captained the Ireland side, and I doubt if he had an equal around that time. He was a strict disciplinarian and brooked no nonsense from his colleagues. He questioned a few of my decisions and suggested that the "Ireland" players were being punished more often than the College players. Such was not the case, and I told him so. I did penalise his county colleague Eamon Mongey, one of the best midfielders for his size in the position, for picking the ball off the ground. Eamon had a very neat trick of putting his hands under the ball before putting his toe to it first. I whistled him early in the match, as indeed I did in the cases where other players infringed the pick-up, but very soon I had no problem in that regard, as all the players picked the ball properly. The Ireland team won the game, which was thoroughly enjoyed by a very big attendance.

In 1952 I was appointed to referee the National Football League semi-final between Donegal and Cork on Palm Sunday at Croke Park. It was a red-letter day for the Ulster county because they were creating history, being the first-ever team to represent Donegal in a major game at Croke Park. The Cork team was captained by Eamon Young, one of the finest footballers I had the privilege to watch around that time, and he was one of the stars of Cork's win. During the course of the game one of the Donegal forwards was "floored" in an attack on the Cork goal. I booked the Cork defender for the foul and went to retrieve the ball to award a free to Donegal. When I looked around I discovered there was an "extra" Donegal man on the field. A supporter had run in from behind the Cork goal and was having a verbal exchange with Cork's John Cronin, and was telling him in no uncertain fashion what he thought about Cork and all Cork men. The Donegal man stood about 5'6" while the Cork defender was about 6'3" so it took a bit of talking up to on the part of the Donegal man. Having assured the "visitor" that I was capable of dealing with any indiscretions on the field of play I steered him gently off the pitch and handed him in charge to an official. As he was being led away, he called back to me, "You'll never be as good as your father!" and with that parting shot he left. Cork won the game convincingly enough and went on to beat Dublin in the League final, which earned them a trip to New York. But trouble arose in Cork over the composition of the travelling party. The team trainer was an Army man, Corporal Jim Behan-O'Brien, but the Cork County Board decided to leave him out of the party making the trip. The team captain was Eamon Young, an Army captain, and he informed the Board that if the team trainer was not brought on the trip he would stand down. The Cork Board refused to budge and Eamon, a highly principled individual, stuck to his guns, and didn't travel with the team to the States. Nobody has contributed more to the advancement of hurling and football than the same Eamon Young, a gifted conversationalist, a prolific writer on the games, and one of the most respected figures in GAA circles in Cork.

I was very busy as a referee in the early part of 1952 refereeing Leinster championship matches. In June of that year I got a phone call from Cavan County Secretary, Hughie Smith, who asked me if I would officiate at the reopening of Breffni Park, Cavan, and referee the challenge match between Kerry and Cavan. I agreed. The official opening of Breffni Park took place on Sunday, 8 June, and I took charge of the first game between Kerry and Cavan, after which Mayo, then All-Ireland champions, played Antrim, and the referee was Tommy O'Reilly of Cootehill. An attendance of 12,000 marked the event and the gate receipts were over £1,000. The blessing was performed by Dr Austin Quinn, Bishop of Kilmore, and he was accompanied by Dr James Moynagh, a native of Mullahoran and Bishop of Calabar, and County Chairman Father Noel Fay. The reconstruction work had begun in 1950, planned by Pat Gaffney, B.E., Cavan and carried out by Messrs P. Clarke and Sons, Newtownbutler. The new stadium covered seventeen acres of ground of which the pitch and sideline covered four and a half acres. The actual playing pitch measured one hundred and fifty six by ninety-one yards, and there was a space of twenty-one feet between each sideline and the sideline seats. The ground accommodated 7,000 in sideline seating, and the whole cost of the reconstruction was £14,000. The only point of note in the Kerry-Cavan game, which Kerry won 1-7 to 0-5, was the fact that I played six minutes over the time in the first half because of a faulty timepiece which I had borrowed from my brother, Michael, one of my umpires. He had assured me that it was one of Clery's finest watches, but as I discovered, it was never intended as a match timepiece. Cavan failed to use the extra minutes even though wind assisted in that first half, and Kerry led 1-2 to 0-3 at the interval.

The Kerry team lined out as follows:
D. O'Neill, G. O'Sullivan, P.B. Brosnan, J. O'Shea, J. Murphy, J. Lyne, C. Kennelly, B. O'Shea, D. Hannifin, P. Sheehy, W. O'Donnell, T. Lyne, J. Brosnan, S. Kelly and T. Ashe.
The Cavan team consisted of S. Morris, J.J. O'Reilly, Phil Brady, P. Fitzsimons, J. Sheridan, L. Maguire, B. O'Reilly, A. Corrigan, Dan McCaffrey, T. Keogan, B. McEnroe, V. Sherlock, J. Cusack, M. Higgins, T. Tighe.

All-Ireland champions Mayo had no difficulty beating Antrim in a one sided second game by 3-8 to 0-4. It was of course, one of the finest Mayo teams ever to grace a playing pitch. The teams lined out as follows:
Mayo: S. Wynne, W. Casey, E. Waters, S. Flanagan, G. Prendergast, H. Dixon, J. McAndrew, J. Nallen, E. Mongey, P. Irwin, P. Carney, M. Mulderrig, M. Flanagan, P. Cannon and J. Gilvarry.
Antrim: M. Darragh, J. Roe, J. McDaniel, A. Bergin, R. Cunningham, P. Murray, T. McGarahan, D. Forde, M. Gribben, S. McDonald, K. Armstrong, T. Best, S. Gibson, H. Gallagher, J. McCallin.

A very informative programme was produced for that historic occasion and browsing through it I came across the following snippet:

> In the issue of the Anglo-Celt dated 13 May 1922, an advertisement appeared under the heading "GAA — Great Challenge match" for a Thompson Machine Gun at Ballyjamesduff on

Sunday 14 May between teams selected from C and D Battalions
No 3 Brigade 5th N. Division. Commandant General Hogan will
throw in the ball at 4. oc new time. Referee Commdt Seamus
McGurran. Admission sixpence. Dance in Hall same night."
The result of the match between these IRA sides was a win for
C. Batt. by 0-7 to 0-6 "before a small attendance".

I doubt if the GAA, so conscious about its "non-involvement in politics" nowadays, would allow a game to be staged for such a trophy in
present times!

My handling of the Breffni Park game between Cavan and Kerry
must have pleased Ulster officials, because I was picked to referee the
Ulster senior football final that year between Cavan and Monaghan at
Breffni Park. In spite of the fact that there was a national newspaper
strike on at the time, Breffni Park was packed to capacity for the final
on that 27 July. When I arrived out on the pitch my attention was
drawn to the fact that the sidelines were overcrowded and spectators
had actually spilled onto the pitch. I spent ten minutes or more, while
the teams had a kickabout, trying to bring a bit of order to the
scene. As soon as I had cleared spectators from one part of the line,
another crowd moved in, so I immediately summoned help from the
Gardai and officials. I told them I was not starting the game until all
those who were not seated were moved from the playing pitch. It
took precious time but it was worth it. By the time I started the
match there was plenty of space along the sidelines in which the lines-
men could operate. Cavan won the game 1-8 to 0-8. It was a real
cracker, very competitive and played in a splendid sporting spirit.
Cavan had Mick Higgins, Tony Tighe, J.J. Cassidy, Johnny Cusack,
Seamus Hetherington and Edwin Carolan in the attack, a great sextet.
Mackey Moyna was the Monaghan placekicker but while he accounted
for five of Monaghan's eight points, he also missed several comparatively easy frees, which was to prove crucial at the finish. Monaghan
were appearing in the final for the first time since 1944, and having
already won the Dr McKenna Cup earlier in the year, had high hopes
that the coveted championship title could be won. But the wily
and experienced Cavan men, led by Phil "Gunner" Brady, Pat Carolan,
Benny O'Reilly and goalie Seamus Morris, were to carry the day. It
was no fault of Ollie O'Rourke, Mickey McCaffrey, John Rice and
Packie McQuaid in the Monaghan defence, while the Moynas, Tom

and Mackey, Hughie McKearney, Paddy O'Rourke and Pat Clarke worked very hard in the losers' cause. There was so little between the teams that day, but Mick Higgins' goal was the real clincher.

I refereed the All-Ireland senior football semi-final on 3 August at Croke Park; it was not covered by the national daily newspapers because of a printing strike. Meath won the game 1-6 to 0-7, and the only incident which stirred a minor controversial note was my decision not to allow a Roscommon goal, after I had blown for a free. It all started with a Roscommon line ball taken by Eamon Boland, who centred the ball to the Meath square, and as it was in flight Meath full-back Paddy O'Brien nudged the Roscommon full-forward, Brendan Lynch, who was backing in. I immediately blew the whistle to award a free to Roscommon. Owen O'Sullivan, who was deputising in the Meath goal for the injured regular 'keeper Kevin Smyth, made no attempt to prevent the ball from entering the net, which he could have so easily done. He picked the ball up and threw it out to me. The Roscommon subs and team mentors were jumping with delight thinking that a goal had resulted; but the cheering died down when I placed the ball on the 14-yards line for a free kick, which was duly pointed. I had no intention of allowing a goal in that particular instance, though an ardent Roscommon fan argued after that I should have done so. He insisted that I should have applied the advantage rule (there is no such rule). I explained I had blown for the free before the ball had entered the Meath goal area, and the so-called advantage hadn't arisen. He still maintained that I should have allowed the goal. I then asked for the sake of the argument, "Had the ball gone wide instead of dropping into the net, what should I have done?" Unhesitatingly he replied, "Given the free, of course."

In truth, the Roscommon forwards lost the match that day. Their midfield of Eamon Boland and Gerry O'Donoghue virtually owned midfield, and the forwards received an ample supply of the ball to win the game easily. Credit had to go to the Meath defence for the manner in which they curtailed the Roscommon forwards. Meath had the best full-back line in the game in Miceal O'Brien, Paddy O'Brien and Kevin McConnell, one of the best I've seen and still unequalled to the present day for consistency, defensive covering and all-round balance. The Meath attack included the wily and most accurate Peter McDermott, Brian Smith, Paddy Meegan, Mattie McDonnell, Jimmy Reilly and Declan Brennan, a great attacking sextet. McDonnell was the Meath goal scorer, bustling defences into making errors and punishing them for doing so, while Meegan (3), McDermott (2) and Reilly (1) had the other scores. The fact that Eamon Boland accounted for four of Roscommon's seven points speaks for itself, because the forwards were confined to a point each from J.J. Nerney, J.J. Fallon and George Scott. J.J. Nerney and Meath's left half-back had a great duel all during the game, though I did warn both for niggling fouls, as I preferred to keep the play flowing. The Roscommon team still contained a number of the great players who had won All-Ireland titles in 1943 and 1944, Bill Jackson, Eamon Boland, Brendan Lynch and J.J. Nerney.

A new face, Gerry O'Malley, was playing in his first All-Ireland senior semi-final that day, and was to go on and add lustre to his name and perhaps emerge as "one of the best players ever not to have won an All-Ireland medal". The Roscommon team was: A. Brady, W. McQuillan, T. English, B. Jackson, Batt Lynch, G. O'Malley, S. Kelly, E. Boland, E. Donoghue, J.J. Nerney, J.J. Fallon, S. Scanlon, G. Scott, Brendan Lynch and G. Murray. The Meath half-back line was Patsy McGearty, Connie Kelly and Christo Hand. Des Taaffe and Brendan Maguire formed the midfield partnership. At the end, Meath fully justified their win, even though Roscommon did show up blemishes which Cavan were to exploit in the final that year. I had the pleasure of refereeing the All-Ireland minor final that year too, between Galway (winners) and Cavan. Gerry Kirwan was the only player from that 1952 minor Galway team to graduate to the senior inter-county side, and win an All-Ireland senior medal, against Cork in 1956. I can find no trace of any of the 1952 Cavan minors making an impact at senior inter-county level in later years.

In February 1953 I refereed the Munster-Ulster Railway Cup football semi-final at Croke Park. John D. Hickey, in his description of the match in the *Irish Independent*, said, "From start to finish it was a thrill a second encounter, and I have seen many an All-Ireland that did not yield as much immaculate fielding. Two incidents — a magnificent swerving 45-yards spring by Iggy Jones and a miracle save by Cork goalie D. Roche, after the Tyrone man had shot a 'Bullet' from inside the square, assured the match an abiding place in the memory of most spectators." The fact that John D. singled out Iggy Jones's solo run pleased me because I had given the Tyrone star the advantage; he was subjected to a lot of pulling and dragging and hefty charges, but he rode them all before unleashing a pile-driver which the Munster goalie saved brilliantly. Iggy was a marvellous footballer — some years previously I had refereed an Inter-provincial Colleges match between Leinster and Ulster in which Iggy had starred, so I knew his capabilities when he elected to go on that electrifying solo run which brought non-stop applause from the 13,933 attendance. Playing behind him that day was his county colleague Eddie Devlin, with Tony Tighe at full forward, Hughie McKearney at right corner and Mal McEvoy and Mick Higgins completing the line. The game itself was productive of many fine spells of football from both provinces. The lead alternated in the closing minutes before Tom Moriarty secured the levelling point for Munster.

Coming up to full time, I awarded Munster a free about 45 yards out from the Ulster goal on the Hogan Stand side of the field. One of the Munster players placed the ball on the spot where I had indicated; I blew the whistle for the free to be taken. Another Munster player reset the ball and was about to kick it when he got instructions from the sideline to move into the Ulster goal, and John Cronin was called from centre back to take the kick. I kept pointing at my watch as big John came ambling down field and I gave a few bursts on the whistle to indicate that I wanted the kick taken quickly. When John reached the ball, he stooped and reset it, so I promptly ran across to him, picked up the ball and gave a free to Ulster. The kick was taken and I blew full time with the teams locked at 2-5 points each. After the game John D. Hickey came into the dressing-room and asked me why I had changed the free decision and given the award instead to Ulster. I quoted him the rule, as best as I could remember, which states: "Once the ball has been placed for a free by the referee, or has been placed on the spot indicated by the referee by a player of the team awarded the free, a player from that team may not reset the ball, except with the expressed permission of the referee. Should a player fail to comply with this regulation the referee shall disallow the free. . ." I explained to John D. that I had awarded the free to Munster with a minute remaining, and a scorable one it was too. But by the time all the resetting had finished, and John Cronin had reached the ball, time was up; I considered the placing of the ball again by John Cronin, without my say-so, a breach of the rule, so I applied the penalty. When the two provinces met later that afternoon to decide on the replay, Munster said they were unhappy with my decision at the end of the game. Padraig O Caoimh told them that he considered my handling of the match the best exhibition of refereeing he had seen for some time. The Ulster representatives said that they would have no other official but yours truly for the replay, and "Paddio" had the last say, when he told Munster that he had already decided that I would be in charge for the replay the following Sunday, which I was.

The infamous "foreign games" rule was to rear its ugly head for the replay, however. On the day before the replay it was reported to the Munster Council meeting that Mick Gould, Denis Bernard and Jim Brosnan, three Munster players, had attended the Ireland-England rugby international at Lansdowne Road the previous Saturday, and all three had been reported by the "Vigilance Committee". For the benefit of those who may not be familiar with the procedure regarding the attendance of GAA players at other sports, the Association had a Rule, 27, which stated that "any member who plays, attends or helps to promote Rugby, Soccer, Hockey or Cricket thereby incurs automatic suspension from membership of the Association." There was also a rule which banned a member from participating in foreign dances or similar entertainments, etc. Some County Boards appointed "Vigilance Committees" to watch or attend at the banned games to see if they were being supported by GAA players. The vigilance committee individual who reported the three Munster players also reported to the Ulster Provincial Secretary, Gerry Arthurs, that Eddie Devlin of Tyrone had been seen at that rugby international. When Munster appeared on the field the following Sunday for their semi-final replay, Gould, Bernard and Brosnan had been replaced on the selection.

Ulster had still to come out on the field, so I decided to hurry them along as it was coming near match time. I went to the Ulster dressing-room and saw a very agitated Eddie Devlin standing on a seat, very nearly in tears, surrounded by the Ulster selectors. Eddie told them he had not been in Lansdowne Road on that date, and he would bring as many witnesses as was required to prove to the Council that he was not at the rugby match. Eddie beseeched the selectors not to deny him the opportunity of playing in the replay. At that point, I told Gerry Arthurs that it was only a few minutes from match time, and I wanted the Ulster team out on the field. I took my leave and when the Ulster team trotted out on to the field Eddie Devlin was not among the players or the reserves. The Ulster selectors had accepted

the "Vigilance" report and replaced Devlin on the side. It could well
have been that the Devlin episode upset the Ulster men, because they
were beaten 1-12 to 2-7 in another great contest, and as I viewed the
game Eddie Devlin was badly missed. The tragedy of that whole unhappy event was that an innocent man had been wrongly convicted of
breaking the "foreign games" rule. Eddie's own account of the hap-
penings that weekend only served to prove the fallibility of the
notorious "Vigilance Committee". The GAA were spared the embarrassment of a High Court action at the time, though the Tyrone star was
approached by a number of individuals who were very keen to have
his name cleared. Eddie Devlin was a staunch GAA man, as too were
all his family, and they were highly respected nationalists. The fact
that Eddie had been accused of attending a rugby match appalled
them, and it was particularly hurtful from their viewpoint as he had
been wrongly accused.

The true facts were that on the afternoon of the rugby international
Eddie had been doing sideline at a UCD-Geraldines Dublin senior
football league game. Eddie was released from the match by UCD,
because he was playing for Ulster against Munster the following day,
and as a precaution against injury the club agreed not to play him in
the League tie. Eddie Devlin left Belfield after the UCD-Geraldine
match, and cycling to his digs in Sandymount Avenue, near Lansdowne
Road, he got caught up with the crowds coming from the rugby
match. As luck would have it he bumped into the three Munster
players, Gould, Bernard and Brosnan, and a discussion took place
about the rugby match and of course, the Railway Cup semi-final
the following day. But the wheels were already grinding and a Vigilance
Committee report was already being formulated for dispatch to the
Munster Council meeting which was taking place after the Munster
Council Convention, held on the day before the Railway Cup replay.
The Vigilance Committee report was read at that meeting and Gould,
Bernard and Brosnan had their three months' automatic suspension
confirmed. They, of course, were ruled out of the Railway Cup replay.
Dr J.J. Stuart of UCD took up the cudgels on behalf of Devlin. He
knew the Tyrone player had been in Belfield on that Saturday in
question and he demanded an apology from the Central Council. He
was prepared to bring the entire UCD and Geraldines teams before
the Council as witnesses on Devlin's behalf. The matter was left in
abeyance. The Combined Universities selectors had met on the morn-

ing of the Railway Cup replay and picked their team to play Ireland on the following Sunday. They had received no official intimation of the suspensions when they sat down to pick their team and accordingly, they included Gould, Bernard, Brosnan and Devlin.

As matters transpired, the three Munster players had to be replaced for the Universities game the following Sunday but rather significantly Eddie Devlin took his place at midfield, and though beaten 4-10 to 0-7 by the Rest of Ireland, Devlin celebrated his innocence with a masterful display for the College side. The fact that Devlin played heightened interest in his case, and more pressure was put on him to bring the GAA to court on a defamation of character charge. Eddie was in an intolerable position. He was in his final year in Dentistry at UCD and had arranged to take up a two-year course in England when he qualified from UCD. While he was extremely annoyed at being made a victim of a horrible mistake, he had to weigh up the consequences a court action against the GAA would have on his career. The extraordinary fact was that Eddie Devlin never put his foot inside Lansdowne Road to watch a rugby match until 1982 when he brought his 17-year-old son to watch an Ireland-England International. He was never suspended for his alleged visit to rugby headquarters in 1953. His only crime was being in the wrong place at the wrong time. I often wondered how many other Eddie Devlins suffered a similar fate, but were never brought to public notice. Thank heavens for the 1971 GAA Congress at Belfast which buried the infamous "ban" once and for all time.

The absurdity of the "ban" came across dramatically in the case of Limerick's hero Mick Mackey, a Garryowen rugby club fanatic in his GAA prime, and one who never missed a game in which the club was involved. Mick was known to attend rugby internationals at Lansdowne Road. That created problems at times for the Limerick County Board, since Mick was an indispensable member of the county hurling team. They resolved the problem by appointing the bould Mick to be the "Vigilance Committee" for the county. Needless to say, no one ever fell foul of Mick — at least as a "Vigilance Committee" man. Then there was the case of another famous player, Tom Cheasty of Waterford, who was suspended for attending "Foreign Dances". It was alleged publicly at the time that there were a dozen other GAA men at the same dance, none of whom was suspended. Naturally, the question was asked why were they let off scot free while the star Cheasty got the hatchet. In the end of the day an informed observer came up with the reason for the apparent discrimination, which was that the other twelve were there in their capacity as "vigilantes".

Chapter 7
Days of Drama

Amateur drama is now firmly established in this country, helped very much by the inauguration of the All-Ireland Drama League many years ago. Amateur groups provide excellent entertainment for their respective communities by staging charity shows, much appreciated by all sections of the public. Little did I know when I joined a Dublin drama group that it would lead to my winning a very prestigious award at the ultimate Drama Festival in Athlone some years later.

It started for me when I attended a meeting in Neil Ryan's house in Walkinstown to discuss the possibility of forming a drama group. Neil Ryan, Noel Dillon (my sister Maire's husband) and Pat O'Shea were civil servants and former Irish Army officers who had served together in the "Emergency", and we had from time to time met on social occasions with their wives. My fiancée, Ann McDonagh, had plenty of stage experience, having sung in the Theatre Royal and the Capitol Theatre in the city. My sister Maire and I had received plenty of grounding in stage work at the Abbey School of Acting. In essence, we had a good base to work from at the meeting. Also present at that inaugural get-together were Mick Roddy, Sean Cunningham, and Mick Breslin. It didn't take long to take the decision to form a drama group. We were fortunate to have the services of John P. Dowling as the group producer; he had served with the "Cairde Fail" Group in that capacity. Our new group was well represented on the male side, so Pat O'Shea's wife Rosaleen, Neil Ryan's wife Maire, Sean Cunningham's wife, Betty and Dr Bob McWade's wife, Noreen helped to strengthen the female end of things in the group.

As we became more ambitious we increased our numbers with the

addition of Noreen O'Carroll, Carmel Tate and Nellie Dwyer. I persuaded an Eoghan Ruadh pal of mine, Paddy Walshe, and his fiancée,
Felicitas Kearns, to join. Mick Roddy and Sean Cunningham looked
after stage management, along with Margaret Dowling, JP's wife, and
Betty Cunningham. As with all new groups, the first production was
crucial. We had a small beginning but a useful one. My brother-in-
law, Michael J. Kearns, who was later to become involved in the
amateur drama movement in Dublin, asked us to participate in a
Variety Concert in the Father Mathew Hall, Church Street, on 31
October, 1952. Michael was interested in having a one-act play on
the programme, a comedy if possible. Our producer, J.P. Dowling,
suggested Sean O'Casey's *Pound on Demand*, a lively little play with
five characters, in which the action takes place in a Post Office. We
started rehearsing immediately. Noreen O'Carroll played the Post
Office girl; Neil Ryan, Sammy; my fiancée Ann was a customer, Noel
Dillon a polisman and I played Jerry. The play went down very well
with the Dublin audience. The guest artiste at the concert was singer
Maureen Breslin, now mother of the Nolan Sisters, who are big stars
on the showbiz circuit.

It was decided to move quickly on producing a full-length play.
The choice fell on B.G. McCarthy's *The Whip Hand*; a very suitable
choice, with six male and four female characters. We needed a spacious
rehearsal area, so I agreed to allow the group the use of a large basement in the sports shop I owned at the time in Talbot Street. We had
great fun during rehearsals of the play and after many weeks of hard
work we were ready to launch it on the public. We were invited to
stage it at the Morning Star Hostel in Richmond Street, which provided food and shelter for homeless people. The cast consisted of
Neil Ryan (Paud), Maire Dillon (Mrs Fogarty), J.P. Dowling (Willie
Brannigan), Mick Breslin (John Fogarty), myself (Larry Fogarty),
Ann McDonagh (Bernie Regan), Paddy Walsh (Peter Kavanagh),
Felicitas Kearns (Maureen Keogh) and Nellie Dwyer (Nora). J.P. Dowling was producer. There is one scene in the play when Paud, after
taking a lot of verbal bashing from Mrs Fogarty, suddenly rounds on
her and lashes her with his tongue. Our Morning Star audience immediately took him to their hearts, and standing up from their chairs,
they roared shouts of encouragement at Paud to "give it to her";
"That's the stuff, give it to the ould bitch". It was really audience
participation stuff, and did they lap it up. Never after was any pro-

duction of *The Whip Hand* greeted with such spontaneous enthusiasm. A good friend of mine, Father Sean Kitt, who administered in Castletown, Co Wexford, asked us to put the play on in the local parish hall, which we did to a very appreciative audience during Lent. Father Kitt belonged to the Dublin diocese, but when you stepped across the road to the Hall, you were in the Ferns diocese. The Lenten regulations in the latter diocese were not as stringent so Father Kitt gave us all a dispensation to enjoy ourselves on the Ferns side, which we did. The fact that we had the opportunity of having another run out with *The Whip Hand* helped us to improve the performance of the play.

We were now ready for a greater test so we entered our production for the Meath Drama Festival in Navan. The Navan Festival was one of the best and most popular occasions on the amateur drama circuit; it was also one of the best organised. We decided to enter a one-act play as well, and the choice was J.M. Synge's *Riders to the Sea*. My sister Maire played the main part of Maurya; Sean Cunningham played Bartley, Ann McDonagh took the part of Nora and Phil Kearns played Cathleen. The women "keeners" were Noreen O'Carroll, Nellie Dwyer, Margaret Dowling, Anne Cleary and Agnes O'Callaghan. The men included Noel Dillon, Mick Breslin, Paddy Walsh and myself. Competition at the Meath Festival was very stiff because it attracted many of the leading groups in the country. The adjudicator was the well-known Abbey actor Ray McAnally, who in his summing up at the end of the Festival, claimed that the standard of competition was the highest he had experienced for quite some years. In the Open sections in which we were involved, the Three-Act prize went to the Clones Dramatic Society for their production of *Vacant Possession* with 92 marks. We came a close second, which was a marvellous achievement for a rather inexperienced group, tasting Festival fare for the first time. We did have the added satisfaction of gaining a special commendation certificate for the part of Bernie, played by Ann McDonagh. We got a further boost to our morale when we won the One-Act (Open) section with *Riders to the Sea* and our producer, J.P. Dowling, was highly commended for both productions. We celebrated very late into the morning in the town that night.

Our successes at the Navan Festival fanned our appetites for more of the same, so we quickly entered for the Father Mathew National Drama Festival at Church Street, Dublin, one of the oldest and longest established Festivals on the circuit, attracting all the top Dublin groups. Competition was really razor keen. Many of the competing groups were very experienced in Festival Drama and their productions were, in the main, of professional standard. They were marvellous groups, British Railways Group, Sundrive Players, Dun Laoghaire Drama Group, Lancos Productions, St Francis Drama Group and the RIAM Drama and Verse Group, just to mention some. We learned a lot from our experience at the Navan Festival and we picked up very useful hints from Ray McAnally's summing up of our performances of *The Whip Hand* and *Riders to the Sea*. Those comments are always invaluable for groups participating in festivals, helping greatly to improve subsequent productions at stage presentation and also at acting levels. We were now more than hopeful of doing well at the Father Mathew National Festival, despite the fact that some of the major groups we were competing against featured plays we would not have attempted because of the demand on players and stage helpers. They were really that good. The adjudicator was Mr John Bourne, BDL, London and for the entire week the hall was packed. We found it very interesting to watch other plays being performed and then to listen to the comments of the adjudicator after every performance. Mr Bourne had a capacity attendance on the final night of the Father Mathew Festival when he stepped onto the stage to give his verdict on all the various productions that he had seen over the two weeks. Even from all the comments he made on the various plays we hadn't a hint on how we were to fare. He then came to the crunch and told the silent hall that the Premier Award, the Capuchin Periodicals Cup for full length plays and the one act play, had been won by the "Walkinstown Players". We couldn't contain our excitement, and it was minutes before the poor adjudicator could complete his announcement. He had awarded us 88 marks for *The Whip Hand* and 86 marks for *Riders*. We also won the *Irish Independent* Cup for Three-Act plays; J.P. Dowling received the Best Producer award, and highly commended certificates went to my sister Maire for "Maurya" in *Riders* and Neil Ryan for "Paud" in *Whip Hand*. No new group could have had a more successful foray into the hard grind of festival competition. We left the Father Mathew Hall on that 17 May evening in 1953 walking on air. One of the perks for winning at the Festival was two free nights at the Father Mathew Hall in which to stage a play of our own choosing. We liked Michael MacLiammoir's *Where Stars*

Walk, which we had seen presented by the Dalta Theatre Group in
Navan. One of the very fine actors in that group was Noel Lynch, a
brother of the more famous Joe, of Glenroe fame.

As it was to be a social production for the group and indeed a test
of our acting abilities, it was decided to stage *Where Stars Walk* in
the Church Street Hall. We didn't realise the trouble the play was to
cause us. It is a mixture of fantasy, comedy and satire with a generous
entertainment content. Most of the parts are cameo parts, so it was
up to each player to make the most of his or her offering. Neil Ryan
and Ann McDonagh played the parts of the mythical lovers, Midhir
and Etain; Princess Etain,

> A Daughter of a King of Ireland, heard
> A voice, singing on a May Eve like this
> And followed half awake and half asleep
> Until she came to the Land of Faery
> Where nobody gets old and godly grave
> Where nobody gets old and crafty and wise
> Where nobody gets old and bitter of tongue,
> And she is still there busy with a dance
> Deep in a dewy shadow of a wood
> Or Where Stars Walk upon a mountain top.
>
> — W.B. Yeats

The part of Rex Dillon was to have been played by Sean Cunningham, but he opted out because of business pressures. We had to call
on the services of another fine actor, Vincent Bradley, who was familiar
with the role, having played it with another group. Vincent remained
with us and his excellence as an actor of quality was of immense help in
later productions. My sister Maire played the part of Sophie Sheridan,
the part of Sheila McCann was taken by Roseleen O'Shea, Pat Dillon
played Bob Twomey, Carmel Tate was Mary Dempsey, Noel Dillon
took the part of Mr Brunton and I played Tommy Millington. The
harpist was Roisin Ni She and the production was very well attended.
The group had good publicity over their success earlier at the Father
Mathew Festival.

The action of the play takes place in the drawing-room of Sophie
Sheridan's house in Dublin. In the opening scene which features the
mythical lovers there are a few exclamations of "Oh God, how beauti-

ful" and "Oh God, what beauty", etc., after which the play develops. After a short period the President of the Hall, Father Celsus, came backstage and said that if he heard one more "Oh God" he would order the curtain down, and we knew he meant it. The cast tried frantically to leave out all religious appellations in their lines in order to comply with the good Father's wishes, and this wasn't at all easy. We decided not to avail of the second free night at the Hall. A few weeks later we brought the play to the Curragh Camp and performed it at the Military Hospital, where it was given a rousing reception.

We didn't rest on our laurels, because we immediately started into rehearsals for our next production, Walter Macken's *Home is the Hero*, a very demanding play with several strong parts. It was felt that we should gear the production for the Meath Drama Festival in mid-March. John P. Dowling, our producer looked a natural for the part of Paddo (the Hero), and the other parts were filled by Maire Dillon (Dalia, Paddo's wife), Mick Breslin (Willie), Ann McDonagh (Josie, Paddo's daughter), Neil Ryan (Dovetail), Roseleen O'Shea (Bid, Dovetail's wife), Carmel Tate (Mrs Green, tragic widow), Nellie Dwyer (Lily Green) and Noel Dillon (Trapper Flynn). I played the part of Manchester (Spiv). The rehearsals took place in the basement of my sports shop in Talbot Street and the whole cast worked very hard. It was ready for our first run-out in March, a charity performance in aid of the Churchtown and Kilberry Schools Improvement Fund at the Town Hall in Athy, a venue we were to visit on a number of occasions with various productions. The weather could not have been worse on 4 March 1954, when we arrived to perform the play. Despite a terrific gale, snow, hail and sleet, theatre lovers in the town turned out in force to see a play about which much had been written in the daily press. The audience reaction to the play was fantastic, and indeed pleasing from our viewpoint. The *Nationalist & Leinster Times* on the following Saturday gave the production a very favourable review, singling out J.P. Dowling, Maire Dillon, Mick Breslin, Roseleen O'Shea, Carmel Tate and Ann McDonagh for special mention. A week later we presented the play at the Meath Drama Festival, along with a One-Act, *Spring* by T.C. Murray. The adjudicator was Miceal O hAodha, Production Director at Radio Eireann. The one-act play is a delightful one and has been performed by virtually all drama groups. There are five characters in the play. I played the part of the old man, Andreesh, Neil Ryan had the part

Wives of well known footballers (from left): Mary Heffernan, Lily Jennings, Ann O Ceallacháin, Maureen Lavin, Maura Ferguson with children (from left) Eimear Jennings, Niall Lavin, Finin O Ceallacháin, Ronan Ferguson.

Walkinstown Players, who won the Capuchin Cup in the National Drama Festival at the Fr Matthew Hall. With cup is J.P. Dowling, producer. Included are Sean Cunningham, Seán Óg O Ceallacháin, Mick Breslin, Maire and Noel Dillon, Felicitas Kearns, Paddy Walsh, Neil Ryan, Ann McDonagh, Nellie Dwyer, Nan O'Carroll, Betty Cunningham, Pat Warren and Mick Roddy.

John P. Dowling, producer, Walkinstown Players, receiving the Capuchin Periodicals Cup from Fr Nessan OFM Cap. Adjudicator John Bourne (London) is in the centre.

The cast of *Where Stars Walk* by Mícheál Mac Liammoir. From left: Vincent Bradley, Ann McDonagh, Neil Ryan, Carmel Tate, Seán Óg, Noel Dillon, Maire Dillon. Seated in front are Roseleen O'Shea and Pat Dillon.

of Seamus, Carmel Tate was Shuvawn, Noreen McWade was a fine Jude and the young girl was played by Deirdre Dillon, the 10-year-old daughter of Maire. Deirdre was to receive special mention at several festivals for her playing of the young girl's role. Once again we found that it takes an exceptional play to win the Open section in the Three-Act at the Navan Festival, but we did finish high up in the marks for production and presentation.

We did have success with *Spring* by taking the award in the One-Act (Open) for the second year in a row, and that gave us a nomination to the All-Ireland Drama Festival in Athlone. We had already gained a nomination to Athlone with *The Whip Hand* in the Three-Act section, which was quite an achievement in such a short number of years for a group. J.P. Dowling was anxious to have a few more run-outs with *Spring*, so our good friends in Athy came to the rescue and invited us down to play *Spring* and *Home is the Hero* in the St John's Little Theatre. That was again a valuable exercise; the reaction of the audience can help a group immeasurably in polishing up a production, and the receptive audience in Athy simply did that. There is a scene near the end of *Spring* where the old man, Andreesh, is carried through the door of the cottage by his son, Seamus. In Navan, Andreesh was carried head first through the door but there were a few titters from the audience, which we thought of no significance. We performed the same direction in Athy, getting a similar reaction, and we then realised something did not gell in a very touching moment of the play. When we talked about both productions after the visit to Athy, someone pointed out that Andreesh should have been carried in feet first, so that the old man's face could be seen by the audience. It was a very small point, but obviously important to the production.

With Athlone over a month away, we decided to enter *Spring* in the One-Act Open section at the County Dublin Drama Festival in Donabate. This was an extremely popular Festival, which most of the Dublin groups supported. We were delighted to win again with *Spring*, and J.P. Dowling won the Producer's award. There was an added bonus for me, as I won the Best Actor award and my 10-year-old niece, Deirdre Dillon, received a special commendation certification for her small but important part in the production. In his summing up the drama critic of the *Drogheda Independent* gave me very high praise, which was very flattering, and alluding to the rest of the cast said: "Carmel Tate as Shuvawn gave a creditable performance, her acting being of a high standard. Of the younger members of the cast, Noreen McWade as Jude, the woman of the house, put over a difficult role with ease and gave a very convincing portrayal. The part of her husband, Seamus, was in the capable hands of Neil Ryan, who made no mistakes. A special word of praise is due to the little girl, Deirdre Dillon, who performed her small but effective part delightfully. Altogether, it was a magnificent play, magnificently handled by all concerned."

We were all set for Athlone and the All Ireland Festival. The important thing to remember about Athlone is the fact that you are competing against the best drama groups in the country, the best plays chosen from all the major festivals throughout the country, and indeed, against the best amateur actors and actresses in the movement. It must also be mentioned that quite a number of groups, in order to enhance their own productions, bring their own scenery, stage sets and props for particular productions, especially if those sets are not available in the Athlone theatre. I would stress that those in charge of staging festivals in Athlone do all in their power to ensure that visiting groups get the best of attention, and no effort is spared in the preparation of the various plays for that evening's production. On Friday 30 April we presented the three-act play, *The Whip Hand*, and the one-act, *Spring*, before a packed house in the Sportex Hall. I played the part of the old man Andreesh in *Spring*, and when we had completed, I quickly had to prepare for the part of Larry, a young medical student, in *The Whip Hand*, two very contrasting roles.

When we assessed our performances later that night over a cup of tea, all were agreed it was our best offering of both plays. There were the usual few nervous hiccoughs but in both productions we felt we had got the pace right, and in the three-act extracted all the humour and fun which the play offered, the audience reacting accordingly. There is a scene between Willie Brannigan and myself in the third act in which Willie lists all the various individuals I would need to canvass for support, if I was to pull off the "eggtesting" job, including the GEE AH AH (GAA). Every time that sentence was said it brought a great reaction from the audience, irrespective of where we played it. Obviously, it was because of my own involvement in GAA affairs. Indeed, I had to show a doubting friend the actual line in the play before he believed that we hadn't put the line in ourselves in order to extract a laugh. Certainly, the audience in Athlone responded very well and it was quite some time before I was able to deliver my reply to Willie.

In that year (1954) the adjudicators were Gabriel Fallon of the Abbey Theatre, the former actor and author, and W. Bridges-Adams, an Englishman, who lived in Bantry, Co Cork. Mr Bridges-Adams had already adjudicated on the Southern Festival circuit. In Britain, he had directed plays at the Memorial Theatre, Stratford-on-Avon but a lot of people held reservations about his suitability for the Athlone Festival, a view not shared by the Festival Director, Brendan O'Brien. He regarded the distinguished man of the theatre as a capture for the Athlone Festival. Gus Smith, in his book *Festival Glory in Athlone* made this interesting observation: "It was soon apparent to those close to the festival scene that the imposing Bridges-Adams wasn't taking altogether too kindly to Gabriel Fallon, his fellow adjudicator. Once after a production in the Dean Crowe Memorial Hall, Fallon remarked to Bridges-Adams: 'Don't you think the team work was very convincing tonight?' 'Teamwork!' repeated the Englishman sardonically. 'You sound, sir, as if you are talking about a football or cricket team.' But, Fallon assured him, 'Teamwork is a popular word in the Irish theatre.' 'Then, sir, you are not talking about the Theatre'." Gabriel Fallon denied that he had any clashes with his fellow adjudicator; however he did admit that there were certain things about Irish plays which Mr Bridges-Adams didn't understand. "The extraordinary thing," reflected Fallon later, "was that he was persuaded that I held a high rank in the IRA and was one of the fastest triggers in the West." Both men survived the Festival and proceeded to enjoy it.

I was unable to be at the final adjudication on the Sunday night in Athlone, but members of the group were present. The results were given out on the eleven o'clock radio news bulletin, just a few minutes before I went on air with my GAA programme. The Three-Act Play (Open) was won by the Clones Dramatic Group with Walter Macken's *Mungo's Mansion* directed by Victor J. Wheatley, who also took the main part of Mowleogs Canavan. Wheatley was undoubtedly a brilliant actor-producer, who was to win many awards for his stage productions and acting abilities. The group specialised in Macken's plays and was a clear example of what a small group can achieve at amateur level. The radio announcer Tommy Cox, went on to give the other category winners, and my heart gave a jump when he mentioned that I had been awarded the Best Actor award at the Festival. I had to wait until the rest of the group had returned from Athlone to learn the details. Our group, The Walkinstown Players, had received a special award for *The Whip Hand* and in addition, Deirdre Dillon had got a special award for the part of the young girl in *Spring*. J.P. Dowling had received a special citation for both the Three-Act and One-Act productions.

After most festivals the adjudicators give each group a written assessment of their productions. In Athlone, each play was assessed under four headings, production, acting, stage presentation and choice and suitability. In dealing with *The Whip Hand* under "production" the adjudicators stated: "The adjudicators confess to having laughed so much at this play that, when it was over, they were unable to give the cast as many notes as they generally do. Their concern must now be to remember that, even if the show had been of an indifferent quality, it would have tended to benefit by contrast with the grimness of the two or three productions which had preceded it. Fortunately, in this case, both the production and performance were admirable in themselves. Over and above his unobtrusive efficiency in the management of the stage business, the producer (J.P. Dowling) seemed to have borne in mind the fundamental truth that in a play of this kind every character must be the sort of person you would like to know. Add this to the rollicking high spirits which he shared with the whole cast and all the ingredients of a jolly show were present." On the question of "Acting" the adjudicators said: "High marks to Mrs Fogarty (Maire Dillon). If she does not mind being compared to Queen Victoria, we would say of her also that she towered in spite of her stature. What is more important, it was on her, most of all, fell the responsibility of sending us away convinced that every person in the play was pleasant. If she had played with a hard heart this would not have been so; as it was, we became very fond of her. At an equal level was Larry [myself]. This part was played with deftness, polish, charm, unflagging vitality and a sense of character that raised it above the level of a commonplace juvenile lead. We admired him the more when we realised that he had played an old and dying man earlier in the evening. It was typical of a production in which all the players were adjusted to each other and to the play, that the timid John (Mick Breslin) seemed exactly the sort of brother Larry might have had and Bernie (Ann McDonagh) exactly the right girl for him; both these parts were well and truly played. No Uncle Paud (Neil Ryan) could altogether fail, but this one deserved praise for the ripe and sure touch with which he took his opportunities. Peter (Paddy Walshe), the one loose thread in the play — he was discreetly made interesting enough to hold his own as he was wanted. Willie Brannigan (J.P. Dowling) had to be seen to be believed in; when seen, he instantly was, to our great delight. Dan (Noel Dillon) and his daughter (Felicitas Kearns) implanted themselves clearly and again, pleasant.

"At the outset the speech was strong, clear and lively, and should dispose altogether of the notion that Irish drama must be spoken in a downhill tone. There was very little fidgeting and people took their cues in professional style without cutting in on each other's laughs. We ought, perhaps, to scold them for small tamperings with the text, but as many of these were actual improvements prompted by stage sense we let them off — with a caution. 'Stage Presentation', entirely adequate for the purpose and 'Choice and suitability of play', Good."

When dealing with the production of *Spring* the two adjudicators were more critical in their views; on production and acting the assessment stated: "Although their work was marred by minor faults, the players scored heavily in both these categories. Shuvawn (Carmel Tate) was rather too monotonous in intonation, and might, indeed, with considerable profit have taken some of the essential rhythm of her dialogue from the very fine speaking of Andreesh, who, on the other hand, might have used more of the whiteness of age in his make up, particularly in his beard. Yet, both performances were effective performances. The players of Jude (Noreen McWade) and Seamus (Neil Ryan) clearly knew what they were about, the first being sufficiently emotional and the second suitably restrained. Yet, the not-too-easy transitions in Jude's part were rather too jerkily taken and might have been coloured by a greater generosity of feeling. Undoubtedly, the most wholly delighting performance in the play was given by the child actress Deirdre Dillon in the part of Nora." For Stage Presentation they felt that setting, lighting and effects were good. The business with the dying lamp was imaginatively contrived, while the choice of play was excellent.

A very extensive review of the All-Ireland Drama Festival appeared in the *Westmeath Independent*, written by J. Kane Archer, who covered the two weeks of the Festival, watching more than thirty amateur companies representing the finalists from a dozen different Festivals.

He also covered the Festival for the national dailies and his comments were avidly read by all the competing groups. Writing about B.G. McCarthy's *The Whip Hand*, Kane Archer said: "Close on the heels of the Clones Dramatic Society production came the Walkinstown Players who have improved immeasurably since last year. Their production of *The Whip Hand* runs very close indeed to equalling the achievements of Clones. Starting with the great advantage that McCarthy's play succeeds in its own aims (where Macken does not) these players delivered their caustically witty lines with a zest and liveliness that carried the play well, and which hardly slackened for a moment. The best performance came from Sean Og O Ceallachain as the slick-alec Larry Fogarty, perpetual medical student threatened with a dismal future as official Egg Tester, whose personality on the stage was highly reminiscent of Ronald Shiner turned Irish, matching the part with a superb impertinence that never palled. The contrast with his performance a half hour earlier as Andreesh, the old man in T.C. Murray's *Spring*, which had a dignity filling old age, marks him as an actor, not altogether to be accounted for by his experience as a commentator. Maire Dillon, as Mrs Fogarty, was a fitting opponent in this battle of wits, and fine performances came from Neil Ryan, Noel Dillon and J.P. Dowling (producer) among others in a fine and technically competent cast."

We were disappointed at not having won the Open section. We genuinely felt that our production of *The Whip Hand* deserved more than just a special award. However, that's the luck of drama festivals. We did respond to a number of requests by putting on plays at various centres, but by then my interest in amateur dramatics was beginning to wane. I enjoyed the experience and the fun associated with productions for charities but the over-emphasis on trying to win at festivals started to detract from the original idea on which the group was founded. The constant demands on personal time, and the travelling, were interfering with my other interests, so I felt it was time to call a halt.

Business had slackened off considerably in my sports shop, due to the depression, and I was forced to dispose of it at a major loss. In September 1954 Ann and I got married and some weeks later I was invited by Paddy Flynn, Sports Editor of the newly launched *Evening Press*, to become Gaelic Games correspondent. I started in November, and I have filled that role ever since. Indeed, I may add I am the only link that remains of the original band of contributors which started out with the new paper in 1954. The "Walkinstown Players" continued to perform with distinction and in late 1954 they started rehearsing Brian McMahon's fine play *Bugle in the Blood*, for a charity performance in the St John's Little Theatre in Athy. This play by the well-known Kerry playwright offers a great challenge to an amateur drama group and has a number of character parts, which gave members of the "Walkinstown Players" an opportunity of displaying their acting skills. Two performances of the play were given on Thursday and Sunday before Christmas and on each showing the hall was packed.

The local theatre critic paid a warm tribute to Vincent Bradley for his playing of Tim Sullivan, a very sensitive performance, while Jimmy McClatchie, another particularly fine actor, who would win the Best Actor award at the All-Ireland Drama Festival at Athlone many years later for the part of Feste in *Twelfth Night*, took the part of Rab. He also mentioned that four of the cast, Neil Ryan, Noel Dillon, Mick Breslin and Rosaleen O'Shea, as Botany Connell, Circus Jack, Joe Trimble and Mrs Monaghan respectively, gave remarkable realism to their difficult roles. Newcomers to the boards at St John's, Jo Bagnall as Maroya Trimble, A.J. Mullarkey as Andy Trimble, Noreen McWade as Evelyn McCann, Maire Fitzgerald as May Bridie Monaghan, impressed immensely. McClatchie's playing of Rab, the coloured pedlar, and Bradley's fine portrayal of Tim Sullivan were the high spots of the evening. Once again J.P. Dowling's production came in for high praise, while stage management was in the capable hands of Sean Cunningham, Alison Curran, Frances Butler and W. Clarke. *Bugle in the Blood* was to win awards for the "Players" at Cavan, Gorey and Meath Festivals, but alas it failed to bring the ultimate prize from Athlone. The "Players" put on two well-known plays for their 1955-56 season in *Friends and Relations* by St John Ervine at the Bernadette Hall in Rathmines, and *Juno and the Paycock* by Sean O'Casey in the Dagg Hall, RIAM, Westland Row, Dublin. The group continued to put on many fine productions until it eventually ceased as a group in early 1957.

Chapter 8

Radio Times

Sports Stadium was the only midweek sports programme on radio when I joined it in the early 1950s. It was an extremely popular programme, embracing all the major and minority sports, and for that reason it had a wide appeal. The programme was conceived by Brian Durnin in 1949 and contained a weekly roundup of views and reports. It was a scripted programme under the editorship of Gus Ingoldsby, the Staff Administration Officer, who was unofficially in charge of sport at the time. The programme was presented in turn by Eamonn Andrews and P.P. O'Reilly and in 1951 it was taken over by Philip Greene. To begin with, Philip was the editor and producer and later assumed complete control as presenter. It was Philip who invited me to contribute the Gaelic games portion.

I had met him some years earlier, not in a radio context, but on the playing fields. I was a member of the Ierne Sports Club in Parnell Square; the club had a sports ground on Richmond Road, Drumcondra, which catered for tennis, soccer and cricket and boasted of a very successful social side. I was working at the time in O Glasain's shop in O'Connell Street and we had our half-day on Wednesday. Dave Keenan was a member of the soccer section and he organised a friendly match on those Wednesday afternoons. The Ierne team was composed of members mostly, Jimmy Little, Jimmy Davenport, Bill Coghlan, father of Eamon, Leo Ward, Paddy Dyer and Pa Daly who all three played with Drumcondra, Jimmy O'Meara (also Drums), Dermot Byrne, Sonny Farrell, Dave Keenan and myself. Phil Greene played on the opposing team; this included many of the leading cross-channel players of the time who were home on holidays, and who enjoyed

127

the Wednesday "crack". The more prominent were Con Martin (Aston Villa), Noel Kelly (Arsenal), Tommy Eglinton (Everton), Paddy Waters (Carlisle), Dave Walsh (West Brom), and there were others who turned up looking for a game, and were always accommodated. When Phil and I renewed acquaintance later on radio, he claimed that I had "kicked the shins off him", in those friendly matches, an accusation I denied, of course. I claimed that Gaelic players had a slightly different approach to soccer, and anyway pleaded ignorance of the soccer rules. I really enjoyed those matches, and to give the visiting team an extra touch of class (I often reminded Con Martin) I sometimes threw my lot in with Phil's side. Con Martin typified the all-round sportsman. A brilliant international soccer player, he was also a fine hurler and an outstanding Gaelic footballer, golfer and cricketer. I played against Con in my college days and I marked him down then as a coming star. He never used questionable tactics. Con made his debut on a Dublin senior football team in the early 1940s and went on to win a Leinster championship medal. When it was discovered that he had been playing soccer at the same time, he was denied his medal. Over thirty years later the Dublin Supporters Club presented him with a compensatory medal which he values.

In 1953 I was invited by Philip Greene to join Hermitage Golf Club, near Lucan, a membership I have always treasured. Five years later Phil and I went on to win the prestigious Hermitage Open Four-ball Matchplay championship. I soon learned about the rules of the game from Phil, but in a way which was not intended. In our semi-final match, we were one hole up playing the 17th. One of our opponents, inadvertently, indicated the line of putt for his partner by placing the flagpole on the surface of the green — which is against the rules. We played out the hole, which was halved in par 4's. As we were leaving the green, Philip, more in an educational gesture, explained to our opponents that they had broken a rule of golf by indicating the line of putt with the flagpole. They were surprised. "Are you claiming the hole, Phil?' asked one of our opponents. "No," said Phil, "I'm just letting you know about the incident in case you didn't know the rule." Our opponent's next remark stopped us in our tracks. "Well, Phil, I'm sorry, I have to claim the hole off you for not applying the proper rule yourself." I was stunned, but Phil was furious, and there was nothing we could do about it. We were now all square, playing the match, going down the 18th which was duly halved in a par four. It was on to the 19th which I won with a par four for the match. We won the final beating two very fine Hermitage members, Kevin Byrne and Dr Jim Gormley.

Phil and I were to win many more competitions in the club for many years after that, which helped to bring my handicap down to 2. I represented the club in Senior Cup, Barton Shield, Junior Cup, Barton Cup and other major competitions. My big thrill was winning the Club Championship in 1963, the same year as another left-hander, Bob Charles, won the British Open championship. In 1977, I led the Press, Radio and Television Society team to victory in the prestigious Dublin United Golf Societies Matchplay competition. The team consisted of Seamus Smith and Shay Keenan (*Irish Press*), John Foley and Brendan O'Farrell (*Irish Independent*), Frank Johnstone (*Sunday People*) and myself. The Society captain was Brendan McKenna of the *Evening Press*. It was the first time for the Society to win this highly coveted matchplay title. Con Martin was also a member of the Hermitage Club and claimed, with some justification, that he was responsible for bringing my handicap down; but I had paid a dear lesson judging from the number of times I had to put my hand in my pocket to pay my fourball bets against the same Con.

He was one of a number of prominent well-known soccer stars who appeared on Philip Greene's *Sports Stadium*, which was, without doubt, a marvellous programme. I brought along leading GAA players for comments on weekend matches and they in turn met leading players from the other codes or athletes who were appearing at the time. All those guest players had a common bond; they enjoyed their respective sports and it was surprising how well versed each was in the other sports. *Sports Stadium* had many notable guests. I can recall meeting Ronnie Dawson, Karl Mullen, Gordon Wood (an excellent hurler) of rugby fame, Christy O'Connor, Harry Bradshaw, Norman Drew, Joe Carr (golf), Billy Morton, Ronnie Delaney, Noel Carroll (athletics), Dr Kevin and Mick O'Flanagan and numerous other soccer personalities; a host of GAA stars, Ring, Nick Rackard and Billy, Sean Purcell, Heffo and the great Dubs of the time. Phil invariably included special visiting guests on the programme and some who spring to mind include Jesse Owens (a wonderful man), Test cricketers Denis Compton and Patsy Hendron, Mike Hawthorne of motor racing, tragically killed later, Stanley Woods and Reg Armstrong, noted motor cyclists, and many more. The *Sports Stadium* team looked after virtually every sport. I covered Gaelic games; Dr Austin Darragh (who brought my son Finin into the world) looked after rugby, along with Liam Browne. Liam also looked after athletics (AAU); Dan Lyons covered the NACA scene; Sean Murphy racing, Frank Johnstone and Kieran Kenneally soccer with Philip; Paddy O'Neill ("Paddy O'Brien"), dogs, Barry Mason motor sport, Stanley Bergin cricket, Harry Thullier fencing and table tennis and Kevin Byrne tennis, while the father figure, Mitchel Cogley, commented on all sports. The provincial scripts for the programme were supplied by Tom Barrett (Munster), Jim Lydon (Connacht) and Jim Davey (Ulster), and those provincial scripts were read by various members of the Radio Eireann Repertory Company, Tomas Studley, Seamus Forde, Joe Lynch, Leo Leyden, Joe O'Dea, Charlie McCarthy and Arthur O'Sullivan, together with a few free-lancers, Gay Byrne included.

Some years after taking over the programme on a permanent basis, Philip Greene decided to change the format slightly. He did away with the morning script rehearsal on the Fridays. We assembled instead in the afternoon and recorded the programme. That system was to change as well. One afternoon, as we were preparing to record the programme for later transmission, Phil took my script, and tore it in pieces, much to my amazement. "You won't need it, you can do it off the cuff," said Phil. And so I did. I previewed all the GAA matches of that weekend without referring to a script. From that afternoon on, Phil dispensed with all scripts, and every contributor had to preview his particular sport without reference to a script. In 1953 Philip Greene was appointed Sports Officer in radio, a decision which was prompted by the decision of Gus Ingoldsby, the Staff Administration Officer, to seek promotion, which was no longer possible if he had stayed in radio. Ingoldsby's tenure in sport was purely temporary but he was very much drawn to it. "There was," he told me recently, " a considerable demand for broadcasts of all the All-Irelands from Irish missionaries in Africa, and I set up the machinery by which those broadcasts were transmitted from Brazzaville, the short-wave station in the French Congo. In time, All-Ireland finals were picked up in Central Africa, much to the delight of exiles in those countries." The practice was to continue very successfully after Philip Greene was appointed Sports Officer in 1953, and he was able to extend the coverage to other continents as well. Phil remained in charge of *Sports Stadium* until 1969 when it was taken over in a different format with

Dublin United Golf Societies Association 1977 Trophy Winners. From left: Seamus Smith, Frank Johnstone, Brendan O'Farrell, Brendan McKenna (Society Captain), Seamus Keenan, Seán Óg and John Foley.

Tea break in the *Irish Press* Wire Room. Overseer Eddie Fitzgerald with Seán Óg.

the redevelopment of the Sports division in RTE.

There has not been a better sports magazine programme produced since the passing of *Sports Stadium*, a very intimate and chatty show, which had a legion of followers. I could not have worked with a finer band of contributors, journalists and otherwise, under the superb direction of Philip Greene. He and I struck up a great relationship and the fact that we represented rival codes was never allowed to impinge on that friendship. Our first assignment was in July 1953, when we headed off to interview the Munster senior hurling finalists, Tipperary and Cork, for the programme. Thurles was our first stop where we met the ever-courteous and helpful Tipperary County Secretary Phil Purcell, a former All-Ireland hurler. The recording machine we used on that trip was a large, cumbersome apparatus, an M5, which is now in the RTE museum. Later that evening at training I interviewed John Doyle, Pat Stakelum, Jimmy Finn, Phil Shanahan and the legendary Paddy Leahy. The recording machine was so heavy that it took the two of us to carry it from interview point to the car. Thankfully, it was later replaced by a neater machine, an L2, which one person could carry and operate. Phil and I moved on to Cork and to my old friend Jim Barry, who needed no encouragement when venturing an opinion on anything. I also persuaded Christy Ring to comment, a feat in itself. Ring shunned publicity but I was more fortunate than most in getting him to commit himself to a chat about a particular match. I completed my interviews with the Cork players on that visit, having spoken to the peerless Tony Shaughnessy, Dave Creedon, Vince Twomey, Paddy Barry and Gerry O'Riordan, whom I had played against in Dublin when he was figuring prominently with the Civil Service club. Phil edited the piece and it went out as a Munster final special the following Friday on *Sports Stadium*.

The final itself was a bit disappointing. I had seen far more exciting games between these two rivals at the famed "Gaelic Grounds" on the Ennis Road. Even though Tipperary led by five points early in the second half, there was no great urgency in their play. Tipp, I thought, made a major blunder by taking off Connie Keane despite the fact that the defender had kept a tight rein on the redoubtable Christy Ring. With Keane's departure, the pressure was off Ring and he gained a new lease of life. Following a great goal from Josie Harnett, Ring proceeded to hit an inspired patch, shooting three points in a row, and Cork were on their way to a second win in a row over their great rivals. Philip decided we should cover the All-Ireland football finalists, Kerry and Armagh, a few months later, and that particular assignment only served to prove the difference between the experienced and the inexperienced. Kerry were no strangers to the All-Ireland scene, but Armagh were. Indeed, Armagh were appearing in their first All-Ireland football final at senior level and the whole county was agog with All-Ireland fever. Collective training was part and parcel of the All-Ireland scene at the time, which in essence meant that an entire squad of players were brought together and trained together during the three weeks training period. That collective training was abolished at the 1954 Congress on the recommendation of a Commission of Inquiry set up by the Central Council. The motion to set up the Commission was initiated by the Civil Service Football Club. The "Service" spokesman at the time was Paddy O'Kelly. Full-time training was held to be inconsistent with the amateur status of the GAA. Kerry moaned loud and long at its passing. How could they, with so many immigrants in the team, prepare without collective training? They blamed the new rule for losing the 1954 final. They have adapted alright!

The Kerry team was based in Killarney for the 1953 final, while Armagh trained in Maghera on the shores of Lough Neagh. Dr Eamon O'Sullivan, the famous Kerry coach, was a legendary figure and could not have been more helpful. I was able to conduct all my interviews with the players, together with a very in-depth interview on football generally with the very knowledgable Dr Eamon, which we were able to use as a special in a much later programme. Sean Murphy, Micksie Palmer, Jackie Lyne and Jim Brosnan gave me plenty of material during the course of the interviews which served to prove that not alone were they good footballers but they were also good talkers. The scene was so different when we eventually reached Maghera, where the Armagh team had their training camp. When I set about rounding up some of the players for my interview piece, trainer and coach John Vallely stopped me. He told me he didn't want me interviewing the players, claiming that it would put them under too much pressure, and that he had banned the press in general from talking to them or annoying them. Despite all my pleadings the bould John refused to budge. Instead, we were allowed to interview the selectors and Board officials, while John spoke on behalf of the team. Incidentally, some of the self-same strictures apply to this very day in some of the counties involved in major finals. The same reasons are being offered: that publicity in the media, be it radio, TV or newspapers, might put too much pressure on the players. That of course, is a whole heap of rubbish, and I can say that not alone as a former player, but as a broadcasting journalist who has been in the business for forty years. Most players enjoy the attention of the media, while the country at large enjoys the comments made by players on the occasion of major games. Perhaps some players outstep the mark in brashness but in the main I have found GAA players to be quite willing to stick their necks out, without appearing to be bigheaded with their comments.

Croke Park hosted its greatest crowd ever for that 1953 football final. The gates at the Canal end were forced in just before the start and literally thousands poured in. If the truth were known it would in all probability reveal an attendance bordering on the 90,000. That 1953 final was won by Kerry but possibly thrown away by Armagh, who were to my mind, having seen them destroy Cavan in the Ulster final, one of the finest teams ever to emerge from Ulster at the time. They had been well and truly beaten in the 1950 All-Ireland semi-final by that superb Mayo team led by Sean Flanagan, but I thought they had a team in 1953 which was quite capable of winning the coveted Sam Maguire Cup for the first time. There were periods during the game when that possibility looked decidedly on and none more so than in the final minutes when that very efficient and excellent referee Peter McDermott (Meath), after consulting with his umpires, awarded Armagh a penalty having deemed that the Kerry goalie had picked the ball off the ground (the rule has changed since). Kerry were leading by two points as Bill McCorry stepped up to take the penalty. Bill was an excellent penalty-taker but to the amazement of the hushed crowd, he blazed the ball wide. Kerry went on to win the title. McCorry's missed penalty is part of the Armagh folk memory.

1954 was a more significant year, for Cork and for Christy Ring. The Leesiders accomplished a notable three in a row run of successes over Tipperary in the Munster final that year. Cork easily beat Galway in the All-Ireland semi-final and were through to the final against Wexford. It produced a great battle between two very well-matched sides; the greater experience of Cork helped them fashion a 1-9 to 1-6 victory, and more important still, an eighth All-Ireland medal for the Cork captain, Christy Ring, the first player to achieve that rare distinction. Earlier that morning I had dropped into Barry's Hotel, where the Cork team stayed, for a chat with the Glen Rovers star. As I was leaving, I asked him whether in the event of Cork winning, he would come into Radio Eireann and chat about the game. My phrasing of the invitation brought a sharp retort from the Cork player. "What do you mean, if we win today? Of course we will win, and you better be here to collect me," he said unsmilingly. After the 1954 final there was only bedlam around the Cork dressing-room and naturally Ring was the hub of all the attention. Everybody wanted to shake his hand and it took me a long time to get to the dressing-room door before I was bundled into the room by a couple of helpful Gardai. I eventually reached Ring and as I held my hand out to congratulate him he said, "What did I tell you this morning, didn't I tell you we would beat them, didn't I make arrangements with you?" I felt at the time he was annoyed that I had actually doubted him in the hotel in the morning visit. After leaving Croke Park I rushed home to prepare my match account for my radio programme. On my way back into town I called to Barry's Hotel and collected my star guest, who was reclining in his bedroom, by no means looking like the man who a few hours earlier had made hurling history by becoming the first player to win eight All-Ireland senior hurling medals.

On the way to the Henry Street studios I explained to Christy the procedure I would follow before inviting him to comment on winning his eighth All-Ireland medal. I told him I would describe the match, after which I would chat to him. During the course of my match review I mentioned that Ring had missed from a couple of scoring chances, and at each such mention, the Cork player would rise from his chair and wag an admonishing finger at me. Thankfully he had the good sense to keep from interjecting whilst the programme was going out live on air! Ring was an ideal subject for an interview, and the fact that I had built up a good rapport with him helped me to elicit information which he would normally withhold. The fact also that I had played the game at top level, and against him on occasions, was another bonus. He loved to talk about the game, but not too much about other players. Many years later, when he filled a selector's role with the county, I approached him after a game in Wexford, which Cork lost, for comments for my *Evening Press* column. After posing some questions, Christy looked straight at me and said, "You know the game; you played it; you saw what happened out there to-

day, why are you asking me?" It was a typical Ringey reaction. After
further pressure he gave me the comment I was seeking.

My interview with Ring on the night he won his eighth All-Ireland
medal was not only historic, but noteworthy for the sincere and
genuine way he answered all my questions. He told me afterwards
that he was very conscious of the fact that he was actually talking to
the nation, and some of his answers gave that impression. He laid great
stress on fitness and made repeated references to practice. He claimed
that a player would never be great unless he was to devote a lot of
time practising the skills of hurling. Practice, practice, practice, he
preached. I asked him would he now consider retiring from the game.
I can still see those steely blue eyes boring into mine when he replied,
"I have no intention of retiring, I'll keep hurling as long as the good
God above gives me the strength." His pious wish was granted; he
kept hurling away until he retired from the inter-county scene in
1965.

The 1954 Cork winning team returned to a marvellous reception.
The streets were packed with delirious supporters, the best reception
ever accorded a winning Cork team for many years. At the meal for
the team in the Victoria Hotel in Patrick Street later, a learned friend
sitting beside Christy was over the moon with the greatness of the
occasion. Ring brought him down to earth with a bang. "Listen,"
he said, "we are still in Patrick Street, where winning Cork teams and
supporters have celebrated through the years, but we are a long way
yet from the Mall." The Mall was, and is, the professional, financial
and business apex of Cork. Little ever escaped the man from Cloyne,
but you really needed to know him. He had a great sense of humour
but he always appeared to be serious. Tony O'Shaughnessy, one of
the finest corner backs it has been my privilege to see, and to my
mind, the real corner-stone of Cork's three All-Ireland winning successes in 1952, 1953 and 1954, always reminds me of an incident
involving Ring, Tony and myself, on the morning of the 1952 All-
Ireland final against Dublin. I had dropped into Barry's Hotel to have
a chat with Christy and I bumped into Tony. He asked me to drive
him to the Richmond Hospital in North Brunswick Street to see
Paddy Downey of the *Irish Times* who was recuperating from an ill-
ness. Tony asked Ringey to go along too. The car I was driving at the
time was a Fiat 600, a small two seater, but it had space behind the
two front seats for another passenger. Ring insisted on sitting in the

front seat, consigning Tony to the back, which was a tight squeeze.

As I drove towards the Richmond, Ring asked me, "Do they pay
you much in Radio Eireann for that programme of yours on Sunday?"
(I hadn't taken over from my father at the time). I told him a lie, and
said the programme paid very well. Said Ringey, "Wouldn't you think
a man of your standing would have a better car?" I told him I couldn't
afford a better one, and it got me around the city. Tony O'Shaughnessy
poked Ring in the back and said quietly, "Shure, you haven't got a
car yourself." Ringey gave him a look. "That's not the thing, I'm
talking to your man here," pointing his finger in my direction. We
drove along in silence until we reached the Richmond. The three of
us walked up to the reception and inquired about our patient. We
were told that we could not see Paddy because the doctor was on his
round and there was no way the matron would allow us next or near
the ward. I asked a passing nurse to carry a message to Paddy, informing him that three visitors had called to see him; even the fame of
Christy Ring wasn't sufficient to persuade the nurse to allow us up to
the ward. A few minutes later, as we were going down the hospital
steps, we heard a shout from one of the ward windows, and there
was Paddy with his neck sticking out of the window, waving to us.
We chatted for a while because he was only delighted to see us, but
he was yanked back into the ward by the matron, who told us to clear
off and not to be giving the hospital a bad name. Even Paddy wasn't
spared a tongue-lashing from the same matron. Christy enjoyed the
situation very much and as we were going out the gate of the Richmond, he looked back and chuckled, "She must be hell to live with."

In all my years presenting the Sunday feature on Gaelic games, I
had relatively few letters of criticism over the way the programme was
compiled. True, I did receive letters from listeners complaining about
omissions of certain results which hadn't reached me, or lack of coverage of some of the provincial matches. There were occasions when
listeners wrote and claimed I was biased towards one particular team;
but you accept all that as being a listener's privilege. The actual games
coverage part of my Sunday night programme was absorbed into a
general sports programme in 1969 but, of course I still retained the
results sequence, which is very much part of the Sunday night radio
service.

I had my first and only disagreement with GAA Secretary Padraig
O Caoimh in 1955, and it arose out of comments I had made in my

report of a Leinster senior football championship game in Croke Park. During the course of my match review I named a couple of players who had incurred marching orders during the game. I also mentioned, when dealing with another match in Ulster, that a prominent player of the time had also fallen foul of the referee, and got his marching orders. The fact that I had mentioned the "sendings off" did not go down well in certain GAA circles; the policy at the time was to refrain from naming culprits. On the following day I got a telephone call from Secretary O Caoimh. He was quite pleasant and spoke about the previous day's matches at headquarters. He asked me was it necessary to mention on my radio programme the fact that players had been sent off. He told me he was concerned with the image of the Association, and how best that image should be portrayed over the airwaves. He took exception to the fact that I had gone out of my way to mention the names of certain players who were sent off the previous day in championship matches. He then asked me if I was going to persist with that policy on future occasions. I told him I had stated a fact; that I was present and saw the players being sidelined for fighting and felt that the fact should be stated. He said that the players had not been named in the afternoon commentary on the game with Micheal O'Hehir, which was more or less the line he (O Caoimh) would wish me to follow. I told him that I didn't see how not naming the sent-off players was helping the image of the Association; at least by naming them, listeners knew who they were, whereas by not naming them, I was compounding a situation where every player on the field had a shadow cast over him. He was very unhappy about my attitude; he thought the Association would take a dim view of frequent references being made on radio to fighting and players being sent off, comments which could easily be left out of my match reports. He then said that if I was not prepared to change my approach, the Association could always get "somebody else" to do the Sunday night GAA programme on radio, and with that parting comment, he put the phone down. I was naturally very concerned about my position. I accepted the fact that the GAA was a very powerful and, on occasions, ruthless body, and with their influence they could make life difficult for me. The question was, would the radio authorities back me if the GAA carried out their threat?

The following day I went into Radio Eireann and spoke to Philip Greene. I told him about the phone conversation with Mr O Caoimh the previous day, and asked for clarification of my position. Philip was extremely annoyed that I should have been subjected to that kind of intimidation and insisted that I accompany him to Roibeaird O Farachain, the Controller of Programmes. I repeated my conversation of the previous day for the benefit of the Controller, and he too became visibly angered over the matter. He assured me that Radio Eireann would not tolerate interference from any quarter in their affairs. He reiterated what Philip Greene had said earlier to me: that I had full control over my programme's content; that I was to use my own discretion in matters relating to it, and under no circumstance was I to tolerate any interference from outside bodies or individuals. Mr O Farachain then directed me to ring Mr O Caoimh and request a formal letter setting out the comments he had addressed to me on the phone the previous day. I did ring the GAA Secretary, who told me he had no intention of writing the letter requested and put the phone down. Padraic O Caoimh was never one to mince words. I continued to make references from time to time about players being sent off in matches and naming them, but I heard no more from GAA headquarters about those references. Of course, the advent of television seven years later changed that whole situation in a big way; viewers could see the culprits who had transgressed the rules leaving the field, and they had to be identified by the match commentator. Padraig O Caoimh never mentioned our telephone conversation in subsequent meetings, nor did I, and we remained the best of friends until his untimely death in May 1964. He was a visionary who lived only for the Gaelic Athletic Association, and through his own hard work built it into the great organisation it is today.

In compiling my match coverage on Sunday nights I had to rely at times on the *Irish Press* reports of various matches. I would attend a game of my own choice, and I would include brief reports of the other matches, courtesy of the *Irish Press*. I could not attend the 1961 Munster hurling final between Cork and Tipperary, but I had arranged to use Mick Dunne's report of the match. I called into the *Press* on my way to Radio Eireann and got a copy of Mick's report of the game. In it, Mick stated categorically that Christy Ring had struck Tipperary's Tom Moloughney during the course of a flare up, 18 minutes into the second half. In my shortened account of the match on radio, I stated that the Tipperary man was felled by a blow from Ring's hurley, an act which had marred the final from a spectator's viewpoint.

At the time I was making that comment on radio, the scenario had changed in the *Irish Press* sports department. Padraig Puirseal, who was working on the subeditor's desk at the time, advised the Sports Editor, Oliver Weldon, that it would be wiser from a legal viewpoint to leave Ring's name out of the copy as having actually struck the Tipperary man. When Mick Dunne's report of the Munster final appeared, Christy Ring's name was indeed left out of the report in connection with the incident, but the rest of Mick's comments were left in. Later in Mick's report, he stated: "At the end of a long and illustrious career, this game added no lustre to Ring's reputation, and as one who has so often been thoroughly enchanted by the artistry of this great forward of them all — and recorded my praise of his achievements, when praise was due, there can only be condemnation of his behaviour yesterday." Even that particular paragraph left no one in doubt about the player who had been involved. Mick Dunne, to this very day, has still very clear recollections of that incident, the events which led to it and the sequel — he has never changed his view on it. John D. Hickey, who was also at the final, did not see Ring strike Moloughney, but was told by those reporters sitting near him in the press box that Ring was the aggressor. John D. named Ring as striking Moloughney in his report of the match in the *Irish Independent* the following day.

The incidents in the game provoked a lot of comment at the time but the Munster Council took no action. The Cork County Board did; they threatened legal action against John D. Hickey and myself unless the allegation against Christy Ring was withdrawn. The Board were probably prompted by two factors: they were aware that I was not present at the game and that I had used the version written by another journalist. They also knew that the actual incident was not seen at the time by John D. I may say that, in my long experience of watching matches from the press bench, it is not possible to watch every moment of the action. A reporter may scribble an item which he wishes to refer to later in his match report; an incident happens, maybe off the ball at that precise moment, so the reporter has to depend on a colleague to fill in the details of something he had not actually witnessed himself. That's what happened in the controversial Moloughney case involving John D. Hickey. Val Dorgan, in his book *Christy Ring*, devoted a special chapter to the Ring affair. He rightly explains my role in the matter but he erred when he said that I apologised immediately for my radio comments on the incident. I certainly did not. On the foot of a threat of legal action from the Cork County Board, I was summoned to the office of the Radio Eireann legal adviser, Fachtna O hAnnrachain, to give him my side of the story. By that time the matter had been taken up by the National Union of Journalists on behalf of John D. and myself.

We attended a very emotive meeting of the union, presided over by the late Michael McInerney, which arose because pressure was being applied on John D. and myself to withdraw the comments made about Ring in our match reports. I had in my possession affidavits from friends of mine who were present at the match and who had stated that they had seen Ring strike the Tipperary player, and they were quite willing to go to court and give evidence to that effect. Radio Eireann were naturally very concerned about a possible court case, and in those days, with money very tight, they wanted to avoid at all costs the risk of such taking place. I explained to Fachtna O hAnnrachain that I would be guided by whatever course of action the NUJ would take in our case. A very militant section of the union were all for confrontation, claiming that a journalist's reputation was being interfered with, and all the evidence put before the meeting only proved that a fact had been stated. The union was directed to talk to the Cork County Board to see if some solution could be found. Those talks went on for some time, months in fact, and it was at that stage that I was asked by the legal department to read out on radio a statement withdrawing comments I had made on the match in question. I was in no position to refuse, and did so on radio the following Sunday night. Unfortunately there were side-effects, with the banning of John D. from the press bench by the Cork County Board when he went to report on the Cork county final. That very nearly led to a far-reaching decision to withdraw all NUJ reporters from attending any games under the Cork County Board, but they were only threats.

After protracted discussions between the NUJ and the Cork GAA a statement of agreement was reached between both bodies in March 1962. I was directed to read the statement out on radio on Sunday night and it was published in the *Irish Independent* at the same time. The statement went as follows:

The Irish Council of the National Union of Journalists has been

conducting an investigation into the facts surrounding the striking of a player at the Munster hurling final between Cork and
Tipperary at Limerick last July. It has received reports from
many journalists, spectators and officials who were present at
the game and who were eye-witnesses of the particular incident.
As a result of this investigation the Council has come to the conclusion that grave doubt existed about the facts as reported
and wishes to extend to Mr Christy Ring, who was mentioned
widely as the player most directly concerned, its sincere regret
for any distress, hardship or injury to reputation which he may
have suffered as a result of his name being mentioned. He is, in
fact, innocent of the offence, and his name should not have been
singled out. At the same time there is full appreciation of the
sincerity of all those who reported the game, but in the light of
the evidence there can be no longer any doubt of the facts. In
this connection this Irish Council believes that there is now full
realisation that reporting of incidents concerning players, where
there is any doubt of the facts, can have wider repercussions on
those players who are, after all, also private individuals who are
workers or employers, and who have their own private social
lives which could be injured by mentioning of their names.
There is need for even greater care in checking the facts, therefore because of the resulting effects on private lives as well as
on playing reputations.

In these discussions the County Board and the National Union
of Journalists agree that generally the standard of sports reporting is high and that journalists have contributed to the success
of Gaelic Games. Both parties agree on full co-operation in
securing the highest standards of sportsmanship on the field of
play in all games. It is agreed also that the publication of this
statement will ensure the withdrawal of all libel actions, the
withdrawal of proposed industrial action by this union and the
withdrawal of any ban on journalists.

That ended the matter, but the tone and content of the statement
was bitterly resented by the journalists who were present at the
particular match and nobody resented it more than John D. Hickey.

I could well appreciate the action of the Cork County Board; they
were defending one of their own. The Munster Council would have

earned the respect of many people had they ordered an investigation into incidents which were talking points throughout the county. It was normal practice in the councils of the GAA in those days to confine investigations to matters mentioned in the referee's report. The referee was the fall guy then for any action taken in the council chamber later. When he was Chairman of the Dublin County Board in the early 1940s the late Sean O Braonain didn't hesitate to carpet culprits who had escaped the eye of the referee. The attendance at the 1961 Munster hurling final was 60,177, but the Council did not act and swept it under the carpet, leaving the onus to fall on the Cork County Board. The ironic part of the whole affair was that there were a number of people who were quite willing to go to court and swear that Ring did strike Moloughney; there were others who would have sworn he did not. For my own part, I had an unsolicited affidavit from a local Garda Sergeant, who claimed he was quite close to the incident when it occurred, and he had no doubt that it was the Cork player who had struck Moloughney and he was willing to go to court and state it.

Years later, Christy and I were being driven to a radio station in Hartford, Connecticut, to talk about the Cushing Games, and on the way the conversation turned to hurling. We discussed the styles and merits of counties both of us had played against. The fact that you had played the game at top level was very important when you got involved in an argument with Christy. For one thing, he respected your viewpoint without necessarily agreeing with it; more often than not he held a different view. Tipperary was mentioned, and I casually asked him what had happened in the 1961 Munster final. Christy kept looking straight ahead and said very quietly, "That's all water under the bridge, I've forgotten about it." I never asked him again. It did recall a story told to me by the great Kerry footballer Paddy Kennedy many years later. Ring and himself were chatting in Gaelic Park, New York. A Cork-born exile cut in to greet Ring as a long-separated friend. When Christy registered non-recognition the exile was taken aback. "Don't you know me, surely you remember our meeting on the steps of Barry's Hotel after the 1942 Final?" was his naive response. Ring's response was equally naive. "I hardly remember the 1942 final at the moment." It ended that conversation. Ring was undoubtedly the master of the put-down. We were discussing a particular game one evening and an innocent bystander happened to throw in a comment. Ring looked at him and said, "What do you know about it, have you played the game?" The poor chap admitted he hadn't played the game and Ring then said, "Well, leave it to the men who have, and listen." The 1961 Munster final is now part of GAA lore. The central figure has passed to his eternal reward, but the doubt still remains.

Chapter 9
American Journeys

The deterioration in Padraig O Caoimh's health in 1963 forced the Central Council to bring in more staff to ease the burden on its ailing top official. A Cork teacher, Sean O Siochain, was taken on and he subsequently was to fill the post on the death of O Caoimh. I was in attendance at Croke Park on the night of O Siochain's appointment as Ard Stiurthoir, and I announced it to the country at large on the live *Thursday Sport* programme on TV which was presented by Micheal O'Hehir. Sean O Siochain became one of the most efficient administrators ever appointed by the Association; not alone was he a superb public relations figure but in the years that followed he streamlined the whole working of the GAA machinery. He had many fine qualities, not the least being the fact that he was most approachable. He became a great friend of mine, and I introduced him to the game of golf. We have played in many Celebrity-Ams in various parts of the country, and one recent such outing had a rather novel sequel. We had to play early in the morning because both of us had other commitments in the afternoon. As we stood up on the first tee in a well-known north city club, we were greeted by the captain of the club, who made himself known to us. He thanked Sean for supporting the charity outing, and Sean in turn said, "And you know Sean Og." The club captain shook my hand and wished us an enjoyable round. Later that night when the captain of the club was saying his "thank you's" to all those present who had supported the outing, he mentioned briefly that he was in the club early that morning and was "delighted to see Sean O Siochain and his son Sean Og teeing off in the first fourball." Needless to say, I have got great mileage out of that particular slip of the tongue, and I never stop reminding my "father" of that announcement. I must hastily add, "father" and "son" continue to support charity outings.

At precisely 3.50 am on Monday 15 June, 1959 the phone rang on the night porter's desk in the *Irish Press*. Paddy Clare, who was on duty answered it; as he was taking the call he looked across at me, and threw his eyes to the heavens. He thanked the caller and put the phone down. "It would be my luck," he said, "a caller just rang to say that there was a big explosion over on the north side of the city." I asked him had the Gardai or fire brigade heard anything; he immediately checked. They had heard nothing. I had completed my rewrite of the previous day's GAA matches for the *Evening Press* and I was waiting to give the Wire Room Overseer, Eddie Fitzgerald, a lift home to Raheny. Eddie was checking the wire machines to ensure that there were no late news stories needing urgent attention. Having satisfied himself that there were none, he started to clear up and tidy the place for the morning staff. By this time the hands of the clock had crept up to 4 am at which time the last edition, the city edition, started rolling off the presses. Paddy Clare was still busy answering the phone as more people called in to report the big explosion, which had by then been located in the Santry area. It was now beyond the stage when a small paragraph could have been inserted in the late box column about the explosion. There was nothing more that Paddy could have done at that stage but to alert the night editor to follow up the story.

Eddie and I decided to drive home by Santry, simply out of curiosity, but also in case the story might have needed checking for the paper. Sure enough, when we got there we saw a lot of Garda activity at Santry Athletic Stadium. A Garda soon put us in the picture. Two huge craters had been blown in the new cycling track which was to have been opened officially that evening. It took an awful amount of persuasion on my part to get the Garda on duty at one of the entrance gates, to let me see the damage to the track. There were indeed two large craters blown in the cycling track and terraced stand; a pavilion was wrecked, and ten dwelling houses in the vicinity were damaged. Happily there were no casualties to people. It was now 4.30 am, so Eddie and I drove straight away to my house, which was only ten minutes away from the stadium. This was a major story.

Santry Stadium had been made world-famous the previous August, when five athletes out of eight, including our own Ronnie Delaney, covered the mile in less than four minutes, a unique feat then. The first four broke the official world record of 3 mins 58.7 secs, and the first two beat the unofficial figure of 3 mins. 57.2 secs set up by Englishman Derek Ibbotson. The winner that night was Australian Herb Elliot, in a time of 3 mins. 54.5 secs, 4.2 secs lower than the world record and 2.7 secs below Ibbotson. Second was Mervin Lincoln in a time of 3 mins 55.9 secs, eight yards behind, with Ronnie Delaney, five yards further back in 3 mins 57.5 secs. All three were inside the world record held by John Landy of Australia (his time was 3 mins. 58 secs). Murray Halberg of New Zealand was fourth in 3 mins. 57.5 secs, and it was his first time to run in the mile. He had already set a world record for the three miles the previous night at the track. It was an historic occasion for athletics in Dublin on that August evening and a triumph for Billy Morton, the father figure of athletics in this country. Billy had billed the famous event the "Millennium Mile" and Billy, as everyone knows, was years ahead of his time.

At 5 am on the morning of 15 June, 1959, I sat down with Eddie Fitzgerald and wrote a piece about the blowing-up of the famed Santry cycling track, including information about the historic mile of the previous year. When I had completed it, I rang the world news agencies, Reuter, Press Association and United Press International and broke the story. When I satisfied them about my credentials they took it eagerly. It made a major impact and within a short space of time, Santry Stadium was again on the world map as the story reached every newspaper office which took the Foreign Press service. It was now 6.30 am. I waited until 7 am and rang the news room in Radio Eireann and gave them first-hand information about the explosions, which they were delighted to get. Ironically, when I eventually looked for payment for my hard night's work (or should I say morning) from the radio newsroom editor, he told me that they had used the agency copy (which was also mine). However, thanks to the intervention of Philip Greene, the Sports Officer, I was paid a handsome fee for my early morning call (before the news room had received the wire service story). I was also paid by the wire services which had distributed the story world-wide.

Billy Morton quickly set about getting the track ready for the official opening that night. The craters were filled in and the cycling track was ready for that evening for an all-cycling programme. The track was officially opened by Dr C.K. Mills, Assistant Managing Director of Arthur Guinness & Co, and all the events were held. Shay Elliott, Ireland's only professional, won the professional 1,000 metres from Brian Robinson and Fausto Coppi, the famous Italian, reputed to be the best cyclist of all time. Elliott was relegated to second place in the 10 laps point-to-point which was won by Darrigade of France. The entire programme was carried out on the new track before a big attendance. Once again Billy Morton's slogan, "It will be all right on the night", came to pass.

In the early part of 1961 a group of Dublin-based GAA sports writers came together and formed the Association of Gaelic Sports Journalists. The Patron was Paddy Mehigan, the father figure of Gaelic writers, better known as "Pato" of the *Irish Times*. The President was Mícheal O'Hehir; the Chairman was John D. Hickey; Treasurer was Con Keneally and the Secretary was Mick Dunne. The rest of the committee consisted of Paddy Puirseal, Paddy Downey, Donal Carroll, Val Dorgan, Gerry McCarthy, Peadar O'Brien and myself. The purpose of this committee was to nominate a leading footballer and hurler at the end of each season, and present the two players with a suitable award at a function later that year. In the inaugural year, 1961, the two players chosen were Liam Devaney for hurling and Gerry O'Malley in football. Engraved statuettes were presented to the players later that year, and the practice continued very successfully for the next four years, when well-known players who had been very conspicuous from a playing and a sporting viewpoint were the recipients of the eagerly sought Association of Gaelic Sports Journalists awards.

In 1965 the Association of Gaelic Sports Journalists became involved in the Cardinal Cushing Games, a charity group set up in New York by John "Kerry" O'Donnell. That year, John "Kerry" invited three Kerry players, Mick O'Connell, Tom Long and Mick O'Dwyer, to play in exhibition games in "Gaelic Park", New York. The games were a huge success and a substantial sum of money was handed to the Cushing Games Charity. The following year, Kilkenny and Tipperary played for the "World Cup" in aid of the fund with similar success. John Kerry was keen to extend the scheme and felt that the GAA sports writers should become involved in some way in the selection of players. There was a problem: Mick Dunne and John D. Hickey wrote critical comments about the New York administration and they were promptly told by John Kerry that they would not be allowed into Gaelic Park again. I got a call one morning from John Kerry's brother, Tim, who told me that John was anxious to make peace with the two journalists. I met him, and we discussed the idea of the Gaelic writers picking players for the exhibition games for the Cushing Charities. John was willing to meet the Committee of the journalists, lift the ban on Dunne and Hickey, and extend the hand of friendship. John Kerry and I had been friends for many years and I had interviewed him on radio in the *Sports Stadium* programme. His brother Tim was a near neighbour and close friend of mine and most knowledgeable on football, having won five All-Ireland medals with his native Kerry. I contacted John D. Hickey and Mick Dunne and explained John Kerry's offer. After a brief discussion it was agreed that they would accept the offer of peace. A meeting of the Association of Gaelic Sports Journalists was called, normal relationships were restored and the meeting further agreed that the Committee would become involved with the picking of players for the Cushing Games. Both John Kerry and his brother Tim, who attended the meeting, were delighted with the Committee's decision.

Guidelines were set out which would govern the selection of the players: (1) To honour players who had given outstanding service to Gaelic games; (2) To include deserving players whose chance of a US trip with their counties was slight; (3) To give representation to all four Provinces. A few weeks after the inaugural meeting, we selected the players for the trip to play exhibition matches in New York, Boston and Hartford, Conn. The full panel was Christy Ring (Cork), Jimmy Duggan (Galway), Tom Neville (Wexford) and Paddy Molloy (Offaly) in hurling. The footballers were Tom Maguire (Cavan), Jim McKeever (Derry), Mickey Kearins (Sligo), Joe Langan (Mayo), Pa Connolly (Kildare), Noel Delaney (Laois), Bernie O'Callaghan (Kerry) and Paddy McMahon (Clare). O'Callaghan had to enter hospital two weeks before the previous year's All-Ireland final against Galway, so he was getting a rewarding trip. A couple of the panel had made previous journeys to the States, but most were travelling for the first time. I was making my first trip. The Cushing Committee (Irish Branch) decided that I would accompany the players on the initial trip, being the link in restoring relationships between John Kerry and the two journalists. I was delighted with the decision.

Weeks before the actual departure date, I was kept busy checking to make sure that the players had got their passports and visas.

A week before we were to leave I got a phone call from Christy Ring to say he was having difficulty getting leave from his job (he was an oil company representative). I rang John Kerry and explained Ring's dilemma. His reaction was predictable. "If Ring doesn't make the trip, we can call it off, he's the big attraction." I got back on to Ring, and told him about the warning I had received from the New York maestro. He gave me his boss's telephone number at head office. I rang him the next day and explained the consequences if Christy Ring could not make the trip. I highlighted the charitable purposes of the whole venture, and stressed the importance of Ring's involvement. I made a good case and was relieved when the necessary permission was granted for Ring to travel. The Cardinal Cushing Games party left on Friday, 21 May, and were to be the forerunners of other panels in subsequent years. The 1965 panel of players was something special, being the first to be chosen. We received a marvellous welcome when we arrived at Kennedy Airport in New York. The welcoming party included John Kerry O'Donnell, the very amiable and most helpful Kerry-born New York GAA President Donal Keating, and Mike Flannery, Board Treasurer. The party immediately left for the Manhattan Hotel, 44th to 45th Street at 8th Avenue. It had 1,400 rooms, each with a private bath, television and radio and was located in the heart of the fabulous theatre and cinema district around Times Square. John Kerry had a very busy pub right opposite the hotel, where we really enjoyed our morning and afternoon meals.

The first series of games in the Cushing Charities took place on the Sunday after we arrived and they were a sell-out, attracting over 8,000 at Gaelic Park. The nett receipts were over 20,000 dollars. The excitement generated by the appearances of Christy Ring, Jimmy Duggan, Paddy Molloy and Tom Neville was reflected in the number of spectators who gathered after the hurling match to meet the visiting players. There was added excitement for the footballers in the party as many fans waited patiently to make themselves known to Joe Langan, Pa Connolly, Noel Delaney, Jim McKeever, Tom Maguire, Bernie O'Callaghan and Paddy McMahon, and to hear news about relatives from the players' home towns. During the interval we had a further surprise when Bobby Kennedy and his electioneering party arrived at the Park, and I had the honour of introducing all the members of the panel to the famous politician. He was very keen to meet Christy Ring, whom he addressed as the "Babe Ruth" of the Irish game of "hurley". He made a short speech over the ground loud-speakers (courtesy of "Lefty" Devine, the commentator who always describes the action of games in the Park, and a great friend of mine) and made a quick tour around the pitch, shaking hands with everybody, before being whisked away by his numerous security staff.

The following day we were taken by coach to Washington DC and a tour of the State capital. We visited the House of Representatives and the Senate where we had a special meeting with the Speaker of the House, Mr John McCormack, who made us very welcome. The party was then taken to Arlington Cemetery; wreaths were laid on the grave of President John Kennedy which was, to my mind, the most touching moment of our whole visit to the State capital. Ruppert Breweries were the major sponsors of the Cushing Games and they laid on a treat for us on the Wednesday: a visit to the multi-million dollar Aquaduct Race Course.

This beautifully laid-out track is controlled by the New York Racing Board, which stages racing there seven days a week during the season. Betting on the Tote exceeds two million dollars on each day of racing. The quickest and most expedient way of getting to the track is by the "Aquaduct Special" which leaves hourly from Grand Central Station. We were among thousands heading for the track and packed like sardines into the carriages. Offaly-born Frank Feighery, Liaison Secretary of the New York Cushing Committee, was our tour guide during our stay and he was most helpful. Tom Maguire and I were fortunate to get a seat on the "track special", seated opposite two typical New Yorkers. Both were Jewish, Nat and Abe, and the conversation during the entire trip concerned the runners on the race card, which could be bought at the departure point. Abe held an unsmoked cigar butt in his mouth and he was able to roll the cigar from one side of his mouth to the other while he delivered judgement on the various racing fancies mentioned by Nat. Nat had some kind of a facial affliction, a nervous twitch, and every word he uttered was accompanied by a twitch and a quick shrug of the shoulders. They really fascinated Tom and me, but we pretended not to notice them. The conversation went something like this:

Abe: "Whaddya fancy in the 'foist'?"

Nat: "I like the look of 'Sunspot'. The guys in the plant gave me a few bucks to put on it."

Abe: "There's better pulling cabs around Central Park. I wouldn't back it with phoney money." (Silence)

Nat: "I got a good tip for 'Stormy Weather' in the second. He won well last week and is well worth a few bucks."

Abe: "Did ya see what he beat, did ya see what he beat, a bunch of ole cripples, that's what he beat, you can forget it." (Again silence)

Nat: "What about 'Blue Orchid' in the thoid; you liked it last time out, but it shure didn't win." (Silence again)

Abe: "You dumb, or something, I wouldn't let my taxman back that, not alone you. It has no class. Ya need class, but he's for the 'boids'. (A long silence)

Nat: "We ain't doin' too well, Abe, are we? We gotta back 'Havana Chief' in the fourth, see the jock on him, Manuel Pedosa, he's good, he's real good."

Abe: "That son-of-a-bitch, he's been throwing races all his life, whadda you think he's got that new Merc for, go on, ask me?"

Nat: "Don't tell me you won't back the 'Black Demon' in the 5th, it's got class, real class."

Abe: "Shure she's got class, plenty of class, but so has my moider but that don't mean she can stay a mile, and she's got breathin' problems as well."

Nat: "Who, your moider?"

Abe: "Dope, the horse of course, the horse." (Silence for a while)

Nat: "Well, my few bucks are going on 'Flying Thunder' in the last. It has won its last four races."

Abe: "See what I mean, see what I mean, I keep telling you, you know nothing about the ponies. Of course, it has won its last four races, but you tell me a horse that has won five on the trot, go on, tell me. Man, they really saw you comin'. You might as well stick your head out of the winda of this train and get it chopped off at the next tunnel. That's what I think of your 'Flying Thunder'." (Again silence for a while)

Nat: "Ya know something, Abe?"

Abe: "Naw, what's that?"

Seán Óg being greeted at Kennedy Airport, New York, on the occasion of the first Cardinal Cushing Games tour to the States. From left: Michael Flannery, Seán Óg, John Kerry O'Donnell and New York GAA President Donal Keating.

Mayo-born jockey Johnny Ruane talking to Seán Óg at New York's Aquaduct Race Track.

Nat: "We're wasting our time going to the track backing losers. I'm
       sorry I didn't drive the wife to Yonkers now to see her moider.
       I'm a dope."

The train arrived at Aquaduct Race Track, undoubtedly one of the
finest race-tracks I've seen for its size and layout. We were greeted
by executives of the track and made very welcome, given a fabulous
lunch and allowed the freedom of the track. Every punter passing
from the enclosure to the stand had the back of his hand stamped
with a special ink, which, when placed under a special light, showed
up a bright purple, that was your pass. Frank Feighery, our guide,
arranged for us to meet Irish-born jockey Johnny Ruane, who hailed
from Westport. Johnny was delighted to meet the Irish players and
gave his fellow countryman Joe Langan a special welcome. I asked
the Mayo jockey about possible winners on the card but he was
reluctant to make any forecasts. However, he did hint to Tom Maguire
and myself that three of his mounts that day stood a reasonable
chance, but beyond that he wouldn't go. Frank Feighery, being the
local man, claimed that the Mayo "jock" hadn't won a race for
years, and we would be throwing good money after bad. Most of the
players rowed in with the Feighery view and backed their own fancies,
but Joe Langan, Tom Maguire and myself formed a syndicate and
pooled our money. We backed Ruane on the American-style Tote of
"Win, Place and Show" which meant that we had covered all of our
options. Ruane did us proud by winning two of his three races and
finishing second in the other. That performance netted the syndicate
a tidy bundle of dollars, much to the annoyance of Frank Feighery.
He couldn't be contained. "That bum," he shouted, "I've lost my
shirt to him in the past, and he comes up with the goods today; he
should be made do a week in Knock." We later met a very happy
jockey Ruane and had our pictures taken with him. He confessed
he had tried that little extra for his countrymen, and invited us back
the next day, but other events had been planned for us and we had
to decline.

On the way over on the plane from Ireland I felt we should make
some little presentation to John Kerry O'Donnell to mark our appreciation in getting the fabulous trip. The players had no objection, so
everybody chipped in five dollars a man and I was delegated to buy a
suitable gift. I was told of a certain store in 34th Street, so Tom
Maguire and I headed off after our evening meal, by subway. The main

problem was to pinpoint its location. As we kept searching in a comparatively quiet street a New York cop emerged from a shop porch, viewing us with a certain degree of suspicion. "Can I help you, sir?" he inquired. He was small in stature as cops go, and kept fingering the holster on his belt; he also carried a night stick. We explained our presence and assured him that our intentions were noble. "You're Irish," he said, "I would know by the brogue," so I introduced Tom as a former Garda back in Dublin and told him the purpose of our trip to 34th Street. The cop's own name was Frank Hollywood, and his grandfather hailed from Wicklow. I asked him which part, quickly explaining that there was a place called Hollywood in that picturesque county. The cop laughed and said, "You know, I remember my grandfather telling me they had named a town after him in the old country, but my dad shattered that illusion many years later when I grew up."

Our New York friend advised us not to buy the intended gift in the store we had been seeking because, he said, he knew of a better place. He gave us a card with the name of another store near 3rd Avenue. He said he would meet us there the following day at three o'clock; he did, and he introduced us to the store owner. Frank was involved with a few other cops in social work and they bought trophies from time to time from this particular individual. Tom and I chose a very imposing trophy, which we felt would fit the bill. I hadn't inquired the price, remembering we couldn't exceed fifty bucks. Frank stepped in at that stage and inquired, "Do you like that one?" I told him we did but it probably would be too expensive. "How would 50 bucks go?" said Frank. "But surely that trophy costs much more than that," I said. Frank smiled and said, "It sure does, do you want it for fifty bucks?" Never one to look a gift horse in the mouth, I accepted gratefully. We wrote out an inscription for the trophy, paid for it, and were told to call back the next day. When I queried Frank on the good value of our purchase, he only laughed and said, "He owes me one, he owes me one." Tom and I thanked him and brought him off and bought him a few jars to celebrate our purchase. He told us he never missed a game at Gaelic Park whenever he was off duty.

John Kerry's trophy was presented to him on the eve of our departure for home in his spacious bar and eatery on 8th Avenue, and Jim McKeever the Derry star footballer made the presentation. It took John Kerry by surprise and he was genuinely touched by the gesture.

He told us that it was not often he was asked to receive something; more often than not, he was on the paying-out side. Many years later John Kerry told me how that particular piece of merchandise saved him a great deal of embarrassment. A certain county won a major competition in Gaelic Park but someone forgot to bring along the official trophy for the winners. John immediately dispatched his son Kevin home and he returned with the trophy we had, years earlier, presented to him, now minus the inscription. The day was saved, and the particular team had their presentation. John later exchanged the proper trophy for the one presented earlier in the day.

During that 1965 Cushing Games trip, an extra match was included in the itinerary in Hartford, Connecticut. The party travelled by coach and we were met by the Foley brothers from Castlemaine, Co Kerry, one of the most remarkable families it has been my good fortune to meet. I remembered big Pat, as he had been a prominent member of the great New York team which had beaten Cavan by two points in the 1949-50 National Football League final. His brother Jim was on the successful New York team in 1964 which beat Dublin in Gaelic Park. Jim epitomised all that Kerry football stands for; he was a lionhearted player and played until he dropped. Eight brothers in all had played with the Hartford team and seven of them with Kerry in New York competitions; but Pat and Jim were easily the more famous of the brothers. When the Hartford team fell on lean times in 1953, John Kerry O'Donnell arranged an evening game against Mayo (New York) at Gaelic Park and the entire proceeds were given to the Hartford club, who were then in a position to fulfil many out of town fixtures in the League which the club would otherwise have had to cancel. The Hartford club included many Connecticut public servants of Irish extraction. Mayor Kinsella and City Treasurer John (Bud) Mahon were members of the Irish club, as indeed were City Councillor John Fitzgerald, a cousin of Michael (Toots) Fitzgerald from Dingle, and a member of the Hartford football club. The Police Chief, John Kerrigan, was also a member of the club.

Undoubtedly the Foleys were a remarkable family, and there were ten of them living in the greater Hartford area — eight men and two girls. Having lived in a country atmosphere at home in Castlemaine, in Kerry, Hartford was a natural, with its great industrial complex and Insurance Home Office Buildings only minutes from the green pastures. Pat was the first to emigrate, in 1947. The others followed,

Meeting Governor John Dempsey in the State Capitol, Hartford, Conn. Back row, from left: Tom Neville (Wexford), Tom Maguire (Cavan), Frank Feighery (New York GAA), John Kerry O'Donnell, Pat Foley (Hartford GAA Club). Front row third from left is Jimmy Duggan (Galway), alongside Governor Dempsey (seated) and Seán Óg.

Tom, Jerry and John in 1949; Tim in 1950, Mary and Dan in 1953, Ellen and Jim in 1956 and Mike in 1960. There were originally twelve in the family but the oldest sister Kitty died at the age of 12, and the youngest, Bridie, stayed with the parents in Kerry. The Foleys were to make it in a big way in the land where they had set their roots. Dan was Secretary of a local Union. Pat was a member of the West Hartford Democratic organisation, worked in various capacities in the Travellers Insurance Co and was a system analyst. Tom, Tim, Jim and Mike were steam fitters, following a four-year apprenticeship, a very lucrative trade, which affords them the opportunity to travel anywhere in the States at a fixed pay scale. Jerry worked in the proof room of a local distillery. John was a member of the Travellers Insurance Co as one of the underwriting staff. The girls were busy housewives, Mary, the wife of Austin Traynor, a printer, originally from Offaly and Ellen married to a Longford man, John Hosey, assistant manager of a supermarket. When I visited Hartford in 1965 the Foley family count, including children, was 37. The older brothers went into the bar and restaurant business as a sideline, and sponsored a softball team, an American football team and a bowling team which participated in local amateur leagues under the bar's name. Since then most of the Foleys have blossomed into successful businessmen, and when I visited San Diego some years ago I met Jim Foley in his high class bar.

When the Cardinal Cushing party arrived in Hartford we were met by Pat Foley, chairman of the Cushing Games fund-raising committee in Hartford which through its own activities had raised in excess of 25,000 dollars for the Cushing Fund. Pat had a busy schedule laid on for us, including a visit to Governor John Dempsey, born in Cahir, Co Tipperary. On this trip we were joined by John Kerry O'Donnell and his son Kevin, and members of Ruppert Breweries, the sponsors of the Tour. Governor Dempsey was only delighted to welcome the Irish party and after an exchange of greetings, he presented each member of our party with a silver tie clip, bearing the State coat of arms. No provision, unfortunately, had been made to present the Governor with a suitable gift from our side and the situation wasn't helped when I was called upon to say a few words on behalf of the visiting party. As I moved forward, I was able to slip my Aer Lingus tie clip (green shamrock on the national colours) off. I said my few words expressing good wishes to the Governor and I ended up pinning on him my treasured Aer Lingus tie clip, which I had got from my school pal, Tom Kennedy, in the Aer Lingus Offices on Fifth Avenue in New York. As we were departing from the Governor's office, my arm was grabbed by Joe Mullarkey, one of the Governor's office staff. Joe had Mayo connections. He pushed me gently into a side office and said, "You did fine, Sean, you did fine, but would you ever tell Aer Lingus to change the design of their tie clips." I looked at him quizzically, so he opened a drawer, and reposing within were about a dozen tie clips, similar to the one I had just given to the Governor. "It's not that the Governor doesn't like getting them," said Joe, "but we could do with a new shape." I made a mental note to tell Tom Kennedy the next day I met him and of course to get a replacement for the tie clip I had given Governor Dempsey.

We moved on to Boston that weekend to complete our itinerary of games, and stayed in the Bradford Hotel. In the coach, Christy Ring asked if he could stay in the coach until all the players had been fixed up in their rooms. I thought it was a rather strange request, but Christy was deadly in earnest. He told me of a previous occasion when he arrived for a game; he was whisked away by a couple of people to a dinner in his honour. Over 250 attended the dinner at 10 dollars a head; but Christy had not given permission for the dinner to be staged in his name. He was lauded by several speakers at that particular function, and given a watch which he claimed actually went backwards. He later found out that the group running the affair had pocketed the proceeds, and had only used him as a means of filling the hall. He had taken a vow that never again would he be used unless it was strictly for charity. As the coach approached the Bradford Hotel, I made a brief announcement to the players and explained Christy's reasons for staying hidden in the coach. John Kerry and his son Kevin were not with us, luckily perhaps for the two Irish lads who were waiting for us when we got to the Hotel. John Kerry would have seen them off promptly. However, they asked for Christy. I told them that he wouldn't be joining the party until much later that night. They became very agitated. "But we must see him, we have a function arranged in his honour," said one of them. I asked them had they his permission to stage such a function. They admitted they hadn't. They claimed they had written to Christy weeks before telling him of the intended dinner, but had received no reply. I invited them to check all the rooms, but again assured them that Christy had delayed in

New York and wasn't due in until later that night. I could see that the two young men were going to have a lot of explaining to do to over 200 guests who had paid to see the Cork star.

When the visitors had left, Christy slipped into his room. When I checked with him later he was certainly enjoying himself. He had got on to room service, ordered a huge meal, and was sitting back enjoying it, watching a baseball match. I told him about the visit of the two admirers and the arrangements for the dinner in his honour. I asked him did he receive a letter inviting him to the dinner, and he replied, "I get them all the time, you would never keep up with them." He dismissed any idea of attending the function which was taking place somewhere in the city that night. "What did I tell you?" he said, "Didn't I tell you they would be around, but I also knew Christy wouldn't, watch or no watch." Christy was of course the big attraction the next day at the charity match, when Cardinal Cushing and his secretary, Monsignor George Kerr, presented all the players with a special trophy to mark the success of the Games which had enabled John Kerry to hand over a cheque for 35,000 dollars to the Cardinal's Charity Fund for the poor of Peru.

Chapter 10
The John Kerry Saga

I was sitting in the Liffey Bar in Jackson Heights chatting to barman Joe Taylor when I got a call from John Kerry to say that Jack Dempsey, the former legendary world heavyweight boxer was at the precise moment in his well-known hostelry on Broadway. A few days earlier I had asked him if he would arrange a meeting with Dempsey, a personal friend of O'Donnell's, so that I could interview him for radio. I wasted no time. I took the subway to Broadway and hired a tape recorder from a nearby store. Armed with the machine, I slipped into Jack Dempsey's Bar which was one of the tourist attractions around Broadway. A quick word to one of the bar staff, and the famous man appeared and greeted me with a big smile. I reminded him that we had met on a previous occasion with the Cushing Games players. "You're John O'Donnell's friend," said the big man and no more introductions were needed. He steered me to a corner booth and had the back-ground music switched off. I started the interview and for about an hour I listened in awe as he went through his whole background and his Irish connections. He told me about the boxing booths where he had earned a pittance at the start of his career, and later talked about the famous knockdown against his very good friend Gene Tunney. The stories were endless and I used up all the tape, assuring him that I would return on another occasion to complete the job. I thanked him for his kind assistance and he assured me that any friend of John O'Donnell was a friend of his. He took the Liffey Bar phone number, "just in case someone else might drop in that you might be interested in interviewing." Little did he know that getting Jack Dempsey was to me a very rare scoop. I wrote an explanatory

161

letter to Philip Greene, knowing that he would be only too delighted
to get such an interview. I placed the letter in the box with the tape,
parcelled it up and headed for Fifth Avenue and the Aer Lingus offices.
My old pal from the *Irish Press* days, Bill Maxwell, was there and he
promised me that he would have the tape on the next flight to Dublin, and delivered to Radio Eireann.

Phil, as I anticipated, was delighted to get the Dempsey interview
and brought it immediately to the tape room to play it. All he heard
was gobbledy-gook. Try as he did, he could not find any legible voice
on the tape, even trying it out at various speeds. When I played it
back on my New York machine it was perfect. Phil and the Radio
Eireann engineer tried every conceivable way in which to get the tape
to work, but failed. They abandoned it, but I was not to know that.
A few days later I got a call from one of the managers of the Broadway bar to alert me that Mickey Walker, former welterweight and
middleweight champion of the world, had dropped in to see his old
friend Jack Dempsey. Walker lived on the West Coast, and it was
rather fortunate for me that he should turn up when I was in New
York. The bar manager, Jack Shapiro, had been told by Dempsey to
call me if anyone of note dropped into the bar when he was not there
himself. I was only stunned when the message was given to me, and
I dropped everything and headed off again to Dempsey's bar and
into the same store nearby, where I again borrowed the tape recorder
for a small fee. Like Jack Dempsey, my new interviewee could not
have been nicer. He told me he seldom went to fights and had only
made infrequent appearances at big promotions. He was one of the
great boxing figures, successful at welterweight and middle in the
late 1920s and 1930s. He was called the "toy bulldog" and was
managed by the famous "Doc" Kearns who had also been manager
to Dempsey. Walker had learned boxing the hard way, and he too
reeled off a litany of great stories concerning himself and his opponents in his battle to achieve greatness. He was very proud of the
fact that he had Irish connections, and had only agreed to do the
interview because I was from the "old country", a phrase which you
come up against very often in the States.

He had a great fear of flying and refused pointblank to travel other
than by boat or car. Sometime in the mid 1930s a very lucrative offer
came from France for Walker to box a French opponent, putting his
title on the line. It was an extremely valuable purse. The big problem

Arriving at the Bradford Hotel, Boston, for the Cushing Games matches. From left: Seán Óg, Tom Maguire (Cavan) and Christy Ring (Cork).

Seán Óg runs into the fist of the great Heavyweight Champion Jack Dempsey, on a visit to Dempsey's Bar on Broadway in 1968.

was how to get Walker to Paris. "Doc" Kearns came up with the
answer. He remembered Walker asking about a trip to Ireland some
time before that, but Kearns had told him it was not on. The French
offer made Kearns think again. He told Walker that the trip to Ireland
was on, but he would have to fly by plane. Kearns also told Walker
that he would ply him with plenty of Irish whiskey on the flight and
he would never know he was in the air. The plan worked. Walker took
the plane, was liberally supplied with Irish and didn't sober up until
he landed in Paris. "When I got off the plane I couldn't understand
one word, and I asked Doc Kearns were the people talking in the
native Irish tongue." Kearns had to own up and explain to Walker
that the whole exercise was a ruse to get him to Paris to fight a leading French contender. Walker easily won. He was never to make that
trip to Ireland and to his Mayo relations.

I had the whole story on tape, and was feeling really chuffed, having secured interviews with two of boxing's greatest personalities all
in the space of a few days. Thanking my gracious visitor from the
West Coast, I headed off once again to the Air Lingus offices and met
Tom Kennedy. He assured me he would see that the tape reached
Radio Eireann on the next flight. Another tape arrived into Philip
Greene; another fruitless hour was spent trying to unravel a tape from
yours truly, and all with the same result. It was only when I returned
to Dublin that I learned about the fate of the two tapes. The fault
was explained to me. Most tape recorders have a bobbin, around
which the tape passes to the pickup spool. The bobbin controls the
speed of the tape. The tape recorder I used in the States had no such
bobbin — it just went straight along a slit in the frame from one spool
to the other. It would play back successfully on its original machine
but once the tape was put on a machine with a bobbin, disaster. Had
I been phoned to bring the tape machine home with me, the interviews would have been saved, but nobody thought of that. I was
never to be caught out like that again. The tapes ended up in the
waste bin.

During my stay in New York for the 1968 National Hurling League
final between Tipperary and New York our cameraman, Sean Kelleher,
and sound operator, Terry Gough, decided for safety's sake to leave
all the filming equipment in Gaelic Park, where John Kerry put it
safely under lock and key. On the way back from the Park we decided
to take the subway to Central Station. It was one of those slow jobs

that stop at every station, and after about four stops, two coloured gentlemen entered the carriage. It was obvious they were the worse for drink. They sat opposite one another, just a few yards from another passenger, who was laden down with shopping parcels. We were well away from all three. After a while, a row developed between the two coloured men, and one of them became particularly nasty. He pulled out what I thought was a knife and threatened the other guy with it. "Do you want this shiv in your gut?" he said to his companion, "do you want the shiv in your gut?" The three of us watched spellbound. The train came to a halt at a station and the man with the parcels was up and out of the carriage like a flash. The row continued, and this time the guy with the shiv stood up in a very threatening pose just as the train began to move. He slumped back into his seat as the other man tried to quieten him. The door of our carriage suddenly opened and in walked a Transit cop. Without even noticing us, he proceeded down the carriage and stopped in front of the guy with the weapon. He was small in stature, as most Transit cops are, and pulled out his baton or night stick. He put the top of the baton on the shoulder of the huge coloured man and said, "Hand me over the shiv." "I ain't got no shiv," said the coloured guy, in a whining voice. The small cop gave him a few taps on the shoulder with the baton and said again in a firmer voice, "Give me the shiv." This time the man, who appeared far more sober than he looked earlier, sheepishly put his hand in his pocket and handed over the shiv. "Up, the pair of you," said the small cop as the train was pulling into the next station. The doors opened and the cop pushed both men out on the platform. "Don't let me find you guys on this train again." Both scampered off. Into the carriage comes the passenger with the parcels and takes his seat, where he had sat earlier. The small Transit cop passed the three dumbfounded visitors from Dublin, who could only look on in amazement at the scene unfolding before us. "Bums, that's all they were, just bums," said the cop as he passed through to the next carriage. Sean Kelleher refused to travel by subway from then on, and always took a cab, which he said would come out of his expenses.

I took the subway out to Gaelic Park in the Bronx, one beautiful sunny morning to see John Kerry to discuss the arrangements for that weekend's Cushing Games fixture. He was sitting out beside the souvenir shop writing one of his famous letters. The three guard dogs, huge Alsatians, were prowling up and down that part of the ground, and I was in fear and terror of them. "Take no notice of the dogs, they'll go away," he said quietly. I wished at the time I had his faith in the dogs, who kept sniffing at me every time they came bounding up the terrace. I kept my eyes closed and we chatted away. I had brought a tape recorder with me, and asked him if he minded if we chatted about his early life in New York and how he became involved with the GAA. John Kerry is a very sensitive man, despite the picture which is painted of him. He is a declared millionaire but he will not talk about that aspect of his life nor will he talk about his family generally. "My life is private and I prefer to keep it that way. I never talk about money, that too is my business, and I like to keep it that way. I'll certainly tell you anything else you would like to know," he said. I respected his wishes.

He got the name "Kerry" from his workmates in New York. "They were, like myself, trying to earn a living in very hard times, and a couple of them started calling me 'Kerry' and the name stuck." Born in 1899, he had emigrated as a very young man, the first of the family to leave home. He headed for Montreal in Canada, to relations, and then became a lumberjack in the north of that country. He made a few bucks and headed first for New York and then to Detroit, where he worked for a spell in the Dodge car factory. While working in Detroit he became interested in baseball. At night he attended school and learned bricklaying and plan-reading; a trade which was to help him greatly when he returned to New York in 1926. He quickly found work, a lot of hard work, and saved sufficient to pay his way home to Gleann na nGealt, near Camp, Co Kerry, his birthplace. He never lost his interest in Gaelic games, and played in the West Kerry League with his more famous brother Tim, who won All-Ireland medals with Kerry in 1929, 1930 and 1937. Tim would have won more but for injuries which kept him out of the successful 1931 and 1932 winning teams. John Kerry returned to New York and worked during the boom period, earning over 100 dollars a week, take home pay, until the Wall Street crash and the Depression. He was out of work for three years, the most traumatic period of his life. He was really down on his uppers and he remembers walking from 96th Street where he lived to 42nd Street and Fifth Avenue, just to see apples being sold. A lot of people went to Inisfail Park, not to watch games but to find some friendly face from whom to borrow ten cents

— things were that desperate.

After the Crash, building work improved. John became involved with the Kerry club in the city and eventually he was able to buy his first saloon bar. Ten years later he had four or five going and, having played with the Kerry club for a spell, got involved in the managing side. Between 1932 and 1972 he steered them to win 22 New York football championship titles, a feat which hasn't been topped since. In 1940 John Kerry became President of the Gaelic Athletic Association of Greater New York, which controlled the New York championships in football and hurling. Fifteen years later he was again voted into the position, and was to hold office for five more years. In 1944, the then President Jim Cotter asked John Kerry and Barney Prendergast, a Mayo man, to take over Gaelic Park. Two previous owners had gone bust and the Park was in danger of being taken over by another sporting interest, far removed from Gaelic games. Emigration from Ireland had virtually stopped during the war years and attendances at Gaelic Park were meagre enough. When Barney Prendergast opted out of his involvement in the Park, John Kerry was left to plough a lone furrow. It proved costly. In order to keep Gaelic Park going he had to sell off his saloon bars, except for the Eighth Avenue premises.

In 1947 the Central Council of the GAA decided to hold the All-Ireland football final between Kerry and Cavan in the Polo Grounds in New York, and John Kerry was delegated by the Central Council to organise the biggest GAA event in the Association's history. John Kerry quickly got to work and sold 136,000 dollars worth of tickets in advance. It was said that without O'Donnell's involvement, the whole experiment would have been a gigantic flop. As events transpired, the occasion was an unqualified success, mainly due to the superb work of General Secretary Padraic O Caoimh in Ireland and his warring adversary in New York, John Kerry. In the 1950s New York, through the persistence of John O'Donnell, were allowed to compete in the National League. New York were pitted against the National League winners at home. On 30 July, 1950 New York came up against Cavan before 33,000 at Croke Park and beat the Breffni men 2-8 to 0-12. It was a marvellous New York side which benefited from the influx of many top stars from Ireland who had emigrated to find work across the ocean. With growing attendances at Gaelic Park, and greater activity among the New York clubs, Gaelic games took

on a new dimension. Relations between John Kerry and the Central
Council remained very strained and even efforts to get New York to
affiliate to the parent body were quickly shot down. There were bans
applied to teams travelling out from Ireland to New York, and for a
long time New York were left to their own devices, staging field days
and charity exhibitions, before normal relationships were again restored. New York celebrated its Golden Jubilee in 1964, and the occasion was marked by many events including the meeting of Tipperary,
the 1964 National League champions, and their great rivals, Kilkenny,
title holders the previous year. Gaelic Park was packed to capacity
for the meeting of the two rivals, and the game was billed as the
"first ever Hurling World Cup", which Kilkenny won in a thriller,
4-16 to 3-13. John Kerry instigated the first world tour by the New
York footballers, which took in visits to San Francisco, Auckland,
New Zealand, Melbourne and Sydney, Australia, and the Jubilee
celebration was concluded by yet another historic win by the New
York footballers, who beat Dublin in the National League final, 2-12
to 1-13, to give the exiles their second League crown.

   During a period when all was not well between the Central Council
and the New York GAA, I remember asking John Kerry, when he was
staying with his brother Tim in Artane, in Dublin's northside, would
differences between the two sides ever be resolved. He told me: "Let
me put it this way. When Tim and I were young we would help with
the threshing, along with the other men. When the men were being
fed in our kitchen during the threshing, they'd have bread and butter
and a bowl of milk. My mother noticed that one young man was not
drinking his milk and she asked the reason why. 'There's a mouse in
it,' he said sheepishly. My mother never said another word, but fished
out the mouse, and threw it over the half-door and went about her
business attending to the other lads. When she went back to the young
fellow, he was still looking at his bowl of milk. He hadn't touched a
drop. 'What's wrong with you,' she asked. 'You don't want your milk
with a mouse in it and you don't want your milk with no mouse in
it.' Well, that's the way I am with the Central Council." On another
occasion he was driving me to Aquaduct Race Track and he was in
one of his mellow moods. I suggested to him that he should retire
and hand the business over to his sons and daughters, and take a good
rest from the pressures and acrimony which he had suffered over the
years. His answer was short and to the point. "If I did that, I would

be dead in the morning, it's what keeps me alive." His big disappointment was in 1981 when he offered himself as a candidate for the
GAA Presidency. He got assurances from a number of counties of
support, but when it came to voting time at that Congress, the same
support was negligible. He threw himself wholeheartedly into the
Cardinal Cushing Games to help the poor of Peru, but that was only
one of the many charities he was associated with and supported for
years. The popular profile painted of John Kerry O'Donnell is of a
man who is constantly at loggerheads with the GAA parent body,
intent on sabotaging all efforts of unity between the two. But John
Kerry keeps looking ahead, assessing the impact changes could make
if the status quo was interfered with. He puts it another way. "I
suppose it's like the ageing couple who had been at each other's
throats from the honeymoon onwards. There arrived on the scene
a parish priest whose concern about ailing marriages was a highly
pastoral priority. In due course he visited this couple. Having discussed at length on the Sacramental dignity of marriage with no
apparent impact he proceeded to dwell on other aspects of the union.
After pulling out all the stops the good priest appeared to have
ignited a spark of reconciliation in the wife. But the husband wasn't
giving an inch. As he was about to call it a day the visitor spotted the
dog and cat lying back to back, in peaceful harmony under the table.
Surely this is providential, says he to himself. Turning to the husband
he said, 'Look at those two animals, deadly enemies in the wild, and
there you see them in perfect harmony. Should that not be an
example and a lesson to you?' Back on the instant came the shatter-
ing reply, 'Ah, that's right, Father, but tie them together and see
what happens. '"

John made his point.

O'Donnell will point out that anything that has been achieved by
the New York body is mainly through its own sacrifices and industry,
without any help from the Association here at home. During my visits
to Gaelic Park over the years I have met quite a number of individuals
who had only the height of praise for John Kerry O'Donnell. They
quickly spelt out the charitable functions he had been associated
with; the number of exiles whom he had helped to secure employment, and the number he had employed himself to help those who
were down on their luck. There have been countless charity matches
played in Gaelic Park for priests seeking funds for their missions in

foreign fields. But John Kerry will not dwell on those events nor will he discuss them. He did get recognition in 1968 when he was made a Knight Commander of the Order of St Gregory, a very rare Papal honour, of which he is proud. One of my personal regrets over the years is that I haven't kept some of John Kerry's letters as memen-, toes of a great Gael and of a man who has never forgotten his roots. He is a prolific letter-writer, and he expresses himself most eloquently. He has descriptive phrases to suit all kinds of situations and individuals, and when he wants to lambast some decision taken which affects his beloved New York, he does so with unconcealed vehemence. His command of the English language is phenomenal but behind the facade of a hard, uncompromising, unco-operative and garrulous person lies a very human individual. We have been firm friends since I first met him with his brother Tim at a GAA Congress in the early 1950s, and he is still unrepentant about his stand on matters relating to New York and the parent body of the GAA. I did ask him once about his feelings towards the Central Council and he summed them up as follows: "Individually they are the most intelligent people you could find; but put them together — and you can have them."

The Cardinal Cushing Games were his prime interest and he was genuinely delighted when the Association of Gaelic Sports Journalists became involved in the selection of players for the trip to America in aid of that charity. He rightly claimed that the Cardinal Cushing tour matches far exceeded in interest any other tour undertaken by the GAA here at home. John Kerry was the trail-blazer in that regard, and the whole concept of bringing out prominent players from counties that had never won, or were likely to win, a major national title added immeasurably to the Cushing Games at the time. "I still get letters from some of those players," he told me once, "they have never forgotten the sheer thrill of that first-ever trip to the United States. Isn't that something?" I was the accompanying journalist when the last Cushing Games trip took place in 1972. He brought out the Kerry and Roscommon teams for that occasion. My old friend and genial character Frank King was the Kerry chairman, while the ever-helpful Michael O'Callaghan was the Roscommon figurehead, and Board chairman. Joe Keohane was a Kerry selector, and he dropped out one evening to meet Bridie McManus and myself and my wife Ann in Jackson Heights. The four of us went for a meal to The Old Barn, a delightful steak house. Naturally Joe was the life

Visiting Mayor Kevin White of Boston on the occasion of the visit of
the Roscommon and Kerry teams to play in the Cardinal Cushing Games
in 1972, the last of the Cushing series. From left: Michael O'Callaghan
(Roscommon Co. Board Chairman), Mayor White, Frank King (Kerry
Co. Board Chairman) and Seán Óg.

Presenting a copy of the Immigration Bill to Cardinal Cushing in Boston.
From left: Seán Óg, Cardinal Cushing, his Secretary, Monsignor George
Kerr and Fr Donal O'Callaghan.

and soul of the party and he regaled us with stories which kept us in
the eating house until near closing time. Bridie asked Joe and me to
accompany the manager to a nearby night safe to lodge money. "How
much is in the satchel?" asked Joe, as we flanked the manager on our
way to the night safe. He told him the amount. Joe looked at me and
said, "The 'boys' back home wouldn't believe me if I told them. Here
I am riding shot-gun on thirty thousand bucks, can you beat that?"

The games in New York, Boston and Hartford produced a substantial sum at the time, and were very well attended. Cardinal Cushing
was very ill with cancer but he still turned up to meet the teams at
the Boston match. When he died later that year it brought an end to
a series which had given so many players in this country so much
enjoyment and pleasure; but it wasn't to be the end of John Kerry's
involvement in staging charity events. Cardinal Cushing was a notable
churchman, but he also had a powerful influence in political life in
Boston and was a close friend of the Kennedys. I had met him on
many occasions during my involvement with the Cushing Games from
1965 onwards. In 1968 I travelled to America with the London footballers whom John Kerry had invited to participate in the Cushing
Games. During that visit I was contacted by John P. Collins, Assistant
District Attorney for the Borough of Queens and Chairman of the
American National Irish Immigration Committee, and his Vice Chairman, the Very Rev Donald M. O'Callaghan O.Carm. They were very
much involved in pressurising political parties for support to increase
Ireland's quota of visas to the United States. There were a lot of
inequities in the 1965 Immigration and Nationality Amendments
Bill, which had resulted in a drastic decline in migration from Ireland.
The Irish Committee asked me would I accompany Father O'Callaghan
on a deputation to Boston to see Cardinal Cushing and seek his support and endorsement for a Bill coming before the Immigration Committee in Washington, which would increase the Irish quota to 5,000
each year. John Kerry O'Donnell was the Treasurer of the Immigration
Committee, and he obviously had played some part in getting me
included in the deputation. I said I would give the Committee all the
assistance I could offer. John Collins was New York-born, but his
father had been born in Ireland and he took great pride in his Irish
roots. He told me that when he was going through law school he had
cited the rules of the GAA as the perfect example of democracy. He
was intrigued with the GAA set-up which his father had explained to

him, where all the fundamental changes taking place in Ireland's largest sporting organisation came from the grassroots, the clubs. He felt that true democracy was served when the smallest units could use their combined strength to make changes in the overall structures of the organisation and change policy if such was necessary.

John Collins and Father O'Callaghan gave me a comprehensive breakdown on the quota situation prior to our trip to the Cardinal. I rang Monsignor George Kerr, the Cardinal's Secretary, who had Co Down roots, and an appointment was made to meet His Eminence in Boston on the following Saturday, 25 May. Father O'Callaghan had brought with him a copy of the Bill, which we intended showing to the famous churchman. I was a little taken back with his initial reaction to our visit. The Cardinal quickly pointed out that the Irish were only one section of a number of ethnic groups who were similarly engaged in securing better visa quotas, while acknowledging Ireland's special position in the matter. I explained to him that I was hoping to get his reaction on tape (I had brought a tape recorder with me) and that I would use it on a special programme when I returned to Ireland. Without saying another word, he just pointed to my tape recorder, told me to switch it on and delivered the following statement without recourse to notes or prompting from his two visitors.

> I am taking the opportunity of the visit of the London Irish Football team to comment upon a Bill that is before the Immigration Committee in Washington, to the effect that Ireland be permitted to send 5,000 immigrants here every year. Under the legislation passed some time ago over 4,000 people want to come here this year, and they cannot do it unless this new Bill that has been introduced before the Immigration Committee in Washington will favour the change. Now, in the light of the millions of Irish Americans in this country, and all the contributions they have made to the welfare of the country, I think they are entitled to bring in at least 5,000 immigrants a year to the United States. Surely, they are not asking for much! So, on behalf of a few million Irish and Irish Americans in this part of the US, I raise my voice on behalf of this new Immigration Bill that will enable Ireland to send 5,000 immigrants here a year. Surely, as I said, that is not asking too much.

Father O'Callaghan was delighted with the Cardinal's endorsement of the Bill, and more importantly, to have his comments on tape. As events turned out, the American National Irish Immigration Committee were able to use the taped recording in their very strong lobby for support. A number of radio stations in New York were canvassed and they played the Cardinal's message on Irish-oriented programmes.

Before Father O'Callaghan and I left Boston that Saturday afternoon for New York, we paid a visit to Tommy Shields, who had a very popular Irish programme on radio. I always made a point of getting on Tommy's programme in order to plug the Cushing Games charity matches on our visit to Boston. Tommy was delighted to entertain us, and Father O'Callaghan and I told his listeners about our visit to the good Cardinal and his endorsement of the new Immigration Bill. The day I was due to leave New York with the London football team in 1968 I got an urgent call from Oona Gormley, Sports Co-ordinator in RTE, to say that I was to stay on in New York to do a commentary on the National Hurling League final between Tipperary and New York, the first leg of which was due to be played at Gaelic Park on the Sunday. The urgent request for my services was due to the fact that Micheal O'Hehir had suffered a slight stroke on his way back from the Epsom Derby, and he had been due to fly out to America the next day. I had already spent three weeks in the States so I had to ring my wife Ann and tell her of the latest developments. Being employed purely as a free-lance journalist meant that I was not being paid by the *Evening Press*, who had to get a staff man to write my three columns; I was also losing my Sunday night GAA programme fee during my period away for the Cushing Games. I had to ring Oona Gormley to explain that I had no money and that I would need some to cover my additional expenses. She assured me that all would be taken care of, which it was.

During my stay in New York I had the good fortune of renewing old acquaintances with Bellew and Bridie McManus, who owned the Liffey Tavern in Jackson Heights, Long Island — great friends of my family when they were living in Fairview Avenue, before they emigrated to the States. Bridie was an All-Ireland camogie star with her native Antrim, and a sister of well-known GAA star Harry O'Neill, whose great duels with Cavan's Phil "Gunner" Brady were a feature in the 1950s. Bellew had been manager of Gaffney's pub in Fairview and was a native of Teemore, Co Fermanagh; they had a son, Bellew Sean. I had stayed with the McManuses during the Cushing Tours, and ever since then it has become my second home whenever I visit the States. The Liffey Bar is the focal point for the Irish around Jackson Heights and I met quite a number during my visits. One such local is Chris "Bliss" Kealy, an old hurling pal, who played along with his brothers, "Budger" and Joe, with the St Vincent's club in Marino. Chris emigrated to the States many years ago, became involved in amateur dramatics and is in rare demand for O'Casey plays, being a marvellous "Joxer" in *Juno and the Paycock*. Chris also doubles as my chauffeur during my visits to New York. Joe Taylor from Drumsna, Co Leitrim, who played with the Leitrim club, and a fine footballer he is too, is the day-man behind the bar, while the night shift falls to Tommy Berry, who hails from East Wall in Fairview. Tommy is a natural wit and goes down a bomb with late-night customers. My wife Ann had developed a liking for a "Screwdriver" (vodka and pure orange) when she visited her brother in Sacramento in California. She claims it is a very nice drink. When we were staying with Bridie we paid a visit to the bar one evening and Tommy asked Ann for her choice of drink. Ann without hesitation ordered a "Screwdriver". Tommy placed my soft drink in front of me (I'm a teetotaller), put his hand under the counter and pulled out an actual screwdriver which he placed in front of Ann. From then on she was more exact when she ordered a drink in the presence of Dubliner Berry. Among a large Dublin contingent who frequent the "Liffey" are Billy and Kathleen Nolan, Joe and Rita Gaynor, Maureen King from North Strand, Tom Morrissey (Cork), Martin Quinn (Connemara), Chris Shaughnessy (Limerick) and Daisy McGregor (London). I met Dorothy Hayden-Cuddihy and her husband John. Dorothy had an "Irish Hour" on radio and I appeared on a few occasions on her popular programme. A frequent visitor to the "Liffey" is Joe Stynes, without doubt one of the great characters you meet from time to time in the States. I interviewed Joe on RTE radio. He was a superb all-rounder and played a major part in helping Dublin beat Kerry in the 1923 All-Ireland football final. Joe also played soccer and figured prominently with Shelbourne; that cost him another All-Ireland, being dropped by Dublin for playing "foreign games". Frequent visitors to the "Liffey" are Gerry and Kathleen Toner, of Belfast stock, who make people proud to be Irish. They own the "Abbey Tavern", "Kennedy's", "Desmond's" and "Jim Brady's", which are very popular meeting places for the Irish in New York. The Toners and partner Dessie Crofton, who hails from Loughrea, are members of quite a number of Irish organisations in the "Big Apple".

Having resettled in the McManuses' hostelry I set off to see the London footballers safely aboard their flight home from Kennedy Airport, and welcome in the Tipperary hurlers who were arriving for their National League final against New York. I had watched the National League home final between Tipp and Kilkenny before going to America for the Cushing Games. It was a stormy affair, laced with a number of incidents which got banner headlines the following day in the daily newspapers. Both counties were severely criticised for their parts in the flare-ups. Candidly, I thought much of the so-called "scenes" looked worse than they actually were, and so I wrote in my match report the following day in the *Evening Press*. The Tipperary County Board were furious with the press reports which had called for an investigation into the match and the incidents. Tipp felt that they were being blamed unduly. The Central Council did launch an investigation into the incidents (three in all) as reported by the referee. Arising out of the investigation, Ollie Walsh (Kilkenny) and John Flanagan (Tipperary) were suspended for six months. When the Tipperary Board discussed the suspensions a few weeks later they blamed the press reports for encouraging the Central Council to investigate the incidents in the League final. A month later the Tipperary Board went one step further by banning six members of the press from that year's All-Ireland training camp. The six men were Mick Dunne (*Irish Press*), Gerry McCarthy (*Irish Press*), Paddy Puirseal (*Sunday Press*), John D. Hickey (*Irish Independent*), Paddy Downey (*Irish Times*) and Donal Carroll (*Evening Herald*). I was not included in the ban; my match write-up must have been considered less damaging. The National Union of Journalists took up the cudgels on behalf of the sports writers, and a ban was placed on all coverage of Tipperary affairs in the national daily newspapers. It had all fizzled out by the end of the year, when both bans were quietly forgotten. However, Tipperary qualified for the All-Ireland final that year and it was suggested that the county should boycott the function arranged for the All-Ireland winners after the match. Wexford spared all their blushes by beating Tipp in the 1968 final so the Tipp after-match function was a rather muted one.

The Tipp party arrived in Kennedy Airport for the League final against New York. I held out my hand in greeting to the Tipperary

Board secretary, but he ignored it and brushed past me. It was obvious the hostility against the press was being carried on many miles from home. Let me hastily add that no such hostility was apparent among the Tipperary players and their most genial trainer Ossie Bennett, a long-standing friend. The same applied to the GAA President, Seamus O Riain, a courteous and highly respected President, who travelled with the team. Travelling with the Tipperary party were RTE cameraman Sean Kelleher and sound engineer Terry Gough, who were filming the League final. Fate, in the shape of the weather, was to step in and change all our plans. The rain started to fall in the early hours of Saturday morning and it continued non-stop until late in the evening. I had never seen anything like it. It looked as if someone had opened a dam and allowed all the water to pour out. John Kerry O'Donnell called me to say that there was no earthly hope of playing the first leg of the League final the following day (Sunday). Gaelic Park was completely covered in water. Sea-gulls were having a ball in some of the hollows on the pitch, which contained over six inches of water. The game was called off on Saturday night. On Sunday morning Sean Kelleher, Terry Gough and I headed for the Park, where I filmed an inerview with New York GAA President Donal Keating, a fine person, putting on film the reason for the abandonment of the match and showing the evidence as well. The game was refixed for the following weekend. Tipperary trained in Van Coortland Park, not very far from Gaelic Park. I arranged with Ossie Bennett, the team trainer, to have some of the team present in Gaelic Park for a few interviews, which they did, along with the Board official who had snubbed me at the airport. He stood at the end of a line of players during the interviews for television but I ignored him; he was dressed in his best bib and tucker. He quickly got the message, and walked away eventually. The filmed interviews were sent back via Aer Lingus for showing later in the week. The League final wasn't played the following weekend either; Senator Robert Kennedy was assassinated and as a mark of respect Gaelic Park was closed. I supplied pieces to radio and TV and to the *Irish Press* on the death of the Senator, having watched the actual slaying on television in the McManuses' apartments. I immediately phoned my wife Ann to explain that I would have to stay on in New York for yet another week.

The presence of GAA President Seamus O Riain resolved the problem about the League final. It was agreed that the first leg would be played on Saturday and the second leg the following day. The weather was perfect for the first leg which produced a thriller. New York took the honours, and deservedly so, winning narrowly 2-14 to 2-13, carrying just one point advantage into the second leg on the Sunday. Tipp were not to be denied. The scoring power of Babs Keating, Donie Nealon, Sean McLoughlin, Liam Devaney and "Mackey" McKenna was just too much for the home side, and the Tipp men won decisively 4-14 to 2-8 (Agg. 6-27 to 4-22). It was to prove some consolation for their subsequent defeat by Wexford in the All-Ireland final. My commentary on the final was relayed live from New York by RTE. Relationships between John Kerry O'Donnell and the Central Council, which were strained at the time, were soon put right by Seamus O Riain, and for once a departing GAA President was seen off at the airport by the New York GAA head. But then O Riain was the kind of man who commanded respect, and John Kerry acknowledged it. The lull in that storm was to last until the end of O Riain's term as President. I got a great welcome home from wife Ann, son Finin, and daughters Caitriona and Sinead. I was sternly reminded that I had missed Finin's Confirmation and Caitriona's Holy Communion, but all was forgiven with the distribution of presents I had brought home from the States.

Relations between New York and the Central Council took a nose-dive again in October 1970, following a vicious attack on Dublin referee Clem Foley after the National Hurling League final between Cork and New York at Gaelic Park. It was a disgraceful incident; Foley, who had refereed the game to everybody's satisfaction, was struck by a spectator as he was leaving the pitch, was hospitalised for three days and had to undergo surgery for a facial injury. GAA President Pat Fanning loudly condemned the incident and following the reading of the referee's report, John Maher and John Lynch were expelled from the Association. The Clem Foley incident was to start a chain reaction of events which saw the banning of all visits to New York by teams from this country until January 1972. Even when the tours eventually resumed New York found themselves out of the National Leagues, quite a hefty price to pay for an unwarranted attack on a referee. In January 1971 the Executive Committee of the GAA granted an application for two teams to play in the Cardinal Cushing Games in May, provided the restrictions placed on games in New York be observed. At the Offaly Convention held in February, the

Board President Father E. Vaughan proposed that they send two football teams to play in the Cardinal Cushing Games and this was passed. Accepting that a ban had been placed on counties playing in New York, I got on the phone to John Kerry O'Donnell and suggested that he take out the Jimmy Magee All Stars plus showband personalities to play for the Cushing Charities in New York and Boston. It proved the way out of the dilemma and John Kerry jumped at the suggestion. I was a member of the Jimmy Magee troupe, which had played in charity matches, raising vast sums of money for local charities, in Ireland and in England. The secret of the Magee All Stars lay in the fact that it was comprised of former great players who had become household words and who were still able to command followings at the charity matches. We also had leading Showband personalities included, and the after-match dances were packed to capacity. The Magee All Stars flew to New York on 21 May that year. The party included Sean Purcell and Frank Stockwell (Galway), Christy Ring (Cork), John Nallen (Mayo), Gerry O'Malley (Roscommon), Frankie Byrne (Meath), Dermot O'Brien (Louth), Larry Cunningham (Longford), Father Mick Cleary (Dublin), Kevin Armstrong (Antrim), Willie Casey (Mayo), John Dowling (Kerry) and Paddy Kennedy (Kerry). The old stager, James Magee, was in charge and Liam Campbell, who had not missed a Magee All Stars game, was there as usual giving his commentary, and a very humorous one at that, on proceedings.

The biggest attendance ever turned up at Gaelic Park on 23 May, billed as "Oldtimers Day", to watch the former stars in action and in the words of John Kerry afterwards, it was a case of "doing it without ruffling the extremely sensitive fine feathers of authority". From Ireland also came Dr Pat McAndrew and Father Peter Quinn (Mayo) to join in the reunion of the New York team that had captured the National Football League title in 1950 at the expense of Cavan. The so-called ban on players flying out from Ireland to play for leading New York clubs in the local championship was honoured more in the breach than in the observance. Later, too, all students leaving for the USA were given special dispensation to play hurling and football during their stay — as if a ban would have prevented that anyway . . . In October 1971 the Central Council approved of a recommendation by the Executive Committee, after consultations with the New York Board officers in Dublin, to lift the suspension imposed on John

Maher for the alleged attack on Clem Foley, to allow him to play
in New York competitions. On 9 January, 1972 John Kerry O'Donnell
was elected President of the New York GAA and in his victory speech
said that they should co-operate with the Central Council in every
possible way in endeavouring to put relations between the Council
and New York on a more harmonious footing. The wheel had come
full circle again.

Chapter 11
Adventures on Television

The Irish television service came into being on 31 December, 1961, but in the twenty years or so that I have been associated with the new medium as a programme presenter, match commentator and all-round contributor, I never lost my love for steam radio. There was great excitement surrounding the setting-up of television. I remember a bunch of us attending at a temporary studio in the Marian College in Sandymount where Phil Thompson, on loan from the BBC, put us through our paces in front of the camera. It was very evident from that particular lesson that those of us who were figuring on Philip Greene's *Sports Stadium* had a much better grasp of the fundamentals of television broadcasting by comparison with our colleagues from the newspapers, who had no experience of radio either. Much interest centred on the person who would head up the Sports Division, since we were entering a new era in sports presentation. The RTE Authorities set up an interview board of three men and applications were invited publicly. There was a generous response; I applied, and was duly interviewed. Philip Greene was the man in possession, as he had been the Sports Officer since his appointment to that position in 1953. We all assumed that he would get the job, and informed rumour, once the Board had concluded its business, confirmed that Greene had indeed got the nod. *Ní mar a síltear bítear.* At the end of the day the person appointed was none other than Micheal O'Hehir, who, by the way, had not presented himself for interview. In fact, he had been a member of the three-man Interview Board. The matter was subsequently raised in the Dail by way of a question to the Minister for Posts and Telegraphs. He gave nothing away and simply said it was a matter for the RTE Authority.

When television started I was one of a number of commentators employed on a free-lance basis, and I must say I enjoyed the experience. I believed that television match commentaries were very different from radio, the prime reason being that the viewer was seeing the action at the same time as the commentator, so there was little use in describing the obvious. I had studied guidelines on TV match broadcasting which were circulated to BBC staff, and it was clearly emphasised that comments should be very much restricted, and used only as a means of complementing the picture on the screen. It stated that too much commentary annoyed viewers, and left little to the imagination. I proceeded to follow that particular course, and my style was favourably commented upon, both inside and outside the station. Later in the year, when the question of live television of the All-Ireland semi-finals cropped up, I was chosen for the job. Live broadcasting can be a bit of a test of a person's character. Naturally, during the course of a television commentary, the commentator has to wear head cans (head phones), which means that he can hear all the instructions being issued by the Director to the cameramen, and it takes some presence of mind to try and ignore those comments while commentating on the game itself. It means you cannot answer back, should the Director issue you with an instruction. You get orders like, "Name that sub who is coming into the game," or, "Why was that free given? Give the reason," or "Name the scorer of that goal again." Phil Thompson, the BBC Director on loan to us in those early years had a great sense of humour and I remember on one occasion during my first live transmission, he asked over the head cans, jocosely, of course, "Would the player be sent off if he headed the ball?" After a while you became used to the Director's voice over the head cans, and got on with the task of describing the match. The Head of Sport, Micheal O'Hehir and I differed from time to time over the amount of commentary I was using. He felt I was not using enough commentary, I felt I was using a little too much. It remained a bone of contention between us. I still cling to the view that our commentators tend to over-indulge themselves when describing action on TV matches, and leave little to the imagination of the viewer.

I was chosen to do the first live commentary on the All-Ireland hurling final between Tipperary and Wexford in 1962, and the All-Ireland football final between Kerry and Roscommon. A decision was taken, however, that I would do a commentary in English for the opening quarter and Miceal O Muirceartaigh would take over and do the next quarter of the game in Irish. It was one of those Irish solutions to an Irish problem. A motion had been passed at the GAA Congress that year suggesting that more Irish be used in the transmission of Gaelic games on television. There was never any suggestion of doing bi-lingual commentary on radio, for obvious reasons, one being that it would not have been tolerated. The experiment of doing the All-Ireland finals in 1962 bi-lingually came in for a lot of criticism at the time, even though the TV critics were favourable in their reviews of my end of things. It was generally felt that a better purpose would have been served had the game gone out in its entirety in Irish or alternatively in English, but not a mixture of both. The following year the Head of Sport decided that he would do a simultaneous commentary on the All-Ireland finals on radio and television, which was, in my view, a more farcical approach still. Listeners on radio, who had no access to a television set, were told to "watch the player on the left of your screen", or "look at the player who is lying on the ground on the right of your picture", and other such comments. I believe some of the comments of radio listeners were quite unprintable. That practice didn't last either. Sanity prevailed and it was back to separate radio and TV commentaries on All-Ireland day.

The director for the outdoor sports broadcasts was an American, Burt Budin, and he was truly excellent. He directed the first live All-Ireland hurling final that I did in 1962. His grasp of hurling was extraordinary, and the skilful use of the cameras brought instant praise from all the TV critics at the time, as well as from the many viewers who wrote in to say how much they had enjoyed the day's output on RTE. Budin's direction during the game was amazing for one who knew very little about the game of hurling before he joined the Montrose sports staff. The camera crew also did a magnificent job and I found it quite easy working with the technical people.

In 1963 I got a call from RTE Sports Co-ordinator, Oona Gormley, who asked me to travel to London to film commentaries on the Wembley Games in hurling and football, an annual event promoted by the London GAA Board. The finals were played on a Saturday before big attendances at the famous stadium, where the FA Cup final is staged. It was a particularly busy week in London because Cassius Clay (now known as Mohammad Ali), had arrived to prepare for his bout with British heavyweight champion, Henry Cooper, tak-

ing place the following week. The cameraman on the trip was RTE
staffman Sean Burke, with whom I had worked on many assignments
for the Sports Department. The sound operator was Michael Francis.
Sean Burke brought his Auricon camera which shot 1200 feet of
film, and lasted 33 minutes. It was ideal for a Gaelic match at the
time. It meant that he could film away without having to reload,
using only two rolls to film an entire Gaelic match, but taking three
rolls to film a soccer game. The daily newspapers were covering the
Wembley matches and most of the leading reporters were on the
flight, including Peadar O'Brien of the *Irish Press*. Peadar told me he
was hoping to get an interview with Cassius Clay before he left London.
I confided to Peadar that I was also hopeful of getting an interview
with the great boxer, as I had a camera crew with me. Peadar and I
contacted the *Irish Press* London Editor, Aidan Hannigan, who after
a lot of phoning around pinpointed Cassius's whereabouts in London.
He was staying with his entourage in the Piccadilly Hotel. My needs
were more immediate than Peadar's, as I had to leave London shortly
after the game on the Saturday, while he was staying on until the
Monday. Sean Burke, Michael Francis and I checked into our hotel
(booked for us by RTE, really a dreadful place, and we were not sorry
to leave it when our job had been completed!). I immediately phoned
the Piccadilly Hotel and asked to be put through to Cassius Clay's
suite. The phone was answered by Angelo Dundee, the boxer's
manager and trainer. I proceeded to give a spoof about being over
from Ireland with a camera crew, hoping to get an interview with
Cassius. I explained that a big boxing following would be travelling
over from Ireland to watch the fight with Cooper and Clay and an
interview with Clay would help to boost the attendance from over
the Irish Sea. I could sense he was very impressed, but he would
have to speak to Cassius. I said I would call around to the hotel later
that evening and discuss matters with the star attraction. Angelo
thought the suggestion made a lot of sense and suggested that we call
around 8 o'clock.

  Sean Burke, Michael Francis and I duly presented ourselves at the
Clay suite on the hour and were ushered in by Angelo Dundee. After
the usual exchange of greetings I again made my proposal about doing
an interview with Cassius. Half-way through my preamble in swept
the man of the hour himself, dressed in a ceremonial robe befitting
an African king. He had in his entourage two striking Swedish blondes,

one of them a masseuse, along with, I presume, a couple of body-guards. We got down to business after a brief exchange of identities (Sean Og obviously didn't ring a bell with him). I explained how a filmed interview with him would help to boost the fight takings enor-mously. He was very impressed. I asked him about doing the interview early on Saturday morning as we were booked to film the games at Wembley in the afternoon. Cassius said he worked out at 6 am if that was suitable. Sean Burke was doing his best to attract my attention. "Does that present problems?" asked Cassius. I shook my head and said no. I wasn't going to miss the chance of a lifetime getting the interview with Cassius. Sean Burke kept shaking his head and blurted out, "It can't be done." "What's the problem?" said Cassius. "The problem is simple," said Burke, "we have no batteries for out-door interviews." Sean was dead right. I hadn't thought about batteries for the camera. Cassius came up with the answer. "What about the gym?" The gym hadn't been mentioned up till then. "What gym?" I asked. "The gym in the White City Stadium where I work out. I will be there at noon." Our problem was solved.

We arrived at the White City Stadium in plenty of time, and Sean set up his equipment. Cassius had a number of boxers helping out in his preparations for the big fight, including Jimmy Ellis, a little-known American, who was in later years to become a victim of Clay's punch-ing power when Cassius knocked him out in a title defence. At twelve noon exactly, Cassius swept into the arena, ready to start his workout with Ellis. I explained to him that I had procured a punchball and tied it to the stand with thread near to us at the ringside; when the interview was coming to an end, I wanted him to unleash one of his big punches, just to demonstrate his awesome power. On the signal from Sean Burke I started the interview with "The Greatest", who proceeded to use all the now famous asides, "I float like a butterfly and I sting like a bee," and "look at my face, smooth as a baby's bottom, I'm the prettiest boxer in the world." During the course of the interview I asked him had he heard of a great Irish battler called "Con of the 100 Fights". Back came the answer, "Yeah, but did he win them all?" I assured him he had. "You find him and I'll fight him," said the bould Cassius; even a small piece of Irish mythology failed to knock him off stride. It was really a great bit of fun, and Cassius entered into the swing of things. Coming to the end of the interview I motioned to him that we were ready to do the piece with the punchball, our "get out" piece. I set him up by asking him to demonstrate his punching power. In a completely unrehearsed action, he leapt over to where the punchball was, drew back his arm and unleashed a punch which sent the punchball soaring high into the air. He then turned and roared, "What kind of a dump is this, Dundee, get me a new gym," and went storming off in a show of high dudgeon. It was the greatest piece of showmanship I had ever witnessed. Sean Burke had captured the whole performance on film, down to the punchball finale. The punchball, incidentally, missed Sean's camera by inches as it took off in flight.

A few minutes later Cassius returned and inquired, "Did you get all that?" We assured him we had. "Where did you guys say you're from?" he asked. I refreshed his memory. "See you at the fights," he said, and disappeared. We had only time to pack up our gear and get a taxi to bring us to Wembley Stadium. We filmed both games, which were played before a very big attendance, but quite honestly, I was thinking more about the Cassius piece and the reaction it would have when shown. Michael Francis intimated that he knew a friend in ITV who would pay handsomely for the Cassius interview. Sean Burke quickly put his mind at rest, emphasising that the film was RTE's property, and that was that. When we arrived back in Dublin on Saturday evening, Sean Burke left the film for processing. The following day I brought it to the editing room just to see it. It was a classic, just as Sean Burke described it. After a while more and more members of the staff began drifting into the small viewing room. The film editor, Danny Donoghue, kept showing it until Esther Byrne, the Sports Production Assistant, was alerted, and she arrived to take possession of the film on behalf of the Sports Department. A decision was taken to show the Cassius interview on the Thursday sports programme. Everybody in the Sports Department was delighted and amused with the interview, but a slight snag loomed. Pope John XXIII was dying; if he passed away on the Wednesday, all TV programmes would have to be cancelled. It meant that the filmed interview would have no relevance if it was not shown before the actual fight in the Wembley Stadium on the Friday. Pope John went into a coma on the Thursday and died peacefully on Friday. The Cassius interview went out as scheduled on Thursday's *Sport at Seven* programme and it made an instant impact. There were numerous phone calls from viewers requesting another showing, and overall the calls were very

Cassius Clay (Muhammad Ali) chatting with the then Taoiseach Jack Lynch, on the occasion of his visit to Dublin to box Al Blue Lewis at Croke Park in a charity match.

Cassius Clay (Muhammad Ali) knocks out Al Blue Lewis in an exhibition bout for charity at Croke Park in July 1973.

complimentary. The Sports Department received many calls in the days which followed asking that the Cassius interview be shown again; most of the requests came from people who hadn't seen the interview but who had been told of its contents. Unfortunately, it was never shown again. The film disappeared a few days after its initial airing and was never found. However, I felt a great sense of achievement having secured the interview with boxing's most colourful personality.

The big fight at Wembley was a dramatic affair. Cassius was dumped on the canvas by a Henry Cooper left hook to the jaw in the third round, but two rounds later Cassius got his decision when Henry had to retire with a cut eye. I played golf with Henry in the Clontarf club some years ago and he told me that but for the cut eye, he would have beaten "The Greatest". It always reminded me of the old boxing story about the guy who staggers back to his corner in very poor shape, to be told by his trainer, "You're doing all right, he hasn't laid a glove on you." Three minutes later, the poor guy staggers back to his corner, this time with a black eye and slight cut on the nose, to again be told, "You're doing great, he hasn't laid a glove on you." To which the boxer replied, "Well, keep an eye on the bloody referee, because somebody is hitting me."

In 1968 the GAA succeeded in getting a special TV programme dealing exclusively with their affairs; it was called *Gaelic Report*. That fifteen-minute programme provided the Association with a very useful outlet in which to propagate its activities. The programme had its limitations, as subjects became very difficult to find; most of those which were covered made an impact. I featured several contentious issues on it, and one such programme gave me particular satisfaction. It concerned a club ground in the West of the country. A friend of mine phoned me; he was involved with a local club, and they were anxious to buy out their local pitch from the County Council and develop it. But all applications for such a purchase had been turned down by the Council and particularly by the Council Chairman. The pitch itself was situated on an eleven-acre site on the Council's demesne, and it was on a yearly lease. The club was very anxious to buy the land, develop it, and put in proper dressing-rooms, but every time they applied to the Council they were turned down. The Council instead, offered them a seven-acre site on another part of the demesne; but it was quickly rejected on the grounds that the land offered was poor; it needed extensive drainage, and it was close to a right-of-way,

Henry Cooper, on left, who had to retire with a cut eye in the fifth round of his World Title bout with Cassius Clay seen here at Clontarf Golf Club with Seán Óg and Bob McGregor, President of the Clontarf Club.

Group taken on the occasion of Shay Smith's Captain's Prize at Clontarf Golf Club. From left: Norman Griffen, Bob McGregor (Club President), Gerry Bambrick, Seán Óg, Shay Smith, Henry Cooper, Mick Devine, Tim O'Connor, Sean O'Shea.

which meant that the public had easy access to it. The situation at Council level was interesting. Seven members of the Council were in favour of the club buying out their pitch; seven other members opposed them, so the casting vote fell to the chairman. He was the central figure in the whole affair, but he was far from being well disposed towards the club. Many years previously, he had broken away from the club and formed a rival one. So there was stalemate.

Armed with all the details, I set off with camera crew to investigate. I interviewed the key club officials who explained their dilemma. They also mentioned that they had collected sufficient finance, through raffles, bingo and public collections, to purchase the land and fully develop the necessary amenities. I paid a visit to one of the dissidents who opposed the club's application and he was very impressed with the idea of appearing on TV. But was he prepared to change his mind about allowing the club to buy out the site? I explained that the programme would be going out the following week and he would be seen as a Council member opposed to progress. My words must have sunk in, because he quickly agreed to change his stand and was willing to say so in the interview, which, fair dues to him, he did. That was a bit of a bonus. It left only the Chairman of the Council next on my filming list. As luck would have it, he was at home when I called. I explained the purpose of my visit. He wouldn't relent, and said he was opposed to the club developing what he considered one of the plum sites on the Council's demesne. Things weren't looking too good. I told him I had interviewed the club officials, who had given very solid reasons why their application to purchase the land should be viewed favourably. I then hinted that one of the dissident members I had interviewed had now changed his mind, and was willing to support the club. He pressed me to reveal the member's name, which I refused to do, but I said he would see for himself when the programme was screened the following week. "It's going to be on TV, you say?" said the chairman. I nodded assent. "Let me think about it, and I'll get back to you," he said. I told him I was tied to time and would be unable to come back for further discussions. He thought furiously. I mentioned that the programme on the club would be going out on *Gaelic Report* the following week and it would be watched by all the GAA people in the county. That statement had a dramatic effect on my man who agreed immediately to an interview on the spot. In the course of the interview he disclaimed any bias against the club, thought they were doing a good job, and would support them in any future venture. The programme duly appeared as I had promised. Some days later the matter cropped up at the County Council meeting and the Chairman suggested they take a vote on the club's application to purchase the playing site. Fourteen hands shot up in favour of the application. The club were able to meet the purchase price of the site; they went on to build dressing-rooms and a clubhouse on the land, and it is regarded as being one of the best-developed club grounds in the county — thanks, I'd say, to the power of television. I believe I am still the club's "unofficial Patron".

I continued to work on the television side of things, doing regular filmed commentaries on Sunday matches under the direction of such excellent producers as Justin Nelson and Michael O'Carroll. Justin and I worked on a lot of TV specials for midweek and weekend programmes. I remember one particular feature we did in Irish on a *Lathair Spoirt* in Kerry. The idea was put to me by a prominent GAA club official who worked in the Kerry Gaeltacht area. Justin and I travelled with a camera crew to Ballyferriter, having arranged all the necessary details with our Kerry club official. We had competition at the time from David Lean, who was filming *Ryan's Daughter* in Dunquin and surrounding areas. Justin had worked on films in Ardmore before joining RTE and he had a flair for the more artistic side of filming. Justin incorporated some of the most beautiful scenery you could find into our feature on a Sports Centre in the heart of the Gaeltacht. When the programme was shown it aroused considerable interest, and was much praised for the manner in which the subject was presented in the native language. The programme didn't do the area any harm either from a tourist attraction viewpoint as we highlighted most of the well-known beauty spots. The "Lathair Spoirt" never came to pass. We learned a long time after that the whole idea was the brainchild of our interviewee, who had taken us in. He explained during the course of the interview that with grants expected from the Central and Munster Councils, the Department of the Gaeltacht, etc, the project would be completed by the end of that year. Unfortunately, our Kerry friend was a visionary and while the idea had been floating around in his mind for a number of years, it was quite remote from reality. It all reminded me of another story told about Kerry folk in the early days of radio. A Kerry blacksmith, told by a customer that he had just heard on the radio "up at Murphy's" that the General Election results to hand assured Fianna Fail of an overall victory, cried out "God blast it, shure you couldn't believe a word from their radio, aren't they out and out Fianna Failers. Would you run up to McCarthy's, they are sound Cumann na nGaelers and get the true results from their radio."

I figured in many programmes for the Sports Department. Most of the actual filming was carried out by free-lance or contract cameramen, Joe McCarthy (Cork), Eamon O'Connor (Limerick), John O'Keeffe, Breffni Byrne, Ken Murphy and Paddy Barron, together with RTE staff cameramen Sean Burke and Sean Kelleher. Each and every one of them took a special pride in his work and was most dedicated to the task on hand. Among matches I commentated on were National League football and hurling finals, All-Ireland camogie finals and, of course, provincial finals. The Cork-based Joe McCarthy was a joy to work with if only for the meticulous way he approached his filming assignments. We were engaged to film a Leinster championship match in Dr Cullen Park, Carlow. We had been assured at the time that we could film the game from an excellent vantage point, which turned out to be a concrete structure behind one of the goals near the dressing-rooms. It was too far removed from the centre of the pitch for our purposes, but Joe solved the problem quickly enough. His motto had always been, "Nothing ventured, nothing gained". Joe espied an ice cream vendor selling his products from a small van which had a flat roof. He talked the vendor into driving the van to the half-way stage of the embankment, and paid him a generous tip for the use of the facilities. When I arrived back from the dressing-rooms, having checked out the teams, Joe had already assembled his filming gear on top of the van roof. I climbed up beside him and we were ready and waiting when the big game started. We could do little about the off-air sound effects during the course of my commentary on film, with cries of "Get your ice cream, get your TV ice cream." The vendor had sold all his stock by half time, and he was quite happy with his lot. Joe and I were able to continue our filming assignment and we were quite happy too.

In the early days of television I was sent to O'Toole Park in Dublin to film a tournament match between the Dubs and Kildare. The appearance of a camera in those days was an open invitation for every kid in the neighbourhood to assemble around the filming area. The camera position was on top of the dressing-rooms, and while ideal for height and filming purposes, it was exposed to the elements. Luckily, the rain held off for that particular game. I had just climbed down from the ladder, having finished my job, when I was approached by a number of young fans for my autograph. I scribbled my name on the back of an extended cigarette packet and began putting my gear away, when I heard a young voice saying to one of the autograph hunters, "Who did you get?" "Micheal O'Hehir," was the reply. "That's not Micheal O'Hehir," said the other voice, "that's your man Greene." It was an awful blow to the ego.

Commentators, cameramen and sound operators have to work in all kinds of weather. RTE invariably employed a firm to erect a filming platform from which we worked. Present-day fixtures are more modernised, with cover for all the working personnel. Indeed, there are several GAA grounds which have provided the proper facilities for filming purposes, but RTE have still to erect their own platforms in many venues where they have to work. In the early days you were stuck with a platform with little or no cover. And so it was when I was asked to travel to the "Mick Flanagan Memorial Park" in Ballinrobe for a National Football League game between Mayo and Roscommon. I checked with the weathermen before setting out that morning and I was told that gale force winds and driving rain were forecast for the West for the afternoon. The weather leaving the city was cold but dry. I brought overpants and plastic jacket with me in case they were needed. When I arrived at the venue I noticed that the platform erectors had put up the structure facing the elements, which was not a very bright thing to do. There was ample room on the opposite side of the field. Joe McCarthy and a second cameraman, Breffni Byrne, were already set up on the platform. They had agreed to film in turn, Joe shooting the opening ten minutes, Breffni the next ten, and Joe the next ten. In between changes the cameramen could change their magazines and stow the filmed parts of the match away safely. The rain started as both teams came out onto the field, and the wind began to freshen as well. Fortunately I had put on my rain gear. There was only a handful of spectators at the match; the bulk of those who came were still to be seen in their cars outside the pitch.

The wind by now was blowing strong and towards the filming platform from the Tourmakeady mountains. Joe McCarthy turned to me and said in his quiet Cork accent, "We're going to be in trouble, boy, with the rain." At that stage there was nowhere on the platform where one could shelter from the elements. The cold was intense, and my match programme had turned into pulp; and I was unable to keep track of the scores or scorers, which I normally jot down after each score. Joe had just changed a magazine and was ready to take up filming again when Breffni said, "It's no use, Joe, I can't go on, the rain is getting into the camera and the lens, and I cannot see a thing." Breffni dismantled his gear in an effort to dry it as Joe took over and finished the first half. Had sanity prevailed, the referee would have called the game off at that point. Roscommon had played against the gale in the first half, but every kickout from their goal blew back to the goalkeeper. Every high kick attempted went back over the kicker's head. I had never seen anything like it before or since. It was pure farce. Even Mayo couldn't direct a kick at the Roscommon posts in the first half, the gale saw to that.

The conditions became even worse when the second half started. Breffni had called it a day. He could not use his camera, but Joe ploughed on. The small stream which flowed on the opposite side of the road to the pitch, and which I could see from my vantage point, had turned into a raging torrent, overflowing its banks. The rain was still bucketing down in torrents, and we were saturated. My teeth were chattering as I tried to put words to the action happening on the field. When the referee finally blew the whistle, with Roscommon as winners, everybody rushed for the exits and the comfort of shelter. A soaked to the skin commentator wound up his piece by saying, "Roscommon the winners then by two points," and I added in total abjection, "And I hope to J..... that I will never have to go through the likes of that again in such 'wain and rind'." Naturally the closing comment was erased when the film was shown that Sunday evening, but the bloop is still on the file in Sport. Full marks to Joe McCarthy, he kept working away, not even knowing if the hard work of his would see the light that night on screen. But it did.

In 1980 the Gaelic Athletic Association presented me with the "Hall of Fame" Padraig Puirseal Memorial Award, in acknowledgement of my contribution to Cumann Luithcleas Gael as a journalist and, particularly, in recognition of the results programme on Radio Eireann every Sunday night. That programme commands a wide audience at home and in Britain, where it has grown even greater in the past

Presenting a cheque to GAA President Pat Fanning on the *Gaelic Report* TV programme. From left: Seán O Siocháin (GAA Director General), Tom Fitzgerald, Seán Óg and Pat Fanning.

Seán Óg being presented with the GAA "Hall of Fame" Award in 1980 by GAA President Paddy McFlynn.

couple of years. That, no doubt, reflects the increased volume of emigration across the Irish Sea in recent years. But the programme can
now be picked up in the strangest places. The advent of VHF has
extended the range of the service together with the installation of a
new transmitter, which has strengthened the signal. Recently, a letter
to Radio Audio Research from a Cork man, a radio officer on the
MV *Falaba*, acknowledged an interesting development. The *Falaba* was
operating off the West African coast between Freetown and Mon-
ravia — a distance of 3,000 miles. Because of freak reception, the
radio officer could pick up the GAA results every Sunday night on
the main receiver, in the ship's radio room. The writer of the letter
claimed that for a couple of years, he had got a strong signal frequently
as far south as Dakar (Senegal) and south of the Canary Islands. He
taped the results, he being an interested Cork man, and later tapped
them out in morse code, where they were picked up by friends of his
working on ships off the Philippines and Japanese coasts. It became
a Sunday night ritual, but at least it provided a close link with the
homeland — even if it was by way of GAA results. There were other
occasions when freak reception brought news of GAA matches to
foreign places; Irish priests in Rome have from time to time acknowledged getting strong signals from RTE and were pleased to hear the
results of GAA games, be they local or inter-county.

I was extremely pleased when the GAA honoured me as their
choice for the "Hall of Fame" award. I felt at the time I was accepting
it on behalf of my late father, who had pioneered sport in magazine
form in the early days of steam radio. It would have pleased him no
end to see his foresight being rewarded in such tangible fashion. The
GAA "Hall of Fame" award also acknowledged the fact that the
Sunday night results programme on radio was celebrating fifty years,
twenty-three years of which had been under my late father's control.
Outside of news, it is the longest running programme on radio, and
unique in that it is the only programme in which a son has taken over
from a father to maintain continuity. I was especially pleased that
the award was named after one of GAA's great sportswriters, the late
Padraig Puirseal. Padraig was a colleague of mine and a very close
friend. We travelled to matches together and I valued his advice and
counsel. He epitomised all that is good in sports journalism and was
recognised as one of the great GAA writers of our time. His sad passing
a few years ago was a major blow to the profession. Radio Eireann

acknowledged the family record too in 1980, when Head of Sport, Fred Cogley, presented me with a beautifully designed and inscribed marble citation which I treasure very much. Fred's gracious and witty accompanying speech added very much to an enjoyable occasion.

It was Fred Cogley who invited me to present *The Sunday Game*, a programme devoted exclusively to Gaelic games. I accepted without hesitation. The programme editor was Castleisland-born Maurice Reidy, a sports addict, who tried to convince me that Mick O'Dwyer, the Kerry team manager, was the true guru of Gaelic football, until I reminded him that but for Kevin Heffernan, the Messiah of Dublin football, there would have been no Mick O'Dwyer or Kerry football to highlight during my *Sunday Game* stint. In truth, Maurice did keep me on the straight and narrow during the two years I was involved in the presentation of the programme. The programme Director was John D. O'Brien, who showed the best features of sport in his radio and outdoor presentations. I was very fortunate in having an excellent team working behind the scenes in Production Assistants David O'Hagen, Joan O'Callaghan, Margaret Costello and Vera Sullivan, along with VTR editors Julian Davis and Brian McSharry. A lot of hard work goes into the preparation of *The Sunday Game* programme and much of it is done in the days immediately preceding the game. In my two years as presenter, I had the valuable assistance of the articulate Liz Howard, who analysed the hurling matches. Liz was an All-Ireland camogie player brought up in a hurling household; her father was the legendary Limerick All-Ireland star Garrett Howard. My football analyst was All-Ireland three-in-a-row winner Enda Colleran from Galway, a very astute and excellent reader of the game.

During those two years we used many well known star players as guests, who summarised matches they had been invited to attend. I suppose one could term them experts in their own right. But the word "expert" can be carried a little too far at times. It amuses me when I hear or watch individuals who have neither taken a hurley in their hands or kicked an inflated ball, setting themselves up as experts, and pontificating on the intricacies and mechanics of the games. There are occasions, I'm sure, when players have a good chuckle, when they read or hear some of our commentators trying to explain an error by the player, or a decision by the referee. In most cases, those references are far removed from the truth and only show how little some of the "experts" know about the rules of our games, and in

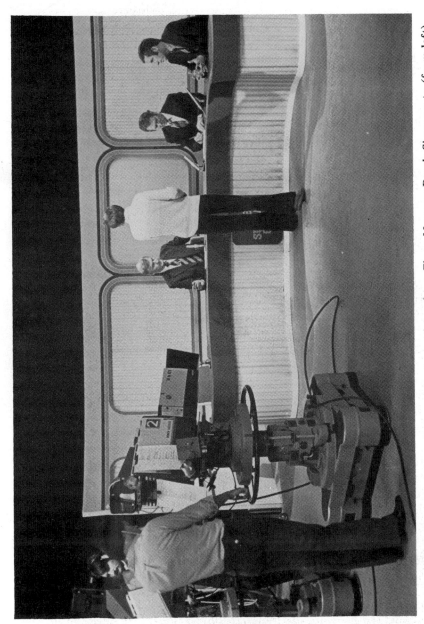

Presenting the *Sunday Game* TV special. Last advice from Floor Manager Derek Simpson to (from left) Seán Óg, Micheál O Muircheartaigh and Enda Colleran.

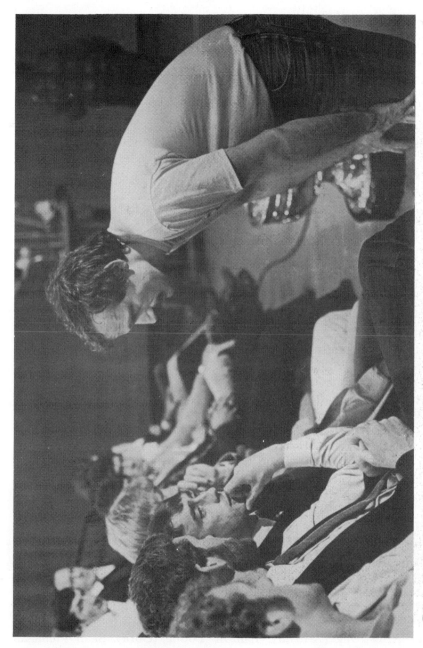

Editor Maurice Reidy chats with Kerry stars before the programme (from left) Jack O'Shea, Eoin "Bomber" Liston and Ogie Moran. At back, Tim Kennelly and Joe Keohane.

some cases, the frailties of players.

It was my practice when presenting *The Sunday Game* to allow the invited guest players or the analyst to give their views on the particular match under discussion, rather than impose my view on the viewer. Those invited to contribute were being paid for their services, and I believed they should earn their fees. Journalism is another field where "experts" are created overnight. There was a practice in newspaper houses where "by-lines" or the names of young journalists were not used over their articles until such time as they served a period of apprenticeship; but that no longer is the case. I listened in amazement one evening to a young journalist of my acquaintance, pronouncing judgement on wayward shots executed by some professionals during a major golf tournament. The young man had only taken up the game of golf at the time, but even at that stage he was rapidly falling into the trap of becoming a so-called "expert". I suppose some things never change. It has always been my contention that only those who have played the game at the highest competitive level can really appreciate the anguish and pain a player suffers when things go wrong on the field. Sport can be very cruel: it can create stars overnight but it can also crush them. A player goes out to play to the best of his or her ability but a number of factors can turn a dream into a disastrous nightmare; the wrong bounce of the ball, a misdirected pass, a momentary lapse in concentration. The prime thing to remember is that players are only human, and it isn't given to humans to command success.

In the two years in which I presented *The Sunday Game* I was able to call on the valued opinions expressed by some of the great players, both active and retired. Eamon Cregan was a natural, having filled the role as player and team manager. He was a marvellous analyst when it came to sizing up a game. Pat Henderson, Eddie Keher and Phil "Fan" Larkin from Kilkenny made valuable contributions to the programme, along with Jackie O'Gorman and Johnny Callinan (Clare), Pat Hartigan (Limerick), whose hurling career was cut short because of an accidental eye injury, John Doyle (Tipperary), and Jimmy Brohan (Cork), all great players and specialists on the field. My football guests were equally famous and their after-match comments helped very much to popularise the programme. They included Mick O'Connell and Mick O'Dwyer of Kerry, Kevin Heffernan (Dublin), Kevin Armstrong (Antrim), Eamon Young (Cork), Sean Flanagan

(Mayo), Jim McDonnell (Cavan), Sean O'Neill and Joe Lennon of Down. The idea of using former great players to evaluate games was an excellent one. Many of our younger viewers, who had heard of those great players, had an ideal opportunity of seeing them on screen. They highlighted some of the game's finer points and some of the abuses as well. They pinpointed weaknesses and strengths; valuable observations in revealing characteristics which were to become associated with certain teams and players of the time. Enda Colleran still remains one of the great thinkers of football and is a valuable contributor to the *Sunday Game* programme. I remember the unsolicited praise Kevin Heffernan lavished on Kerry team manager Mick O'Dwyer and the team after they had achieved a four-in-a-row run of successes in All-Ireland finals in 1981. Kevin was only too well aware of the effort that was needed to win even one All-Ireland, and his tribute to his old adversary on that occasion was typical of the great individual he was himself. "Heffo" and "Micko" may have been great rivals as team specialists but, off the field, they are the best of friends.

There were two occasions when it was necessary to hire a helicopter to transport those of us working on the programme to venues within a couple of flying hours' time from Dublin. That mode of transport enabled the VTR editors who were at the match to get back quickly to base in Montrose, and start editing the film for the *Sunday Game* programme later that night. We used the helicopter for one particular match, a Munster hurling final between Tipperary and Limerick at Semple Stadium, Thurles. Security is always a priority when a 'copter is pressed into service. The Gardai have to be alerted and a guard has to be mounted while the machine is parked. The most adjacent parking spot for the "chopper" was the local church car park, and I got permission from the parish priest to land and take off from the car park on that particular Sunday. On board with me were editor Maurice Reidy, Liz Howard, and VTR editor Julian Davies. The pilot, Colin, was an American, and he was very anxious to see a hurling match. On the morning of the match we arrived at our destination, and the good priest, making sure we were landing in the right spot, insisted in standing in the middle of our landing area, waving his umbrella frantically at us, and it took a few minutes for us to indicate that we knew where we were actually landing; but he got the message. Colin had decided to leave the helicopter in the car park and join us at the match. He set us down amid great excitement. Thousands on their way to the match gathered to see us arriving: the word had got around that President Hillery was attending. I hopped out of the chopper, along with my colleagues, and noticed a Garda Sergeant heading in my direction. "He can't park that there," said the sergeant, pointing towards the chopper. "I'm sorry, Mr O Ceallachain, but he'll have to park that vehicle somewhere else." He was in dead earnest. "Where would you suggest, Sergeant?" I asked. Back came the reply. "I would suggest the Greyhound Track across the way, it would be secure there." The dog track was adjacent enough, so Colin took off and duly parked the chopper in the centre of the track. A Tipperary man of my acquaintance slyly suggested afterwards, on hearing of my earlier experience, that parking the chopper in the safer confines of the Greyhound Track left the local Gardai free to see the match in peace; they would have had to stand guard over the "vehicle" had it remained in the church car park. But I think he was pulling my leg.

The All-Ireland final that year between Galway and Limerick was a real thriller, and it was historic for a number of reasons. Galway captured the title, having tasted a bitter setback the previous year against Kilkenny, also in the final, but 1980 wiped out all those memories as the coveted Liam McCarthy trophy was held on high by Galway captain Joe Connolly, after he had delivered one of the most emotional and best after-match speeches by any winning captain. We had arranged with the teams before the game that the winners would travel out to the Montrose studios soon after the match to interview them, the normal practice on All-Ireland day, for the *Sunday Game* programme. Colleague Jim Carney took on the responsibility of bringing the Galway party to the studio; but the arrangements broke down. The Galway players decided that they would travel back to their hotel for a snack before appearing on the TV show. Instead of arriving at 6.30 pm, the party arrived at 8 o'clock. All our pre-programme plans had to be abandoned. We had after-match interviews; a special interview with John Connolly, who had announced his retirement from inter-county hurling immediately after the game; we had comments from the beaten team as well, which were to be inserted in the recorded part of the night's programme.

We were now pressed for time as we had to be out of the studio before news time at 9 pm. All our prepared scripts had to be abandoned as well, so floor manager Tom Flanagan and I jotted down the sequence of inserts that were to go into the programme and numbered them. The Galway officials reminded us that they had to be away immediately to attend a victory function. There was just no time for re-takes, it had to be a first time or nothing. The recording started. I did the introduction, and I must confess I was quaking. One wrong word, one fluff, and the whole thing would have to be scrapped. After the opening few words, floor manager Flanagan held up his finger to denote insert One, which I introduced. Director John D. O'Brien and Editor Maurice Reidy were relying on me to give them the cues to bring in the various inserts. At the end of each insert I chatted to the players in the studio audience until manager Flanagan again held up his finger directing me to introduce the next insert, and so on till the end of the programme. The whole operation went without a hitch. At 8.55 pm, the Galway party left for their victory dinner while yours truly was stuck to the chair in a lather of sweat. The second part of the programme showed highlights of the match, but our earlier studio piece was now safely on tape and ready to go out after the 9 o'clock news. It was perhaps the only occasion in the two years that I presented *The Sunday Game* that our programme personnel were faced with such a daunting challenge; happily for me, it worked out to everyone's satisfaction.

Galway's victory was a historic one as they were capturing a title last held in 1923. The Connolly brothers joined the ranks of the elite with Joe, John and Michael matching the feat of the famed Rackards, Bobby, Nicky and Willie, three other brothers who were All-Ireland medal winners on the same team, on the same day. Kerry won the All-Ireland football final that year, beating Roscommon. It was to be Dermot Earley's last opportunity of winning an elusive All-Ireland senior medal and he thus joined the ranks of those other great players who sadly depart the scene without achieving football's most cherished prize. Kerry retained the crown the following year but at least a new face appeared for the first time in the winner's enclosure, in hurling, when Offaly deprived Galway of their senior crown in a real thriller. That game will be best remembered for Johnny Flaherty's late goal, when he handpassed the ball to the Galway net, and two quick points from Danny Owens and Paraic Horan gave the gallant midlanders a 2-12 to 0-15 victory. Offaly became the first county since Limerick, in 1897, to win an All-Ireland in their first appearance in the final. We had no problems with the Offaly party from a *Sunday Game* view-point; we devoted the entire programme to the Offaly win, paying them due credit for an historic achievement.

I enjoyed my work on TV sport, being associated with many programmes stretching over a twenty-year period. I was particularly pleased to have hosted *The Sunday Game*, a programme which gave me a lot of enjoyment, as its presenter, but more importantly the number of people I met during the course of my two-year stint. I may have ruffled a few feathers, not too many I hope, but in the main I felt I helped to show that our native games are as good and as skilful as any seen on today's screens. If I am judged on that alone, I feel I was worthy of the choice.

Chapter 12
In My Father's Time

Irish radio was launched at 7.45pm on 1 January, 1926, by Dr Douglas Hyde, *An Craoibhin Aoibhinn*, co-founder along with Professor Eoin McNeill of the Gaelic League. The call sign, Dublin 2RN, was allocated to the new Broadcasting organisation by the British Post Office, who at the time, it seems, had a claim to allot the Irish station their call signs, wavelengths and power. Maurice Gorham, in his book *Forty Years of Irish Broadcasting*, states that the "RN" was intended to be a gesture to Erin! It was known internally as the Dublin Broadcasting Station but it was normally referred to by the public as 2RN. Dr Hyde's opening speech on that auspicious occasion was delivered initially in English.

> Our enterprise today marks the beginning not only of the New Year, but of a new era — an era in which our nation will take its place amongst other nations of the world. A nation has never been made by Act of Parliament. A nation cannot be made by Act of Parliament; no, not even by Treaty. A nation is made from inside itself; it is made first of all by its language, if it has one, by its music, songs, games and customs . . . so while not forgetting what is best in what other countries have to offer us, we desire to especially emphasise what we have derived from our Gaelic ancestors — from one of the oldest civilisations in Europe, the heritage of the O's and Mac's who still make up the bulk of our country . . . This much I have said in English for any stranger who may be listening in. Now I address my countrymen.

He continued in Irish. Dr Hyde's speech was relayed by the BBC from its new high power station, Daventry 5XXX. From the feedback later received, listeners across the water enjoyed it all, and with the enthusiasm of the time, were tickled even hearing the Irish language that they couldn't understand. The new station was able to make a proud boast: 2RN broadcast running commentaries on sporting events before the BBC did. The claim was more than justified, as the "Beeb" was barred from doing commentaries by its obligation not to broadcast news before 7pm, which lasted through 1926; by this time sporting commentaries were already popular with listeners to 2RN. It was claimed, and rightly so, that P.J. Mehigan's commentary on the 1926 All-Ireland hurling semi-final between Kilkenny and Galway was the first commentary on a field game to be broadcast, and it was brilliant. Mehigan, who used the pseudonym "Carbery", was a well-known athlete and sportswriter, who died in 1965. I brought him to many matches in his latter years, a marvellous sports journalist and a most kind and affable friend. He was for years the regular GAA commentator for 2RN and did boxing broadcasts as well. He was the GAA sportswriter for the *Irish Times* and worked in that capacity until his death. He was also the author of many books on the national pastimes, and wrote a column for the *Cork Weekly Examiner*.

The Station Director was Seamus Clandillon, a native of Gort, Co Galway, well known as an Irish singer and as an organiser of feiseanna and concerts throughout the land. He was a very flamboyant character and was in constant trouble with the Department of Finance, who challenged him on the way he was spending his budget allocation. Finance looked with grave suspicion on all aspects of the new service, and constantly queried the Director on the amounts paid to various artists. When Mairead Ni Ghrada joined the new station as Woman Organiser and relief announcer, she was to prove a major asset to the service. She had been Earnain de Blaghd's secretary in the Republican Dail when it was proscribed by the British authorities. She was a fluent Irish speaker and she became very popular with listeners; she was made a full-time announcer in 1929.

From the initial broadcast of the 1926 All-Ireland hurling semi-final, the GAA owed a lot to the enthusiasm generated by the radio commentaries of P.J. Mehigan, who being a hurler, footballer and athlete of note, brought a great sense of audience participation to the events he covered on air. He had a vast knowledge of the games and did at times, it is said, let his feelings get the better of him especially

Sean Seán O Ceallacháin, who launched sport in magazine form on Irish radio in 1930.

when Cork were playing, being himself a Corkman. During one such commentary, a Cork player was reputed to have missed a vital point in front of the posts, and "Pato" exclaimed in horror: "Good Jesus, he's missed it." However, the general acceptance of "Pato's" commentaries was proof positive of the colourful way in which he described some of the major contests of the time. Even though the GAA began to attract bumper crowds to their matches, the Association was finding it hard to make ends meet, even with increased gate receipts. But that situation was to improve with the advent of more subsidiary competitions, which helped to generate more income. Yet, from the foundation of the state the GAA refused to pay income tax. For one reason or another the Revenue Commissioners didn't pursue the matter. It is only fair to say that the GAA had little if any taxable income up to the mid-1920s.

A significant improvement in the finances of the Association occurred from around 1926, the year in which Kerry and Kildare attracted record crowds in the All-Ireland final and replay. The inauguration of the Railway Cups then generated new income. Following pressure from the Central Council the government granted the GAA special exemption from entertainment tax under the 1925 Finance Act, a fact which greatly displeased it because the "foreign games" listed under the infamous "ban" were included in the exemptions. In his *History of the GAA*, Marcus de Burca records that as a result of sustained GAA pressure, the first de Valera Government re-imposed the entertainment tax on the other sports in the 1932 Finance Act, and confirmed the exemptions for the GAA and the National Athletic and Cycling Association of Ireland. Both bodies enjoyed this privileged position until the early 1960s, when the other sports organisations caught up. The Finance Act (1962) extended the entertainment tax exemption to all sports and the Finance Act (1963) did likewise in regard to income tax. Oddly enough, when entertainment tax was introduced initially by the British regime under the 1916 Finance Act, the GAA was given favourable treatment. Following representations made on its behalf by Mr J. O'Connor, MP for Kildare, who had been briefed by the GAA, the Chancellor of the Exchequer introduced an amendment following the Committee stages of the Bill, to exempt "any society or institution founded with the object of running national pastimes." It was only when the Act had become law that an embarrassed Chancellor — he pleaded that he had never heard of the GAA previously — learnt that he had promoted an exemption for a society that had more on its plate than the revival of national pastimes. In the course of angry exchanges in the House of Commons he was told that he had granted a special favour to "an organisation whose membership is open to men who are in open rebellion against this country and closed to all men who join any of His Majesty's Forces." The hapless Chancellor got over his dilemma by assuring the House that it would be a matter for the Revenue Commissioners to decide if the GAA was eligible for benefit in the circumstances alleged. Predictably, the Revenue Commissioners decided against the GAA in due time. However, the GAA never paid a penny.

Before Padraig O Caoimh took over the position of GAA Secretary in 1929, the organisation itself was riddled with disputes and internal wrangling. There were rows between the Central Council and the Provincial Councils, and there were frequent clashes between individual counties and the ruling body. There was a far more serious rift between the Connacht Council and the Central Council for at least four years, from 1926 to mid-1930. Connacht were struck out of the Railway Cup series in 1929, leaving Leinster and Munster to contest the hurling and football finals. The appointment of O Caoimh as the new Secretary went a long way towards ending that whole unhappy position. O Caoimh was to prove over the next three and a half decades that the Central Council could not have chosen a more able, industrious or more efficient person to run the organisation. Indeed, he was to build it into the finest sports organisation in the country.

Perhaps the greatest blow the GAA suffered in the 1920s was the collapse of the *Freeman's Journal* which had devoted a lot of space to the Association's activities and events. In those days the space devoted to sport in the national press was minimal by comparison with today's allotment. The GAA in particular got a significant injection of publicity with the coming of radio in 1926. In the early years of that medium relatively few houses had radio sets; I'm told that the possession of one then was quite a status symbol and neighbours gathered to hear broadcasts of big games in "radio" homes. That kind of community linkage of itself fermented interest in the GAA. I'm reliably informed that for the replay of the legendary 1926 All-Ireland football final between Kerry and Kildare, upwards of a thousand people assembled outside Benner's Hotel in Tralee's main street to hear the broadcast of the game. At half time and with things looking blue for Kerry, every man, woman and child in the crowd marched into St John's Church nearby and said the rosary for a good result. They weren't let down, and so the perception that football is a para-religious ideology in Kerry is backed by a long tradition. In that year Kerry played Cavan in the semi-final of the All-Ireland senior football championship in Tralee. At the conclusion of the game a group of Cavan supporters present were seen to release carrier pigeons to take the result of the game home to Breffni.

It wasn't until the early 1930s that coverage of GAA affairs and games in the national press got a major boost — the appearance of the *Irish Press* in 1931 with its heavy emphasis on sport saw to that. The sports editor of the new paper was Yorkshire-born Joe Sherwood, whose talents in the field of sports coverage had few equals. He was later to become synonymous with the *Evening Press* in 1954, when the "Joe Sherwood" column became compulsory reading for all sport addicts. From then on coverage of GAA matters in the press became competitive. The prominence that the *Irish Press* gave to Colleges competitions fermented interest considerably at that level of games. The spin-off in attendance as a result of the greater exposure was spectacular. The attendance at the 1932 All-Ireland final was 25,000, as against 68,000 six years on.

My dad was quick to realise that there was genuine interest in GAA results and GAA affairs generally throughout the country. He began collecting local results for the Dublin *Evening Mail* and often as not, included any inter-county result he would have as well. Radio Eireann confined themselves to broadcasting major fixtures, Railway Cup finals, All-Ireland semi-finals and finals. Dad believed that the use of GAA results on radio on Sunday evenings would prove a boon to followers of the games. He had built up a solid friendship with the GAA Secretary, Luke O'Toole, who had given him a special pass which gained him entry to Croke Park for all matches. Luke O'Toole's sudden death in 1929 was a big blow to dad, who found him a very efficient official and very obliging in matters dealing with the press. He had met Padraig O Caoimh many times before he was appointed to the onerous office, but those meetings, according to him, had nothing to do with GAA affairs. He was impressed by the new GAA official's attitude towards the use of the media in the promotion of Gaelic games. In October 1929, he told O Caoimh that he had made an appointment to see the Director of Broadcasting, Seamus Clandillon, with the view of getting results of GAA matches included in the news bulletins. The new GAA Secretary was very enthusiastic about the idea and said that he could count on his support. Dad's meeting with Clandillon was very encouraging; the Director told him about his own interest in traditional music and in national pastimes generally. He told him that the idea of having the results of GAA matches included in news bulletins had a lot of merit but he needed time to think about it. The Director made it clear that Radio Eireann would in no way be responsible for the collection of such results, nor would they be in a position to pay for such a service. The radio authorities were still very rigidly under the thumb of the Minister dealing with radio.

Dad was to hear no more from the Director until early in 1930. In the meantime he started to increase the number of local results for the local *Evening Mail*, which had professed no great interest in Gaelic games originally but agreed to pay a small sum towards the service. Interest began to mount in the results in the paper. One morning, as dad was leaving the *Evening Mail*, he was summoned to the Editor's office. The Editor asked him would he contribute some notes on the matches for inclusion on the following day's paper. He gladly accepted the assignment and was paid accordingly. The extra money was a definite help at the time but it also meant a boost of a different nature. He was now in a position to take his place with the other working journalists at major matches at Croke Park with P.J. Mehigan ("Pato" of the *Irish Times* but far more widely known as "Carbery" of the *Cork Weekly Examiner*) and Jim Bolger (the "Recorder" of the *Irish Independent*). Sitting also on the press bench was Paddy Devlin, later to join the new *Irish Press*; he had written his first contribution on GAA affairs in the 1880s. Devlin and Mehigan had both been friendly in their youth with the ageing Michael Cusack, so they had first-hand knowledge of Gaelic games and events right back to the foundation of the Association. I remember Devlin well, as I was brought to Croke Park as a small boy and sat on the steps of the Hogan Stand beside the press seats. Devlin had a small beard and smoked cigarettes non-stop. I watched fascinated as the ash of his cigarette grew longer and longer without falling, before it was stubbed out and another one lit. Devlin spoke very little but looked out over his glasses at the match in progress, making a few notes. The press seats also included Frank McCarragher and Sean McKeon, both old-time Antrim footballers, whose knowledge of Ulster GAA affairs was unsurpassed. McCarragher always brought a few packets of Gallagher's Blues cigarettes to dad, and that prompted good-natured banter about "Protestant cigarettes" being smoked at GAA matches.

Dad combined work as a commercial traveller and a contributor of GAA notes to the *Evening Mail* successfully enough, but the idea of getting details of GAA matches on radio was never far from his mind. He had received no further communication from Seamus Clandillon on the matter and the Railway Cup semi-finals of 1930 were approaching, so he again went along to Radio Eireann and met Clandillon. The Director admitted that he hadn't discussed the results matter with anybody but he suggested that dad have a chat with Mairead Ni Ghrada, to see if results could be accommodated in news bulletins. He again warned that the station could not pay any money for such a service. Mairead Ni Ghrada could not have been more helpful. She was a native of Kilmaley, near Ennis, Co Clare, with a deep interest in Gaelic games, and was married to a Kerryman, Richard Kissane. Mairead suggested putting in results of inter-county matches at the end of news bulletins but only if they could be included in the time allotted to news. She emphasised that she could not drop news items in order to include GAA results.

The first GAA results started at the end of news programmes in late February, 1930, but they did not appear in every news bulletin on those Sundays. Mairead was very unhappy about the omissions, especially since dad had gone to a lot of trouble to get the results. On a sudden impulse, she asked him to sit down at the microphone and read the results of the games for her. She went into another studio and asked the sound operator to let her hear dad's voice on a transmission line. Dad read the results for a couple of minutes and Mairead came back to him and said his delivery was excellent. She arranged with him to be back in the studios the following Sunday. Mairead told Clandillon that dad had an excellent voice for radio and she recommended that he be given time to read the results of GAA matches, after the news bulletins. Mairead also succeeded in wheedling five shillings (25p) as payment for him for his time on air, a considerable achievement in view of the financial constraints which applied at the time (they still remain!). The sum was increased to ten shillings (50p) some years later and remained so for a long number of years.

In those days of the 1930s, communications were positively primitive by our modern standards. A phone call from a rural area to Dublin could take an hour to get through, provided you could get access to a phone. Dad set up his own personal and unique communication system, using Gardai stations, clergymen and local GAA officials who had phones or means of getting the use of phones. He was able, as the months went on, to get additional time, and that stretched to fifteen minutes when he was in a position to include the results of other sports as well. All the results of the day and accounts of matches were a popular feature of his Sunday night programme and it became compulsive listening; the daily newspapers the following day didn't reach some parts of the country until late on Monday evening. The programme grew in popularity as he devoted time to games he had attended on that Sunday, also making reference to other games played as well that day. My mam played her part in ensuring that he was supplied with the results of local matches on the occasions that he had to travel out of the city. He had a press colleague in Ned Hayes, who collected results of Dublin matches for the morning or evening papers, and dad gave him the results of inter-county games in exchange. When dad travelled to Belfast or Thurles or to other GAA venues, my mam brought all the results she had collected from Ned Hayes to the Henry Street studios, and they were ready for him when he arrived. Portable radios were unknown then but had there been a TAM rating in operation, his Sunday night GAA programme would have had a ninety-nine per cent listenership. Indeed, to miss Sean O Ceallachain on a Sunday night was almost unthinkable, and tantamount to missing Mass on a Sunday morning.

The inclusion of soccer results in the Sunday programme rankled with some GAA officials, and criticism began to mount at Central Council and local Board levels. Dad simply ignored the comments and the criticisms, believing in the necessity of having a programme which embraced all kinds of sports. Admittedly, the programme had started with the prime purpose of giving GAA results air-time, but he felt that there was no lessening in the amount of time devoted to Gaelic games. The extra minutes had enabled him to cover other codes, whose results were supplied to him by the Football League of Ireland. The League did complain when soccer results were dropped, which happened occasionally, but while they were given they helped to build up his listening audience. He remained steadfast in his view that sport was sport, and politics should have no place in it — a sentiment I shared and continued to observe even during my own playing days, when I played and attended "foreign games", in spite of the infamous "ban" which was in operation at the time.

The *Evening Mail*, in November, 1933, contained a reference to the programme in its "Jottings", as follows: "Sean O Ceallachain's Sports broadcast used to be given as late as 11pm on Sunday night. A few weeks ago the hour was changed to 10pm and this has given general satisfaction. It is a broadcast that no sportsman, young or old, would think of missing, for it covers the whole field of sport from end to end of the country, and is given with singular clearness. For good reasons it was thought to begin the broadcast earlier. No longer have very young sportsmen a good excuse for staying up till nearly midnight. The news broadcast comes rather late for many a household, but it cannot be said that Dublin is fond of early hours." The GAA had no editorial involvement in the Sunday night programme, but Padraig O Caoimh did make it clear to my dad that the Association would prefer if the name or names of players sent off in matches not be given in the course of his match round-ups on air. O Caoimh felt that such references should be avoided at all costs as he was concerned with preserving the good name of the Association. As dad and he had established a very good relationship, he agreed. As no such conditions were laid down for me when I took over the programme in 1953, I proceeded to mention the names of individual players who had incurred "marching orders", and came into conflict with Padraig O Caoimh over it.

As chief executive officer, Padraig O Caoimh quickly began to make his presence felt in the organisation, travelling the country to attend meetings and conventions and helping to promote better administration. He was very unhappy with the amount of coverage the organisation was getting from radio. He believed that the GAA, which had strong roots in all thirty-two counties, deserved more coverage than the radio authorities were prepared to give, and he was concerned about the standard of commentators being used for the major games broadcast by Radio Eireann. Comments in the daily papers at the time seemed to bear out O Caoimh's concern. On 14 August, 1933 a letter appeared in the *Irish Independent* from "Enthusiast" (Ardara): "Could some improvement be made in the running commentaries on Gaelic games? Many of us here in the North are very interested in Gaelic games and can only hope with the aid of a good commentary to visualise the play. Can't we have announced to us the flight of the ball in its principal movements — movements that count in the game? Can't we be told who plays the ball, to what side frees etc are given, who takes them, and the result?" (If some of the points raised by the letter writer were not included in the so-called commentary at the time, the end result must have been boring for the unfortunate listener.)

The GAA was a very powerful organisation, and felt they had a right to nominate the GAA commentators for the radio transmissions, but that was vigorously opposed by the Director of Broadcasting. It was bad enough to be operating under the shadows of the political parties in power without having to be dictated to by sporting organiations outside. The conflict between the GAA and the Radio Director was to continue for a long time on the subject of commentator selection and suitability. It came to a head in August 1933 when, because of differences over the choice of commentators, the GAA refused to allow a commentary on the All-Ireland senior football semi-final between Galway and Dublin at Mullingar. A Mr P.J. Smith of Shercock, Co Cavan, in a letter to the *Irish Independent* protested against the failure of the authorities to broadcast the game. He suggested that all GAA supporters who owned receiving sets should make a united demand to the authorities to have all matches broadcast where possible. Letters continued to appear in the papers condemning both the GAA and the radio authorities for the failure to provide coverage of major matches. A letter appeared in the *Irish Independent* on 23 August, 1933, as follows: "Do the people at fault for the non-broadcasting of GAA games realise there are invalids who were once ardent followers and spectators of these games. I am one such person, and I am sure, there are others (not many, I hope) who by the will of the Almighty, are no longer able to see those games. I make a special plea to the people responsible to come to some agreement and grant the afflicted ones and all other listeners and licence holders, the broadcasting of the remaining semi-final and final. Signed: Invalid Licence Holder". The letter must have struck a chord somewhere because the second semi-final between Cavan and Kerry at Breffni Park on 27 August was broadcast.

My dad was not beyond getting a ticking-off either from the letter writers and one soccer follower in Cork, "Wireless Soccerite", took him to task for not including his favourite results in the Sunday night programme. The letter went thus: "I beg to protest against the action of the Broadcasting authorities in omitting from the sporting news on Sunday night's (20th) broadcast, any reference to the results of games played under the Association Football code." The letter went on: "Detailed accounts were given of practically all the matches played under GAA auspices from Antrim to Cork and surely wireless licence holders who are interested in other codes of sport are entitled to equal privileges. Now that the soccer season is opening I hope that the Broadcasting authorities will give followers of that code an equal opportunity to hear results of the game in which they are interested." Unfortunately, when the volume of GAA news took up most of his programme, my dad had from time to time to drop, or curtail, the soccer results, and news of other sports such as athletics, swimming, cycling and clay pigeon shooting. The GAA season was in full swing at that time and he did devote a lot of time to county championship results.

The All-Ireland senior football championship final of 1933 between Cavan and Galway was unique because it was the first meeting of the counties in a final, but it was to be remembered for a more bizarre reason. On 10 January, 1926, the two counties had contested the special championship final after the 1925 All-Ireland series had been declared null and void. That year all four provincial representatives, Cavan, Kerry, Mayo and Wexford, were involved in a series of objections and counter-objections brought about by the "Declaration Rule", which was in force at the time. Counties fielded players who were technically illegal, and the offshoot was that Kerry and Cavan were dismissed from the championship. Mayo, nominated to represent Connacht (because the provincial competition had not been concluded in time), survived an objection by Wexford, whom they had beaten in the semi-final, and that left Mayo, for the time being, All-Ireland champions. Mayo were later defeated by Galway for the Connacht title, so the Central Council declared Galway the 1925 champions. The first meeting of the two counties, Galway and Cavan, therefore held a lot of interest. Neither county had actually won the title on the field of play.

My dad was to remember the 1933 All-Ireland football final for a reason which had nothing to do with the actual result. It was his practice to check the two competing teams before the game in case of late changes, and he always paid a visit to the dressing-rooms at half-time to re-check for possible alterations on the sides. The dressing-rooms in Croke Park at the time were under the old Hogan Stand (I was to use them when I started playing with Dublin). Dad would write out any team changes or substitutes and hand them to the commentator who was describing the match on radio. A shock awaited him on that Sunday. As he attempted to rise from his seat at half-time at the Galway-Cavan final, a hard object was poked at his back and a voice whispered, "Stay where you are, don't move." He thought it was somebody playing a joke, so he tried to look around to see who the joker was, when again he felt a hard thrust of a gun barrel in his back, the voice repeated: "Don't move, and do what you are told." Dad complied smartly. He had been sitting on the outside seat of the press bench; P.J. Devlin sat next to him. He heard a commotion around the broadcasting box but he remained in his seat, afraid to move. As the teams were coming back onto the field, some people with seats near the broadcasting box side of the stand were peering over the side of the stand. When dad looked behind him, there was a vacant seat; obviously the occupant had taken his leave. Cavan went on to beat Galway 2-5 to 1-4 to capture their first All-Ireland title. After the match dad went to Padraig O Caoimh and told him about the incident on the Stand and it was only then did he hear from O Caoimh what all the commotion earlier had been about. The daily papers the following day gave the details. The headlines screamed: "Raid on Microphone at Croke Park", "Amazing Incident During Gaelic Football Final". The *Irish Independent* headlines read: "A Big Match Broadcast Sensation — Dramatic Interruption of Comment on Game. Thrill for Listeners". The *Daily Mail* had banner headlines too: "Raiders Appeal for Free State Prisoners. Men Seize Radio Announcer. Scuffle Heard Through Microphone. Amazing Incident at Gaelic Match". Eamon de Barra had been giving the half-time summary of the match when the door of the Broadcasting box was forced open and a number of men entered the box. The *Irish Independent* gave this account of the dramatic events of the day: "Thousands of radio users listening in to the broadcast of the All-Ireland Gaelic football final from Croke Park, Dublin yesterday, had an unexpected thrill. The interval had arrived. Clearly over the air came the voice of Eamon de Barra, Editor of *An Caman*, the official organ of the Gaelic League and the GAA, describing certain phases of the hard fought game. Abruptly his voice ceased. There came stamping noises, an excited cry of 'Stop, Stop' and then another voice, the voice of a stranger, clear, calm and polished. He spoke unhurriedly. This was the message: 'Fellow Gaels! While this match is being played I would ask all listeners to remember that Republicans are on hunger strike at present in Mountjoy Jail, because of the attitude of the Free State Government in refusing to recognise them as political prisoners. The Government responsible for this, claims to be a Republican Government. We protest on behalf of the hunger strikers in Mountjoy against such treatment by a Government posing as Republican. We call on all the citizens of Ireland to support the prisoners in their fight. We make no apology for taking over the apparatus in the interests of the prisoners. Slan De Libh.' The latter part of the message was cut off at Athlone. After five minutes the announcer continued his broadcast without comment."

The *Irish Independent* was told the day after the game that the broadcast was cut off more quickly by the Athlone Station than by the Cork and Dublin Stations. Some versions were that the men got their message through by the Dublin and Cork Stations and did not cease until they had finished. In Athlone, it appears, it was immediately realised what was happening and the broadcast was cut off. "I have nothing to say about it," said Eamon de Barra, when asked by the *Irish Independent* reporter what exactly happened. The Garda authorities also refused to comment on the matter, except that no arrests were made in connection with the matter, but inquiries were being made. Mr Seamus Clandillon, Director of Broadcasting, said he was on leave, and all he heard about the affair was purely hearsay. The same paper carried a further statement on the matter, issued by the Political Prisoners Committee, which went on to say: "Realising the necessity of drawing attention of the Irish people to the action of the Free State Government in forcing Republican prisoners to adopt the most extreme methods of passive resistance, i.e. hunger strike, a number of men, representing the Political Prisoners Committee, commandeered the microphone and apparatus during the interval in the All-Ireland final at Croke Park. The persons concerned wish it to be clearly understood that there was no interference whatsoever with the relay of the match." That particular broadcasting box, situated between the old Hogan Stand and the Long Stand, was used extensively by the various commentators until the new Hogan Stand was opened in 1959, when a special radio and television box was incorporated in the new structure. A takeover of a similar nature would be impossible at the present day because of greater security and technical barriers. Following that incident at the 1933 final, a special guard was placed at all venues where there were live GAA broadcasts of matches, and it applied to soccer and rugby as well.

Dad continued to produce his weekly sports programme. With more demands on his time from other sports bodies, his appeal for an extra five minutes was turned down. He had increased his number of GAA correspondents, which now embraced all four provinces. A decision had been taken to change the Director of Broadcasting in February 1934 but his successor didn't take over until May 1935. Seamus Clandillon was in poor health and that, it seemed, prompted the decision to seek a replacement. In January 1935 an Acting Director was appointed to replace the ailing Clandillon; he was a civil servant, John McDonnell, from the Department of Posts and Telegraphs. He was also a director with a sporting background and that fact pleased my father very much. John McDonnell had been a noted soccer star with Bohemians, capped four times for Ireland between 1911 and 1913. In these years he captained Bohemians, won an international amateur cap in 1910, and played on Inter League teams. During his term as Acting Director of Broadcasting he was a member of Bohemians Management Committee and filled the Assistant Treasurer position in the 1940s, later becoming Vice President. He was very much interested in sport and felt that more could be done to improve the service. Dad and he got on very well and he was shocked to learn of the pittance dad was being paid for putting on his weekly sports programme; he increased the fee to ten shillings (double what he was getting) and better still, made arrangements to increase the running time of the programme to twenty minutes. Unfortunately, the Acting Director's tenure of office was to be short-lived, with the appointment of Dr T.J. Kiernan on 1 May, 1935. The loss of McDonnell was a bit of a blow because many felt that he would have given sport a far greater emphasis and input than it had received previously. Dr Kiernan had been Secretary in the Office of the High Commissioner in London and was on secondment to broadcasting from the Civil Service. He was married to Delia Murphy, a ballad singer who was very popular throughout the country and abroad.

Dad broke new ground when he gave a fifteen minute talk on Michael Cusack on radio in July 1936, in a series entitled "Great Irishmen". The talk got great prominence in the *Irish Independent*

and it also went down well in GAA circles. Another member of the
family was heard on the airwaves around that time when my sister
Maire made her debut on the *Children's Hour* programme, reading
Irish stories; she was to become a regular contributor for many years
after when she produced "Siamse Cois Teine" plays in Irish, and
special features on Irish historical figures in which I too figured. The
range of sports events covered by radio took on a new dimension in
1936 when the *Irish Press* carried a note which said: "Radio Eireann
makes a new departure in broadcasts this evening when the Irish
Greyhound Derby is relayed from Harold's Cross, with a commentary
by Mr Mick Byrne; this is the first time that a greyhound race has been
relayed by Radio Eireann, and it is sure to bring pleasure to many
'fans' who are not able to attend the meeting." Changes in the times
of the News led to the Sunday night "Gaelic Games" spot being
changed to 10.50 pm and that was to continue changing from time to
time before it was brought back again to around 10.30 pm.

Letters continued to be published by the daily newspapers about
the poor standard of match commentaries, and while Dr Kiernan was
unhappy about the position, so too were Padraig O Caoimh and the
GAA. There was frequent correspondence between the Association
and the Director and in 1936 Padraig McNamee, chairman of the
Ulster Council of the GAA and Runai Comhaltas Uladh — Conradh
na Gaeilge, was appointed commentator for the All-Ireland football
final between Mayo and Laois. My dad came up with the idea of
bringing representatives from both camps into Radio Eireann on the
Saturday night before the big game, to talk about prospects. Dr Kiernan
thought it a novel departure and gave his consent. The *Sunday Independent* the following day reported that: "the prospects of the football finalists were reviewed in a broadcast from Radio Eireann last
night by Paddy Mullanny, Treasurer and Acting Secretary of the Mayo
County Board, and Mr Lar Brady, ex-TD, chairman of the Laois
County Board. Sean O Ceallachain was the interviewer. Mr Mullanny
spoke of the contrasting styles of the contestants and of Mayo's great
victories against Galway and Kerry on their way to the final. He said
that Mayomen believed that the margin in today's match would be in
their favour. He added that they had not had the best of luck in Croke
Park in previous years. Mr Brady said that knowing the football ability
of the Mayo men, he realised the big task set Laois. Nevertheless, he
was still confident of victory for his team." Mayo won the match that

Sunday. The idea of bringing representatives of teams figuring in major games to the microphone the evening before the match was to prove very popular; sometimes it was not feasible, because some teams and officials did not reach Dublin until the day of the match. There were other occasions when counties refused to participate believing that it might prove unlucky.

There was a lot of agitation between Dr Kiernan and the GAA over the standard of match commentators, and frequent letters to the papers by fans tended to exacerbate the row between the two bodies. Dr Kiernan suggested to Padraig O Caoimh that they try out new voices. Tests were held but nothing by way of a promising match commentator emerged (that situation was to change later with the advent of a young schoolboy, Micheal O'Hehir). One of the prime concerns of Dr Kiernan was the fact that the commentator had difficulty identifying the players on the field, a difficulty referred to in letters both to the Director and to the daily newspapers. In February 1937 Dr Kiernan made a decision which was to have severe repercussions and which led to the widening of the rift between the station and the GAA. He appointed Eamon de Barra and my dad as the commentators for the Railway Cup football and hurling finals, and the decision was conveyed by letter to Padraig O Caoimh. Some days later the GAA wrote to Dr Kiernan expressing regret that they had not been consulted about the appointment of the match commentators for the Railway Cup finals; the GAA had had another commentator in mind for the finals, and unless he was used, no broadcast of the finals would be allowed. Dr Kiernan replied that he had given the matter a close study, and pointed out that it was Radio Eireann's function to appoint commentators and not the GAA.

The decision to employ de Barra was not surprising; he was pressed into service as a broadcaster a few years earlier in quite unusual circumstances. He had travelled to Cork's Athletic Ground to report for his paper, *An Caman*, on the Munster hurling final between Cork and Clare. The radio commentator for the occasion was Corkman P.J. Mehigan ("Carbery"). As a broadcaster and a journalist, "Carbery" was then part of the permanent furniture in GAA houses throughout the land. He came across with equal fluency on paper and on the airwaves. That day in Cork he fell among friends long — too long — before the match, with the result that he was "maith go leor" by the time he was going on air on the sideline from where the commentary was given. As the game wore on spectators nearby were startled by quite earthy language from the man on the podium. Padraig O Caoimh soon got wind of the word and it did not take him long to decide that very swift measures had to be taken. Hastening to the press table, he quickly explained his dilemma to Eamon de Barra and entreated him to take over the match broadcast. It was a very awkward situation for de Barra, who was a personal friend of "Carbery". After a further plea from O Caoimh the reluctant de Barra took over the "mike" and continued with the match commentary. The reaction to de Barra's commentary was very good and led to him being appointed for other games. Unfortunately that one indiscretion was to end "Carbery's" radio career, and in spite of many pleas made on his behalf, the radio authorities refused to relent. While de Barra had broadcast commentaries on earlier Railway Cup games, it was a first attempt for dad at an actual commentary on that March date in 1937. De Barra had complained to Dr Kiernan about the arduous nature of doing two matches on the one day, and in addition, commentate on Step Dancing competitions which were held between the games. In order to ease the burden, Dr Kiernan decided to allow dad to commentate on one of the Railway Cup matches.

The GAA's refusal to allow the games to be broadcast by de Barra and my father meant that there was no coverage of the Inter-provincial matches in 1937. By that time the St Patrick's Day programme in Croke Park was second in public interest only to the All-Ireland finals, and failure to provide a broadcast caused intense and widespread public reaction. Naturally the GAA being the largest sporting organisation in the country had always taken a rather proprietorial attitude towards broadcasts, and a very keen interest in how the games should be portrayed by its commentators. The feud between the GAA and Radio Eireann over the right to select match commentators continued right through the 1937 season. It featured a number of public statements from the respective camps, with neither side prepared to give an inch. The impasse was still unresolved by the time the All-Ireland semi-finals came round; they were not broadcast. Public interest and disquiet in the conflict mounted with the All-Ireland hurling final over the horizon. Additional complications arose from the fact that Croke Park wasn't available for the All-Ireland finals in hurling because the Cusack Stand hadn't been completed in time, due to a builders' strike at a crucial stage of the construction. It was decided to play the games in Fitzgerald Stadium, Killarney.

As it was evident that the GAA wouldn't relent, Radio Eireann set in train an alternative arrangement to ensure that listeners would get the best service possible. Dr Kiernan sent for dad and Eamon de Barra and told them that he had made arrangements to cover the finals in Killarney on the Sunday. On the day before the game the national papers carried a statement from Dr Kiernan which read: "In view of the widespread interest in the match the Broadcasting Authorities have now decided to alter the original arrangements of having eye-witness accounts broadcast at 6.15 pm. Sean O Ceallachain will attend the minor match and wait for the first half of the Senior game, and commencing at 4.15pm he will broadcast his impressions from Killarney Post Office, where a microphone will be ready. He is expected to conclude at 4.45pm and from then until 5pm Eamon de Barra will give an account of the second half of the Senior game. There is no question of having a description of the match rushed in relays from the Stadium to the Post Office. While the arrangement is immeasurably less satisfactory than a running commentary from the ground itself during play, the Broadcasting authorities feel that it is the best they can do in the circumstances."

Eamon de Barra and dad performed their duties and brought the news of the 1937 All-Ireland minor hurling final (Cork 8-5 Kilkenny 2-7), and senior (Tipperary 3-11 Kilkenny 0-3) to an avid listenership. It certainly was novel but at least those fans who could not make it to Killarney didn't have to wait until 11 o'clock that night for a report on the games. Dr Kiernan had made his point, without the co-operation of the GAA. But there was still a further assignment to be carried out by dad before the day ended — he had to compile his *Gaelic News* programme. A special train, laid on to take followers from Killarney, did not arrive back in Dublin until near midnight. However, Dr Kiernan had made special arrangements to extend the programme times to facilitate him, so his "Sports News" went on the air well after midnight. The programme included all the other results of the day and a comprehensive account of the disappointing Tip-perary-Kilkenny All-Ireland senior final. Dr Kiernan was highly pleased with the day's work and he endorsed it with a personal letter of thanks to both commentators. Indeed, the steps taken by the station brought matters to a head with the GAA. For the All-Ireland senior football final a few weeks later, the GAA agreed to accept the station's suggested commentator, Fr Michael Hamilton of St Flannan's College, Ennis, who was also chairman of the Clare County Board. It was a tactful ending to a strife in which both sides gained little but lost much. The cold war had ended and normal relationships were restored between the two parties. I must say that the Radio Eireann stance was the proper one in the light of modern-day relations between sporting bodies and the broadcasting service.

The old question of mixing soccer results with GAA games on his Sunday night sports programme gave dad endless trouble in his efforts to pacify both parties. But soccer, admittedly, did lose out on occasions. Dad was invited to meet Mr Joe Wickham, President of the Football League of Ireland, and the Secretary, J.L. Brennan, and they expressed concern at the number of times the soccer results had been dropped from the Sunday programme. Dad explained his dilemma — pressure of GAA content. Mr Wickham told him that his Association was anxious to have its own programme and that they had been having discussions towards that end with the Radio Director. Those meetings eventually bore fruit when the Director informed them that he had appointed Mr Seamus Lavery to broadcast soccer results on Sunday nights starting from January 1937 at 8.35 pm. The arrangement was to last until the end of the soccer season. When the programme recommenced in October it had a new presenter, J.L. Brennan. He told the Management Committee of the League that he had been appointed by the Director of Broadcasting to take over the Sunday evening results slot, and the Committee agreed. J.L. Brennan's *Soccer Survey* programme proved very popular and he was to continue in that role until his untimely death in January 1950. His successor Philip Greene established himself as a very fine and able commentator, and he brought his own distinct style to the Sunday night soccer scene. My father continued to provide his GAA listeners with a regular Sunday night programme of results and comments and after the 1937 All-Ireland series of events, there was no more friction with the GAA and radio.

The arrival of Micheal O'Hehir as a GAA commentator brought a new dimension to the sport. Micheal, an 18-year-old schoolboy, wrote to Radio Eireann requesting an audition to do match commentaries. He was given a test, with the result he was appointed match commentator for the All-Ireland football semi-final between Galway and Monaghan at Mullingar in 1938. He never looked back. Micheal

O'Hehir's commentaries brought a new dynamism to GAA matches; his pace, colourful descriptive narratives and general excellence made the armchair listener feel he or she was present at the big game. Make no mistake about it, from the time O'Hehir came on the scene, GAA matches received a major uplift; when All-Ireland finals were relayed to far-flung outposts around the world, it was O'Hehir who made these matches an event not to be missed. No one has equalled O'Hehir's flair or undoubted brilliance for capturing the mood and atmosphere of the big occasion. I would add too, that no two individuals contributed more to the advancement of Gaelic games in this country than Micheal O'Hehir and my dad in the roles they filled.

Radio itself was to benefit in a big way through increased listenership for the afternoon commentaries and again for the late round-up of results and comments on Sunday evenings. I would also mention that the launching of that Sunday night sports programme in 1930 gave the GAA a platform which helped to popularise the games, at a time when coverage at newspaper level was pretty scant in relation to the important role the Association filled in the lives of the people. The results programme which I carry on to this day has now a far greater audience than that ever envisaged by my late father. The Sunday night programme was transmitted initially from the Henry Street studios, situated on the top of the General Post Office building. Those studios were still used for some time after the new TV Complex opened in 1962, before they were eventually incorporated in the TV site.

Dad was often asked how he was able to gather all the results for his programme. He got great fun out of telling some of his friends that his main method was through the use of carrier pigeons. He was able to convince some of his unsuspecting friends that he had a pigeon loft on the roof of the Broadcasting building, into which pigeons would arrive with results for his programme. A friend of his who had been "sold" the pigeon story was invited into the studio one night as dad presented the programme. The roof and window sills of the old studios in Henry Street provided roosting perches for literally hundreds of sea gulls and were at times a major nuisance. Midway through the programme the gullible visitor tried vainly to attract dad's attention to the fact that there were three pigeons sitting on the studio windowsills. He pointed in the direction of the pigeons but dad waved his hands at him to remain quiet. His visitor whipped out a pen and scrawled on a piece of paper, "They may be important results, will I take them in?" Needless to say, dad learned a good lesson from that episode and rarely after did he bring a visitor into the studio during an actual transmission.

Dr Kiernan spent six years as Director of Broadcasting; during that period he helped to transform the entire operation, raising its status and providing programmes of high quality content. It was a remarkable achievement for a man who had had no experience of broadcasting when appointed originally to the position. In 1941 he took up a diplomatic appointment to the Holy See and that was followed by postings to Canberra, Bonn, Ottawa and Washington, before he finally became Director of the American-Irish Foundation with headquarters in New York. He was succeeded by Seamus O Braonain, a man who had a very imposing sporting background, and the first such sporting person since the earlier John McDonnell. O Braonain had enjoyed a phenomenal career as an athlete of high repute apart from being an oustanding rugby player with St Mary's club in Dublin, whom he captained. On joining the Gaelic League he took up football and hurling, though he never lost his interest in the oval ball code. He went on to win All-Ireland football medals with Dublin in 1902, 1906, 1907 and 1908, before an injury forced him out of the game. He was a very popular Director, and it was he who asked me in 1946 to announce the main GAA results of the day in Irish on my dad's programme. The thinking behind the idea was to allow students in boarding schools to stay up to listen to the GAA results.

O Braonain had very strong views about the propagation of Irish on radio and he felt that the inclusion of the GAA results was just a small step in that direction. O Braonain and my father were very good friends and met constantly at major games at Croke Park. O Braonain was very much interested in Dublin, whom he had represented in football and hurling for many years. It was he who instructed dad during the war not to mention or make reference to the weather during the course of his match reviews on radio. The reason was that weather information would have been invaluable to the "warring factions" at the time and the authorities were very strict in the application of that ban. O Braonain never lost his love for sport—and that meant all sport. Despite the financial constraints imposed on the station, O Braonain always ensured that sport did not suffer. I continued to give the GAA results in Irish for three years after O Braonain had retired in 1947. It was Francis McManus, the General Features Officer, who decided that the Irish and English results were over-lapping and he decided to drop the Irish input.

My dad's health became of some concern to the family. He had developed an irritating cough which forced him to take sips of water when he was reading his Sunday night script; he just struggled through it. There were occasions when he over-indulged for "medical purposes" in order to ease his discomfort and that brought him to the notice of the radio authorities. In 1953 Francis McManus asked me to drop in for a chat. He said he felt unhappy and concerned about my father's health and suggested that I take over the programme on Sunday nights. He increased the programme fee substantially and suggested that my father be paid a fee for helping in the compilation of the programme. He made the arrangement for the change on the spot. I had to break the news to my father but he had by then accepted the change. So, after 23 years my dad bowed out. It was the end of one era but the beginning of another.

Thirty-five years have now elapsed since I took over the Sunday night GAA results slot from my dad. I suppose I could also claim I inherited his distinctive voice to some degree, as I'm quickly identified through the spoken word when in company. It doesn't always help to be recognised in that respect as I found out one night. The phone in the radio Sports Department rang and when I picked it up I knew immediately from the background noises, clinking glasses and hubbub of voices that the caller was in a "pub" or club. We get frequest calls seeking results of matches played that day or perhaps it may be someone who had missed the racing results, and had an interest in some race. Most sporting queries are directed to the Sports Department and the one I got on that particular night was no exception. "Would you ever settle a bet?" the caller asked. "What's the query?" I asked. "It's in two parts," the caller said. "I'll do my best, fire away," I said. "Where did Manchester United win the European Cup; and in what year?" Ironically, I have always been a Manchester United fan, so naming the venue for that European Championship Cup win was not too difficult. "I can tell you the venue," I said. "The final was played in Wembley Stadium, but I am not too certain about the actual year. It could be either 1967 or 1968. If I was having a bet myself, I would say 1968 but if there is big money involved, you will have to try somewhere else." There was silence at the other end of the phone. "Hello," I said. "Are you still there?" The caller said, "Is that Sean Og?" I said it was. "How in f..... would you know?" and slammed down the phone.

Having a recognisable voice has its compensations too. I was travelling to Tullamore to cover a game for the Sunday Sport programme. Six miles from Kinnegad a red light started flashing on my dashboard and I stopped immediately. Steam was rising from under the car hood. I discovered the fan belt was in ribbons. I was in a right pickle: where was I going to get a replacement fan belt at noon on a Sunday, and miles away from the nearest garage? I allowed the radiator to cool off and walked towards a distant house in the hope of finding a phone. On the way I saw a water pump in a disused yard. I decided to refill the radiator, and slowly drove the car into the yard. It was only then I noticed a caravan parked opposite the pump. I started drawing water while filling a bucket which had been hanging on the spout of the pump. "Can I help you?" cried a girl who was standing in the doorway of the caravan. I explained my problem quickly, apologising for my intrusion. "You're the radio man, aren't you, I'd know that voice anywhere," she said. It was nice to be recognised but I was more concerned with my situation and getting back on the road. "Come out here, John," the young lady called into the caravan. John appeared. "Listen, say a few words and see would he recognise the voice," she said. Again I explained about the fan belt. John just looked at me and said quietly, "You're Sean Og, and you never said a good word about Westmeath in your life." I started to explain why, when he grinned and added, "They didn't give you much to talk about, anyhow. Let's see what we can do about the fan belt." He walked down the yard to another caravan and arrived back with a box of tools and a couple of old fan belts. "I'll stick one of these on and it will take you to wherever you're going and back."

John duly carried out his repairs, and the fanbelt worked like a charm. I was able to travel on to Tullamore for my radio assignment and return safely to Dublin afterwards. Despite all my efforts, my very obliging "mechanic" would take no money for the running repairs. The only promise I had to give was to say a few kind words about Westmeath the next time I saw them play. I carried out my promise. My very good friend, Paddy Flanagan, the Westmeath PRO to this day cannot get over the high praise I lavished on his county in a subsequent match report, because, as he said himself, "I thought they were bloody awful." But then, Paddy was always a hard man to please...

So, as I mentioned, the Sunday night GAA results programme still goes out over the airways every Sunday night, finding very receptive listeners in many countries, and in strange places. I can only pray that the good man above will allow me present the 3,000th edition of the programme in February 1989. We certainly have come a long way from the crystal set days.

Chapter 13

My Outstanding Teams

A popular practice from time to time is to pick what is considered "Best Football or Hurling Teams" and it is an exercise one approaches with great trepidation. Recently I was asked to name my best fifteen players in their playing positions, and what looked an easy proposition at the outset turned out to be a bit of a nightmare. I came to the conclusion that no matter how many teams you settle on, there would be always someone left out who had strong claims to a place. I fared better in hurling because I was able to designate certain players who had unimpeachable claims to a place on my chosen fifteen. But I did have great difficulty filling some of the other positions. In order to give credibility to my chosen team, I settled on the period from 1940 to 1980, and even when I had finally decided I still felt that I had not done justice to a lot of other contenders.

My choice of goalkeeper fell to Noel Skehan (Kilkenny) from a list which included such superb net minders as Jimmy Donegan (Kilkenny), Kevin Matthews (Dublin), Tony Reddan (Tipperary), Ollie Walsh (Kilkenny), Dave Creedon (Cork) and Seanie Duggan (Galway), to mention just a few. Noel's uncanny anticipation, and his eagle eye which saw danger long before his colleagues around him realised it, made him a special goalie in my book. Goalkeeper is not the best position to be in on a team because he could be the first player to get the blame for mistakes elsewhere on the field. I just couldn't single out any particular game in which Noel excelled; all his performances were top class. I doubt if there are any other players who could boast of being awarded seven Bank of Ireland All-Stars awards in the one position.

Celebrating 100 All-Ireland Hurling Finals at Croke Park in 1987. From left: Seán Óg, representing Dublin All-Ireland team of 1948; Mick Daniels, captain of Dublin All-Ireland Champions 1938; Noel Drumgoole, captain of Dublin, All-Ireland team of 1961.

After match chat: from left, Kevin Heffernan, Tony Hanahoe and Kevin Moran.

The right corner-back spot had many candidates too — Billy Murphy (Cork), Mick Byrne (Tipperary), Phil "Fan" Larkin (Kilkenny), John Doyle (Tipperary) and Brian Murphy (Cork) — but I settled in the end for Wexford's Bobby Rackard, for his courage and scrupulous sportsmanship in a position which demands great patience and forbearance. Bobby had a height advantage over most of his opponents, and like his brother Billy, was the first I saw using his hurley as cover, as he grabbed a high dropping ball. It is not a practice I would recommend and I'm glad to say not too many of our present-day hurlers use it. My choice of full back is Limerick's Pat Hartigan, a lion-hearted player who relied only on hurling skills to beat opposing full forwards; a model for any young player wishing to aspire to hurling greatness in the position. My left corner-back is Tony O'Shaughnessy (Cork) for strength and acute positional sense. He figured on successful Cork teams and naturally the spotlight tended to focus on the out-the-field stars, but I believe Tony was the real cornerstone of the successful Cork teams of the 1950s. Jimmy Finn (Tipperary), for his dashing runs and the quick recovery, is my choice at right half-back: he played in an era of really great wing forwards, household names at that, but he was an inspiring figure and a player to be respected. The centre back spot did present many problems because of the number of candidates available to me, and no matter which player I chose, I still would not be doing justice to the talent available. Some of those names were John Keane, Martin Og Morrissey and Vin Baston (Waterford), Pat Stakelum, Mick Roche, Tony Wall (Tipperary), Vince Twomey (Cork), Pat Henderson (Kilkenny), Willie Rackard (Wexford) and many more. After a lot of soul-searching I finally plumped for Ger Henderson (Kilkenny), for his marvellous positional sense and bravery, when attempting a high catch amidst flying hurleys. As I mentioned, it is not a gambit I would teach a young player because of the risk involved but the few players who get away with it, like Ger, are the exception.

My choice at left half-back was automatic and while there were numerous others capable of filling the berth, the player I chose was the one I admired most, Seamus Cleere of Kilkenny. Hurling is a very skilful game. It has certain features lacking in other stick games, and in order to see it at its best it must, needless to say, be played by skilful players. Seamus Cleere was one of a small band of players who had a special gift, a grace, an elegance on the field which a lot of other players lacked, and which made him stand out above the others. His special combination of flair and movement in the playing of the ball made him a joy to watch. All the attributes I mentioned equally fitted my midfield choice of Harry Grey (Laois and Dublin), whom I played against for so many years on Laois teams and later played with on Dublin teams. I learned a lot from Harry: I have never seen a more stylish player since, in a midfield role. He had the advantage of being lean and tall, and his undoubted artistry in the way he picked and hit the ball made him stand out. I remember he was whistled for a foul in the 1946 Leinster final for a legitimate stroke. Obviously, the referee that day felt that he must have fouled the ball before striking it, such was the confined space available to him. Had Harry been born in one of the more successful counties like Cork, Kilkenny or Tipperary, he would have been one of the most successful players of all time on award lists. I chose Joe Salmon of Galway as Harry's partner, again for the simple reason that the elegant and stylish players will always command attention, and Joe was one of those special players. He was very dedicated and like all great players he didn't have to resort to unsporting tactics to win the ball. He too was the stylist supreme who helped to make hurling the prime attraction it is today. I didn't have to spend much time deliberating over my choice of forwards. The reputations of my three half-forwards were such that I just typed them in, Christy Ring (Cork), Mick Mackey (Limerick) and Jimmy Langton (Kilkenny), and I'm certainly not going to make cases for those three, all of whom I played against, and sadly who have passed to their eternal rewards.

I mentioned grace and elegance on the field earlier, and I could apply that to my choice of right corner forward, Jimmy Doyle, the sweetest striker of the ball one could find, and uncanny in marksmanship. Jimmy belonged to that rare school of left-handers, gifted men, who gripped the hurley right hand down (I was of the more orthodox type, left hand down). There were a number of candidates for the full forward position, but I waved them aside and plumped for Wexford's Nicky Rackard. His huge hurling heart and his propensity for scoring goals made him an easy choice. My final position, left corner-forward, also presented problems because of the number of players who graced the position down through the years. Weighing up all the requirements and the assets needed to make it successfully in the berth, I opted for Kilkenny's Eddie Keher, who won five Bank of

Ireland All-Star awards from the inception of the scheme in 1971. He surely would have been an automatic selection for even more of the coveted awards in his earlier years before the advent of the scheme.

So my "Best Team" for the period 1940-1980 is:

Noel Skehan
(Kilkenny)

Bobby Rackard   Pat Hartigan   Tony O'Shaughnessy
(Wexford)   (Limerick)   (Cork)

Jimmy Finn   Ger Henderson   Seamus Cleere
(Tipperary)   (Kilkenny)   (Kilkenny)

Harry Grey   Joe Salmon
(Laois/Dublin)   (Galway)

Christy Ring   Mick Mackey   Jimmy Langton
(Cork)   (Limerick)   (Kilkenny)

Jimmy Doyle   Nick Rackard   Eddie Keher
(Tipperary)   (Wexford)   (Kilkenny)

My choice of the best fifteen footballers presented a number of problems because of the vast wealth of talent available to me. The prime difficulty was the fact that there were so many players of equal merit vying for particular positions. I decided, therefore, to impose some restrictions on myself to make my task a degree simpler. It helped only partially. I decided to limit my choice to the years between 1950-1980, and to make for as great a spread as possible, to give only one position to a county on a line. How often the temptation arose for me to break those rules or guidelines.

Goalkeepers are a special breed of player and only the really success-ful survive. I had a rich harvest to select from which only accentuated my problem, names like Paddy Flaherty (Dublin), Johnny Geraghty (Galway), Martin Furlong (Offaly), Charlie Nelligan (Kerry), Seamus Morris (Cavan), Kevin Smyth (Meath) and Paddy Cullen (Dublin). I settled for Johnny Culloty (Kerry), who was to my mind, one of the most consistent net minders in the game over a long spread of years. Johnny had the added advantage of playing outfield as well, and winning highest honours there, but he did play on four winning

A meeting of the Bank of Ireland All Stars Selection Committee in 1982 in the Burlington Hotel. From left, seated: Tony McGee (UTV), Michael McGeary (*Irish News*), Jim O'Sullivan (*Cork Examiner*), Mick Dunne (RTE), Micheál O'Hehir (RTE), Micheál O Shea (Radio na Gaeltachta), Sean Óg (*Evening Press*), Ard Stiurthoir Liam Maolmhichil, John Neiland (Bank of Ireland), GAA President Paddy McFlynn, Vice President Paddy Buggy. Standing at back, from left: Donal Carroll (*Irish Independent*), Mick Ellard (*Cork Evening Echo*), Paddy Hickey (*Evening Herald*), Liam Kelly (*Sunday Independent*), Liam McDowell (BBC), Eugene McGee (*Sunday Tribune*).

All-Ireland senior teams. He was a fearless keeper and had sharp reflexes. Enda Colleran got the right corner-back spot simply because of the way he dictated play from his side of the field, and when the big effort was needed, he was always the first to respond. He was a no-nonsense defender; honest, he played it hard, and sporting.

The full back position offered me many choices and it took some time to come to grips with a final one. My man for the No 3 shirt was Paddy O'Brien (Meath), a gentle giant. I refereed a number of matches in which Paddy played and I often marvelled at his wonderful high catching and amazing anticipation of the high ball. The rules governing the game were not as restricted as they are now and because of that, I finally decided on the stylish Meath man. He was ahead of his time in full-back technique. Paddy Prendergast, the "springboard" Mayo full back was a hot contender. Prendergast probably was the first full back in the game to come to terms with the roving full forward. His exceptional mobility saw to that. Sean Flanagan of Mayo was my choice at left corner-back, and I didn't dally too long on that one. Sean personified the true corner back with his aggressive approach and great recovery powers. Rarely was he beaten to a ball in a straight challenge, and he had that great rallying quality that made him a highly respected leader. I gave the right half-back berth to Sean Murphy of Kerry, who was, to me, an automatic choice for the position. He was one of the game's stylists and when other heads were dropping around him, Sean was the marshalling force. He kicked excellently with both feet. There were many contenders for the centre back spot, a truly key position on any side and again my choice was wide, from such as Liam Maguire (Cavan), Jack Mahon (Galway), Jim Crowley (Dublin), Dan McCartan (Down) and Sean Meade (Galway), but in the end I settled for Kevin Moran (Dublin), who in his three years on the Dublin team, proved to be the most exciting player I have seen in the position.

Kevin was indeed something special. He was one of the great readers of the play. He had the ability to move back or forward at crucial stages of a game to avert a dangerous situation or launch a lethal attacking movement. His sally upfield in the opening seconds of the 1976 All-Ireland when he flashed through the Kerry opposition like a hare through a gate was just poetry in motion. His bullet shot at the end of that memorable run missed the net by a couple of feet. Had it gone in, it would have been the score of the century! Kevin has a record no other is likely to match. He won two senior All-Ireland football medals and two National League medals with Dublin in the centre back position and he holds two English FA Cup medals with Manchester United at centre back. My wife Ann and I were privileged to be invited to Kevin's Testimonial Dinner early in 1988, a glittering affair with over eleven hundred guests. Kevin's Manchester United team mates came straight from Old Trafford, after a good win over West Ham, and just made the connection by plane to Dublin to be present at his dinner. One of the guest speakers at the function, along with Kevin Heffernan, was former Assistant Chief Constable of Manchester, John Stalker, whose book on his abortive investigation into the modus operandi of the RUC was a 1988 best-seller. In a fine tribute to Kevin Moran, John Stalker said that among his friends in Manchester Kevin stood forward while others stood back when he was being targeted for his outspoken comments on North of Ireland policing. It was a wonderful occasion and I couldn't but think that it was doing more for Anglo-Irish relations than half a dozen much publicised Anglo-Irish political meetings.

I selected Joe Lennon (Down) at left half-back because of his great ability to lead by example. There are few players in the game at present who can kick balls to unmarked colleagues with the precision which characterised Joe's play. He was also a very difficult defender to get round, as many leading forwards of the time found to their cost. Joe never played on a losing side in an All-Ireland senior final. Uniquely, for a current player, he wrote a book on the science of Gaelic football.

Having restricted myself to having one county represented on a particular line, I ran into serious trouble at midfield, where I had a great number of candidates. Both Mick O'Connell and Jack O'Shea of Kerry had special claims, but which of them should I choose, O'Connell, with his true artistry and impeccable football, or O'Shea with his all-round industry and rallying qualities? I settled for O'Shea, mainly because his competitive edge appeared to be sharper with the chips down and because of his superior and sustained work rate. I suppose you could describe O'Connell as the artist exceptional, O'Shea as the artist cum artisan. Some players tend to lose the head when greatness is thrust upon them; it can never be said of O'Shea, who still remains the unassuming player he was when he first hit the senior scene in the mid-1970s. Finding a partner for him was tricky.

There were John McAndrew (Mayo), Paddy Connell (Meath), Jim McKeever (Derry) and Colm McAlarney (Down). My choice rested with Brian Mullins (Dublin); he personified the comprehensively competitive player, who never acknowledges defeat. He never accepted second best nor was he prepared to bow the head when faced with a major challenge. His surging power on the ball gained him the respect of his opponents.

Forward positions in Gaelic football have produced many exciting players over the years, some of whom walked on to my team without any real challenge. I picked Matt Connor (Offaly) at right half-forward because he was an exciting player to watch but also because he could produce goals out of nothing at crucial stages of games. Allied to that, he was a superb free-taker; but in the main, his ability lay in creating or finishing off for scores. My centre forward was an automatic choice; indeed, I could have selected him in any position on the field, and he would have filled it with the distinction I have accorded him in attack. He is Sean Purcell from Galway, one of those rare jewels who flashed across the football firmament, excelling for many years in defence, midfield and attack, where I have included him. He had power to burn and like Cathal O'Leary (Dublin), Willie Bryan (Offaly), Jim McKeever (Derry), Paddy Prendergast (Mayo), or the great Mick O'Connell himself, he had tremendous "spring" for a dropping ball which gave him an edge over opposing players. He had marvellous positional sense and could cross a ball to an unmarked colleague with precise accuracy. My left half forward is Pat Spillane (Kerry), for his great industry and ability to pick off scores, sometimes under stiff pressure. He also had the uncanny knack of being in the right place at the right time to pick off vital scores — surely the hallmark of a great forward.

My full forward line, I feel, is a very lethal one and includes three players who represent the best in three different decades of fotball respectively. Mick Sheehy (Kerry) at right corner is one of the supreme marksmen of Gaelic football and one of the deadliest opportunists in the game. His ability to pick off a score from the slightest chance has been proved many times. His amazing goal from a quickly-taken free in the 1978 All-Ireland final against Dublin remains a vivid memory for those who saw it. It came from a controversial referee's decision — as Paddy Cullen had left his goal to plead with the referee, Sheehy swooped with the speed and precision of a diving hawk. (Incidentally, that Sheehy goal nearly sent an 85-year-old Kerry woman to a pre-